America's Most Wanted Recipes

Sweet Indulgences from
Your Family's Favorite Restaurants

JUST DESSERTS

Also by Ron Douglas

America's Most Wanted Recipes

More of America's Most Wanted Recipes

America's Most Wanted Recipes Without the Guilt

America's Most Wanted Recipes

Sweet Indulgences from Your Family's Favorite Restaurants

JUST DESSERTS

Ron Douglas

ATRIA PAPERBACK

New York   London   Toronto   Sydney   New Delhi

ATRIA PAPERBACK

A Division of Simon & Schuster, Inc.
1230 Avenue of the Americas
New York, NY 10020

First Atria Paperback edition August 2012

ATRIA PAPERBACK and colophon are trademarks of Simon & Schuster, Inc.

For information about special discounts for bulk purchases, please contact Simon & Schuster Special Sales at 1-866-506-1949 or business@simonandschuster.com.

The Simon & Schuster Speakers Bureau can bring authors to your live event. For more information or to book an event, contact the Simon & Schuster Speakers Bureau at 1-866-248-3049 or visit our website at www.simonspeakers.com.

Designed by Davina Mock-Maniscalco

Manufactured in the United States of America

10 9 8 7 6 5 4 3 2 1

Library of Congress Cataloging-in-Publication Data

Douglas, Ron.
    America's most wanted recipes just desserts : sweet indulgences from your family's favorite restaurants / Ron Douglas.
        p. cm.
    1. Desserts. I. Title.
    TX773.D6956   2012
    641.86—dc23   2012009319

ISBN 978-1-4516-2336-9
ISBN 978-1-4516-2337-6 (ebook)

Behind every great man, there's a great woman:
To my best friend and the love of my life, Nilaja.

CONTENTS

INTRODUCTION

My grandma used to always say that desserts are actually good for you because they make you happy. With all the stress of everyday life, I guess that's not too far from the truth.

When I think of the happy times in my life, I realize most of them were celebrated with some kind of dessert. Birthday parties, weddings, baby showers, holidays, job promotions, anniversaries—you name it—there was always dessert, a special treat to cap off a great day and put a smile on everyone's face.

Well, it's my hope that this cookbook will help brighten your day and put a smile on your face with the secret recipes from some of the top dessert makers in the country.

My team and I have been reverse-engineering restaurant recipes and publishing them on my website, RecipeSecrets.net, since 2003. What started out as just a hobby has evolved into one of the best-selling cookbook series in America. Since then, we've shared our results with over a million curious home cooks just like you.

And after nearly a decade of doing this, the number one question we're asked over and over is . . . "Where did you get all those recipes?"

People can't believe how easy it is to re-create dishes that taste just like you'd experience them at a restaurant.

Our answer is simple: It's been a collective effort.

I am fortunate to have a great team of contributing chefs at Recipe Secrets.net. I couldn't do it without the help of Chef Tom Grossmann of ChefTomCooks.com, Chef Todd Mohr of WebCookingClasses .com, and Marygrace Wilfrom (aka Kitchen Witch) of MamasSecret Recipes.com.

And, most important, we would be nowhere without the help of our legion of over 300,000 RecipeSecret.net subscribers, who contribute recipes that they've mastered and provide valuable feedback to help us improve our copycat creations.

If you've ever wondered how to make the amazing desserts served at your favorite restaurants, you're going to love this cookbook. Inside you'll find copycat recipes for hundreds of popular restaurant desserts that you can easily prepare in your own kitchen. Just imagine how impressed and downright amazed your family and friends will be when you tell them you made these desserts yourself. And when you *wow* your guests with these spectacular desserts, we want to hear about it. Please find us on Facebook or on RecipeSecrets.net and share your experience. That will make all our hard work worthwhile.

Enjoy!

BASIC BAKING TIPS AND FREQUENTLY ASKED QUESTIONS

Source: The Recipe Secret Forum, www.recipesecrets.net/forums

Helpful Hints for Baking Angel Food Cake

Bowls and beaters used for beating egg whites should be grease-free.

Egg whites should have no trace of egg yolk in them.

A tube pan without a removable bottom should be lined with waxed paper.

For improved flavor and a moister texture, allow the cake to "ripen" for a day after baking.

Angel food cake keeps well at room temperature if well covered. Freezing is not recommended.

Brownies and Bars

For easy removal of brownies and bar cookies (and no cleanup!), line the baking pans with foil and leave at least 3 inches of foil hanging over each end of the pans. Grease and flour the foil. When it is finished baking, remove the brownie or bar out of the pan by lifting it up by the over-hanging foil ends. Place the brownie or bar on a cutting board, remove the foil, and cut the treat into pieces.

Default Butter Measurements

¼ stick = ¹⁄₁₆ lb = ⅛ cup = 2 tbsp = 6 tsp = 28 grams

½ stick = ⅛ lb = ¼ cup = 4 tbsp = 12 tsp = 57 grams

1 stick = ¼ lb = ½ cup = 8 tbsp = 24 tsp = 113 grams

2 sticks = ½ lb = 1 cup = 16 tbsp = 48 tsp = 227 grams

3 sticks = ¾ lb = 1½ cups = 24 tbsp = 72 tsp = 340 grams

4 sticks = 1 lb = 2 cups = 32 tbsp = 96 tsp = 454 grams

Great Substitute for Buttermilk

If you don't have buttermilk, just add 1 tablespoon lemon juice or vinegar to 1 cup milk. Let stand for 10 minutes.

Baking with Chocolate

Q: Can chocolate that has seized be restored to its smooth texture?
A: Yes. Add 1 teaspoon cooking oil or solid vegetable shortening (not butter or margarine) per ounce of chocolate and stir. Repeat until the chocolate has regained its smoothness.

Q: Can burned chocolate be saved?
A: No, once the taste has been altered, it can't be rescued.

Q: When should chocolate baked items be chilled and when should they be stored at room temperature?
A: Anything made with tempered chocolate should be stored at room temperature. If untempered chocolate has been used, place the finished product in the refrigerator immediately to harden the fat crystals and maintain the glossy finish.

Chocolate Do's and Don'ts

Do cut or break up chocolate into even-sized pieces for best control when melting.

Don't rush the melting process by turning up the heat under a double boiler. The higher heat will cause the water in the bottom pan to boil and to create condensation on the bottom of the upper pan. This will, in turn, create too hot a temperature for the chocolate and it will burn.

Do partially melt chocolate, then remove the pan from the burner and continue stirring until the chocolate is completely melted and smooth. This will keep it from burning and works especially well when melting larger quantities (over 8 ounces) of chocolate.

Don't cover the saucepan or bowl while melting chocolate. Even the smallest drop of condensation will cause the chocolate to seize.

Do watch milk chocolate and white chocolate carefully while melting. They burn and seize more quickly and easily than darker semisweet or unsweetened chocolate.

Do prep. Have the rest of the ingredients ready to go at room temperature before starting a recipe containing chocolate.

Don't substitute semisweet or milk chocolate in recipes calling for unsweetened.

How to Prepare Chocolate Garnishes

Grated chocolate: Rub a hard chocolate square against the largest blades on a hand grater. Sprinkle over a mug of frothy hot chocolate, a cake, or a tart.

Chocolate shavings: Pass a vegetable peeler over the surface of room-temperature baking chocolate bars. Shave over waxed paper to prevent melting.

Chocolate curls: Using a flat spatula, spread a thin layer of melted chocolate over the backside of a cookie sheet. Refrigerate for 10 minutes. When the chocolate is firm but still flexible, cut it into strips, then place the spatula underneath the chocolate. Push firmly lengthwise along the cookie sheet. If the chocolate is too firm, allow it to sit at room temperature. Carefully lift each curl with a toothpick and refrigerate for 15 minutes. Use toothpicks to secure curls to the top of desserts, if needed.

How to Melt Chocolate

Place on top of a double boiler and melt over hot, not boiling, water.

Or place in a custard cup and set in a pan of hot water.

Or place in a heavy 1-quart saucepan and melt over low heat. If the pan is too thin, it will transfer heat too quickly and burn the chocolate.

To speed melting, break up the chocolate into smaller pieces; stir frequently. If melting the chocolate in a double boiler or in a custard cup set in a pan of water, do not boil the water to speed melting, as this will only thicken or curdle the chocolate.

If melted chocolate thickens or curdles, add vegetable shortening (not butter or margarine) a little at a time and stir until it reaches the desired consistency.

Storing Chocolate

Tempered chocolate, wrapped tightly or placed in an airtight container, will stay fresh for at least a year in a cool, dry place, preferably below 75°F and above 65°F.

Don't store chocolate in the refrigerator unless the room temperature is above 75°F. If you are going to keep chocolate in the refrigerator or freezer for any length of time, wrap it tightly. Any moisture that seeps inside the package is likely to change the chocolate's texture. Chocolate becomes hard and brittle when cold, so let it stand, tightly wrapped, at room temperature before using.

Milk chocolate and white chocolate should not be stored for longer than 9 months due to the milk solids they contain.

When stored at temperatures warmer than 78°F, the cocoa butter in the chocolate will melt and rise to the surface, creating a gray film called bloom. This film affects the appearance, but not the quality or flavor, of the chocolate. The chocolate will regain its original color when it is used in baking or cooking.

Chocolate Substitutions

One 1 oz unsweetened chocolate square = 3 tbsp cocoa + 1 tbsp vegetable shortening, hard margarine, or butter

Six 1 oz semisweet chocolate squares = 1 cup semisweet chocolate chips = 6 tbsp cocoa + 7 tbsp granulated sugar + ¼ cup vegetable shortening, hard margarine, or butter = two 1 oz unsweetened chocolate squares + 7 tbsp granulated sugar + 2 tbsp vegetable shortening, hard margarine, or butter

Four 1 oz sweetened chocolate squares = ¼ cup cocoa + ⅓ cup granulated sugar + 3 tbsp vegetable shortening, hard margarine, or butter

One 1 oz square semisweet chocolate = one 1 oz square unsweetened chocolate + 1 tbsp granulated sugar

4 oz German sweet cooking chocolate = ¼ cup unsweetened cocoa powder + ⅓ cup granulated sugar + 3 tbsp vegetable shortening, hard margarine, or butter

Egg-Beating Basics

The trick to beating egg whites successfully is knowing how much to beat them. Most recipes refer to two critical stages: soft peak and stiff peak.

When beating egg whites to the soft-peak stage, turn your electric mixer on medium speed and beat until the foam turns white and the tips of the peaks bend in soft curls when the beaters are removed. Gradually add sugar to the egg whites after soft peaks form.

With additional beating, the foam continues to thicken, becomes even whiter, and forms glossy peaks that stand straight when the beaters are removed. This is the stiff-peak stage. The egg whites at the stiff-peak stage contain all of the air they are capable of holding. At this point, do not overbeat. Further beating will produce dry, brittle peaks and reduced volume.

Measuring and Combining Flour

Q: I never seem to need as much flour as bread recipes call for. What am I doing wrong?

A: I suspect that you are getting too much flour in your cup. Accurate measuring makes a big difference. Flour compresses and packs easily. If you are scooping packed flour into your cup, you'll have a lot more flour, as much as 25 percent more. The best practice is to sift your flour. Sifted flour is light and airy. So if the recipe requires soft and fluffy flour and you use densely packed flour, you will be adding considerably more flour. That's one of the biggest reasons recipes don't turn out quite right.

If you don't own a sifter, I suggest using a scoop or whisk to churn the flour in the bag until it is light and airy. Then spoon the flour into the measuring cup and level it with a straightedge.

Q: Can I mix all-purpose and pastry flours together?
A: Yes, you can, but every flour has a purpose. Pastry flour has a low protein content to make tender pastries, while bread flour has a high protein content to make chewy bread. (Protein forms gluten and the gluten strands make the bread chewy. In pastries, we want to avoid these strands.)

All-purpose flour is a compromise between pastry and bread flours. By mixing pastry and all-purpose, you will have a further compromise, but it should be a satisfactory one for muffins, cookies, and pastries. It would not be good for bread.

DIY Self-Rising Flour
Q: Can I make my own self-rising flour? I don't have room to store an extra type of flour in my refrigerator, and I don't use it often.
A: Yes, you can. Self-rising flour is essentially all-purpose flour with salt and a leavening agent added. You can make your own self-rising flour for biscuits and pancakes by mixing in 1½ teaspoons baking powder and ½ teaspoon salt per 1 cup of all-purpose flour.

Types of Flours
There are basically four types of wheat flours used in a professional bake-shop. They range from "soft" weak flours to "hard" strong flours. They are classified as cake, pastry, bread, and high-gluten flours.
Cake flour is used to make cakes because of its delicate gluten (protein) structure.

Pastry flour has a little more gluten structure and can be used to make pie dough, biscuits, muffins, cookies, and tart dough.

Bread flour has a stronger gluten structure. It is used to make white pan bread, rolls, and hamburger buns.

High-gluten flour is the strongest of all white flours. It is used in making chewy bagels, pizza, and hard-crusted breads.

Whole Wheat Flour in a White Bread Recipe?

Q: I have a white bread recipe that I have used for years with great results. I would like to try it with whole wheat flour. Can I convert my white bread recipe to a whole wheat recipe?

A: Sure. Most commercial recipes and many others call for 40 to 60 percent whole wheat flour. I would start there. The whole wheat flour may mix a little differently than your white flour. Be prepared to adjust the amount of flour slightly. It's easier to add a little flour to a wet dough than to dribble water into a dry dough, so start out just a bit wet. Since the sharp edges of the bran in whole wheat flour will damage some of the gluten, you may want to add a couple of tablespoons of wheat gluten to your recipe. Also, a good dough conditioner will help.

Freezing Bar Cookies and Brownies

Q: I have several bar cookie and brownie recipes that I bake regularly. Can I just stick my leftovers in a plastic bag and freeze them? What is the best way to freeze bar cookies?

A: Most bar cookies freeze particularly well. There are two ways to freeze bar cookies: Wrap them individually, or wrap and freeze the whole pan after it has cooled completely.

Bar cookies should last for months in the freezer (not the freezer section of your refrigerator, which is not as cold). We've kept bar cookies in our freezer for 6 months with no noticeable loss of quality.

Fruit Pies

To thicken the juices of the fruit, mix some flour with the sugar used for sweetening the pie. When using a bottom crust, sprinkle the lined pie pan with a bit of combined sugar and flour before pouring in the fruit, and cover the fruit with a pinch of flour and sugar before putting the top crust on the pie.

For an average-sized double-crust fruit pie, use 2 to 3 cups of prepared fruit and a total of ½ to 1½ cups sugar with 2 to 4 tablespoons flour (measurements will vary according to the sweetness and juiciness of the fruit).

For added richness and flavor, dot bits of butter over the sweetened fruit before placing the top crust. Use 1 to 3 tablespoons butter for an average-sized pie.

Deep-dish fruit pies should use alternate layers of the fruit and the sugar-flour mixture in order to assure even sweetening and thickening of the fruit juices. Most call for about 4 cups of fruit, with sugar, flour, and butter increased proportionately.

World's Easiest Piecrust

2 cups pastry flour
¾ cup vegetable shortening,
  softened
2 tablespoons margarine,
  softened

½ teaspoon salt
½ teaspoon baking powder
¼ cup plus 2 tablespoons water

Place all the ingredients in a plastic bowl with a lid, and cover. Place one hand on top of the lid and the other hand on the bottom of the bowl, then shake until a dough ball forms. Remove the lid, scrape the sides of the bowl, and replace the lid. Repeat until all the ingredients are incorporated. Remove the dough from the bowl and place on a lightly floured surface; divide into 2 pieces. On a lightly floured surface, roll one piece at a time into an 10- or 11-inch circle. Place in a pie plate and fill with your favorite filling.

Makes two 8- or 9-inch piecrusts

Perfect Pie Dough

When rolling out my pie dough, I roll it on a lightly floured plastic place mat with a wet dishcloth underneath to prevent sliding. I place a large dinner plate on top of the rolled-out dough and cut around the edges (or just pull the excess dough off). This creates the perfect size for a 9- or 10-inch pie plate. And no matter what the recipe says, I never, ever refrigerate the dough.

Pie Shell Shrinkage

Q: How do you keep a pie shell from shrinking while baking?
A: There are two conditions that will cause shrinking of an unbaked pie shell during baking: too much gluten in the flour and too much water in the water-to-shortening ratio. As the shell bakes, the gluten tends to tighten and pull the shell together. Also as the shell bakes, water evaporates and causes shrinkage.

Here are some suggestions:

1. Use a low-protein flour. It's the proteins that form the gluten. An all-purpose flour will work, but pastry flour is better.
2. Don't work the dough too much. Working the dough develops the gluten.
3. After you have rolled the dough, let it sit for 5 minutes. That gives the gluten a chance to relax.
4. Check your water-to-shortening ratio. The shortening will inhibit gluten development and will not evaporate and cause shrinking as water does.
5. Don't stretch the dough to fit the pan. Stretched dough tends to have a memory and slips back into the original shape during baking.
6. Use pie weights. You can buy pie weights at RecipeSecrets.net or in specialty shops.

Fresh Pumpkin vs. Canned

Q: I love fresh pumpkin in my recipes and don't care for the taste of canned pumpkin. Can I use an equal amount of fresh pumpkin puree in place of canned?

A: Yes, I do it all the time. Sometimes our fresh puree has a little higher water content, especially if the pumpkin was not quite mature, and we have to adjust the water content a little in the recipe. If we bake the pumpkin instead of steaming, we rarely have that problem.

Incidentally, we use winter squash and yams interchangeably with pumpkin. In most recipes, we can't tell the difference between winter squash and pumpkin. Yam puree (usually we just mash it) is a little different but very good in most recipes calling for pumpkin.

Flaming a Fruitcake or Other Dessert

To flame a fruitcake or other dessert, dip several cubes of sugar in a small amount of lemon extract, then place them on top of the dessert. Ignite immediately, and you'll get a lovely blue flame.

Working with Yeast

When using yeast, less is better. Too much yeast tends to make crumbly bread, which won't stay fresh as long. If you have too little yeast, the dough may take longer to rise, but the longer rise will give the bread some complex flavors that are more sourdough-like and delightful. Great bread bakers are patient.

When using instant yeast, remember that it takes less instant yeast to equal 1 tablespoon of active yeast, about 2½ teaspoons. Don't over-yeast your bread. If your bread rises faster than it should and has a yeasty, beer-like odor, you've probably added too much yeast.

AMERICA'S MOST WANTED RECIPES

Sweet Indulgences from
Your Family's Favorite Restaurants

JUST DESSERTS

1900 PARK FARE
Bread Pudding

AN EXCELLENT ENDING TO ANY MEAL, THIS CLASSIC DESSERT IS RICH IN BUTTER, CINNAMON, AND SAVORY PUDDING. VANILLA SAUCE (PAGE 2) IS THE PERFECT FINISHING TOUCH TO THIS WELL-KNOWN FAVORITE.

1 loaf day-old white bread, crusts trimmed, cut into 1-inch cubes
6 eggs
2 cups sugar
1 teaspoon vanilla extract
1 cup heavy cream

½ teaspoon kosher salt
1 teaspoon ground cinnamon
½ cup golden raisins (optional)
8 tablespoons (1 stick) unsalted butter, softened and cut into pieces

1. Preheat the oven to 325°F.

2. Layer the cubed bread over the bottom of a 5 by 9½-inch loaf pan.

3. Beat the eggs and sugar until well blended. Add the vanilla extract and stir.

4. Whisk in the heavy cream, salt, and cinnamon. Include the raisins, if you are using them.

5. Pour the custard over the bread cubes and lightly press the bread down with the back of a wooden spoon to ensure all the bread is completely covered.

6. Dot the top of the pudding with the pieces of butter.

7. Set the loaf pan in a larger pan of hot water. The water level should come halfway up the sides of the loaf pan.

8. Bake in the hot oven for about 1 hour, or until the top of the loaf is golden brown and the custard is set.

Serves 10

For an elegant presentation, unmold the bread pudding and serve it on a warmed platter surrounded by some vanilla sauce.

1900 PARK FARE
Vanilla Sauce

THIS IS ALSO KNOWN AS CRÈME ANGLAISE, A DESSERT SAUCE BASED ON MILK, EGGS, AND CREAM, WITH THE DISTINCTIVE ESSENCE OF VANILLA.

1 cup milk
1 cup heavy cream
2 tablespoons vanilla extract

3 egg yolks, at room temperature
½ cup sugar

1. Combine the milk, heavy cream, and vanilla extract in a medium saucepan and bring to a boil; remove the pan from the heat.

2. Whisk together the egg yolks and sugar.

3. Ladle ½ cup of the boiled milk mixture into the yolks and sugar, whisking constantly. Continue with the remaining milk mixture, pouring slowly and whisking constantly so that the yolks don't cook.

4. Return the combined mixture to the saucepan and cook over medium heat, stirring constantly. Do not let it boil.

5. Half-fill a large bowl with ice and cold water. Pour the custard into a smaller bowl and set it in the ice bath. Let the sauce cool, stirring occasionally.

Makes about 2 cups

Store any remaining sauce in a covered container and refrigerate.

'21' CLUB
Eggnog Soufflé

THE '21' CLUB IS A PREMIER NEW YORK ESTABLISHMENT WITH A VIBRANT MENU SPECIALIZING IN THE BEST OF AMERICAN CUISINE. THE RESTAURANT PAYS HOMAGE TO ITS DECADES-LONG HISTORY WITH SEVERAL MENU ITEMS FROM THE PAST. THIS EGGNOG SOUFFLÉ IS A SEASONAL SPECIALTY.

8 tablespoons (1 stick) cold unsalted butter, cut into small pieces
½ cup bread flour
4 cups milk
½ cup sugar
2 teaspoons ground cinnamon
1 teaspoon ground nutmeg
¼ cup spiced rum (optional)
6 eggs, separated
2 teaspoons vanilla extract

1. Preheat the oven to 350°F. Coat a 2-quart soufflé dish with butter and sugar.
2. Cut the butter into the flour with a pastry cutter, or using your hands, until it resembles small peas.
3. Combine the milk, sugar, cinnamon, and nutmeg in a saucepan over medium heat and bring to a boil. Add the spiced rum at this stage, if using.
4. Reduce the heat and whisk in the flour-butter mixture, adding a little at a time and whisking after each addition. Continue whisking over low heat, stirring constantly until the mixture thickens and begins to pull away from the sides of the saucepan.
5. Let the mixture cool to room temperature, 5 to 8 minutes.
6. Add the egg yolks, one at a time, whisking after each addition. Add the vanilla extract.
7. Whisk the egg whites to soft peaks, then use a rubber spatula to fold the whites into the batter—do not overmix the batter.

8. Spoon the mixture into the prepared soufflé dish and bake in the center of the hot oven for 12 minutes—the soufflé will be doubled in size. Serve immediately.

Serves 4

A vanilla cream sauce with spiced rum or the same spices as in the soufflé can be prepared ahead of time and kept warm, then spooned over the hot soufflé when serving.

'21' CLUB
Flourless Chocolate Torte

THIS RICH, FUDGE-LIKE TORTE IS NOT LARGE, SO EVERY WONDERFUL BITE IS WORTH IT. TRY RASPBERRY SYRUP IN ADDITION TO THE DARK CHOCOLATE GLAZE.

Cake
8 ounces semisweet chocolate, chopped
½ pound (2 sticks) unsalted butter, softened and cut into pieces
5 eggs
¼ cup sugar
¼ cup dark corn syrup

Chocolate Glaze
8 ounces semisweet chocolate, chopped
¾ cup heavy cream
1½ tablespoons unsalted butter, softened
1½ tablespoons light corn syrup

1. Preheat the oven to 350°F. Butter and flour a 9-inch cake pan. Tap out any excess flour and line the bottom with a round of parchment paper.

2. To make the cake, set a bowl over a pot of simmering water, being careful not to let the bottom of the bowl touch the water. Add the chocolate and butter pieces and stir until they melt and are blended.

3. In a separate bowl, beat the eggs and sugar with an electric mixer until the eggs are light and fluffy.

4. Slowly add the corn syrup, beating until slowly dissolving ribbons form when the beaters are lifted.

5. Fold the chocolate mixture into the beaten eggs until well blended.

6. Pour the batter into the prepared pan and bake for about 1 hour. A knife inserted in the center should come out clean. Let the cake cool on a rack, then invert it onto a 7½-inch cardboard cake round and peel off the parchment paper.

7. To make the chocolate glaze, combine the chocolate and heavy cream in a medium saucepan and warm the pan enough to melt the chocolate,

stirring constantly. Whisk in the butter and corn syrup. Remove the pan from the heat and let the mixture cool.

8. Put the cake on a wire rack with paper towels underneath to catch the drips while glazing.

9. Pour the glaze over the cake, then spread it with a spatula to evenly cover the top and sides.

10. Refrigerate the cake overnight. Cut into thin slices and serve cold.

Serves 10

'21' CLUB
Rice Pudding

A BIG HIT IN ANY WEATHER, THE SOFTLY COOKED RICE ABSORBS THE DEEP FLAVORS OF A SINGLE VANILLA BEAN BLENDED WITH CREAM AND SUGAR. RAISINS ARE A SWEET OPTION.

4 cups milk
2 cups heavy cream
½ teaspoon kosher salt
1 vanilla bean, split lengthwise
1 cup sugar

¾ cup long-grain rice
½ cup raisins soaked in brandy (optional)
1 egg yolk
1½ cups whipped cream

1. Combine the milk, heavy cream, salt, and the vanilla bean in a medium saucepan. Stir in ¾ cup of the sugar and whisk until it starts to dissolve.

2. Bring the milk mixture to a boil and stir in the rice. Let the rice simmer, covered, for 1½ to 1¾ hours over very low heat. The rice should be soft but not overly gummy.

3. Remove the pan from the heat and remove the vanilla bean. Stir in the soaked raisins, if using. Let the mixture cool slightly.

4. Whisk in the remaining ¼ cup sugar and the egg yolk. Continue to let the pudding cool down.

5. Preheat the broiler, and position the rack as far as possible from the heat source.

6. Fold in all but 2 tablespoons of the whipped cream.

7. Spoon the rice pudding into one large baking dish or eight 8-ounce ramekins. Spread the remaining 2 tablespoons of the whipped cream in a thin layer over the top of the baking dish or individual ramekins.

8. Broil the pudding just until the whipped cream on top is lightly browned. Remove from the broiler and either serve immediately or chill before serving.

Have this impressive dessert ready to go by making it ahead.
It will keep for up to 3 days in the refrigerator.
Broil it at the last instant for a true restaurant experience.

2BLEU
Everything Mud Pie

USING A FEW PURCHASED ITEMS MAKES THIS A QUICK AND EASY DESSERT FOR EVERY DAY OR A SPECIAL OCCASION.

One 3½-ounce package instant French vanilla pudding mix

One 3½-ounce package sugar-free instant chocolate fudge pudding mix

2 cups low-fat milk

One 8-ounce package reduced-fat cream cheese, softened

2 large ripe bananas, thinly sliced

1 chocolate graham cracker piecrust

One 8-ounce package Cool Whip Lite

¼ cup chopped unsalted raw peanuts

2 tablespoons chocolate syrup

2 tablespoons caramel syrup

1. Combine the instant pudding mixes with the milk in a large bowl. Using an electric mixer on low speed, beat the ingredients until well blended. Add the cream cheese and beat until smooth.

2. Increase the speed to medium and continue to beat the mixture for another 2 minutes, or until it is fluffy.

3. Layer half of the banana slices over the bottom of the piecrust. Pour the filling mixture into the piecrust and smooth the top. Layer the remaining banana slices over the top. Sprinkle the chopped peanuts evenly over the pie.

4. Spread the Cool Whip over the top of the pie. Drizzle the chocolate syrup in a zigzag pattern over the Cool Whip, then do the same with the caramel syrup in the opposite direction.

5. Refrigerate the pie for at least 4 hours before serving.

Serves 6

You can easily substitute chopped walnuts, pecans, or almonds if you would prefer not to use the peanuts.

AKERSHUS ROYAL BANQUET HALL

Princess Cake

DELICATE LAYERS OF SPONGE CAKE ARE FILLED WITH RASPBERRY JAM, THEN SMOTHERED IN A RICH PASTRY CREAM.

Cake

3 eggs

1 cup sugar

1 cup all-purpose flour, sifted

4 tablespoons (½ stick) unsalted
butter, melted

Pastry Cream

½ cup plus 1 tablespoon
cornstarch

3 cups milk

3 eggs

¾ cup sugar

2 teaspoons vanilla extract

8 tablespoons (1 stick) unsalted
butter, cut into pieces

1 cup seedless raspberry jam,
slightly heated

1. Preheat the oven to 375°F. Lightly grease an 8-inch cake pan.

2. To make the cake, combine the eggs and sugar in a medium bowl and beat on high speed with an electric mixer until the mixture is light and foamy.

3. Gradually fold in the sifted flour. When the flour has been well blended, fold in the melted butter.

4. Pour a thin layer of the batter into the prepared cake pan; it should be about ¼ inch thick. Bake the cake until golden brown, 8 to 10 minutes. Carefully remove the cake from the pan and set it on a plate to cool.

5. Repeat this process with the remaining batter until you have a total of 4 cake layers. Remember to lightly grease the pan each time you pour in the batter.

6. While the cake layers are baking, prepare the pastry cream. Whisk together the cornstarch and 1 cup of the milk. When the cornstarch is dissolved, add the eggs to the mixture and mix until smooth.

7. In a medium saucepan, combine the remaining 2 cups milk, the sugar, vanilla extract, and butter. Bring the mixture to a boil, stirring constantly.

8. Reduce the heat to medium and whisk in the cornstarch mixture. Whisk until the pastry cream is thickened and smooth. Remove from the heat and let cool.

9. To assemble the cake, place the first cake layer on a cake plate. Spread a portion of the raspberry jam evenly over the first layer of cake. Top with the second layer and repeat the process until all the layers are used.

10. Place the stacked layers in the cake pan and refrigerate for 5 minutes, or until the jam on the top layer is set and not runny.

11. Pour the cooled pastry cream over the cake, making sure it goes down the inside of the pan. Refrigerate the cake for at least 4 hours, then cut into slices and serve.

Serves 8 to 10

*Strawberry jelly works just as well as the raspberry jam.
Just make sure it isn't cold and spreads easily,
so that it doesn't tear the thin layers of sponge cake.*

THE AMERICAN CLUB
Three-Nut Torte

THE AMERICAN CLUB RESORT IN KOHLER, WISCONSIN, IS A LUXURY DESTINATION AND DINING EXPERIENCE OFFERING TWELVE RESTAURANTS AND LOUNGES. THE MENUS CHANGE WITH THE SEASONS AND OFFER SPECIALTIES OF THE REGION.

2½ cups granulated sugar
1 cup heavy cream
1 cup coarsely chopped walnuts
¾ cup slivered almonds
¾ cup chopped pecans
½ pound (2 sticks) unsalted butter, softened

1 egg
½ teaspoon vanilla extract
2¾ cups all-purpose flour
1 egg white
Powdered sugar, for garnish

1. Preheat the oven to 350°F. Spray the bottom and sides of a 10-inch springform pan with cooking spray.

2. Combine 2 cups of the granulated sugar and the heavy cream in a medium saucepan over medium heat. Stir until the sugar dissolves. Stir in the walnuts, almonds, and pecans, then set the mixture aside and let cool.

3. Cream the butter and the remaining ½ cup granulated sugar until light and fluffy. Add the whole egg and the vanilla extract and beat until well blended.

4. Gradually stir in the flour, and mix until well blended. Measure 2 cups of the dough and spread it over the bottom and up the sides of the prepared springform pan, pressing gently to even it out.

5. Roll out the remaining dough between two sheets of waxed paper into a 10-inch circle and set aside.

6. Spoon the nut mixture evenly over the dough in the pan. Top with the circle of dough and pinch the edges to seal the torte.

7. Whisk the egg white with 1 tablespoon water and brush it over the top of the torte. Bake the torte in the hot oven for 1 hour. Let the torte cool before releasing the sides of the pan. Dust with powdered sugar, and cut into slim portions for serving.

Serves 16

ANTHONY'S
Chocolate Soufflé Torte

THIS DESSERT IS SHORT ON INGREDIENTS BUT LONG ON RICH CHOCOLATE FLA-VOR. FOR BEST RESULTS, USE A SPRINGFORM PAN AND NONFLAVORED COOKING SPRAY.

8 ounces bittersweet chocolate chips
8 tablespoons (1 stick) unsalted butter, softened

5 eggs, separated
1 cup granulated sugar
Powdered sugar (optional)

1. Preheat the oven to 350°F. Coat an 8-inch springform pan with cooking spray.

2. Combine the chocolate chips and butter in a bowl set over a pan of simmering water. Stir until melted and well combined. Remove the bowl from the pan and keep warm.

3. In a separate bowl, with an electric mixer on high speed, beat the egg yolks with ½ cup of the granulated sugar until light and foamy.

4. Using a rubber spatula, scrape the chocolate mixture into the whipped yolks. Beat on medium speed until well blended.

5. With clean beaters, whip the egg whites in a stainless-steel or glass bowl on high speed until they turn foamy. Gradually add the remaining ½ cup granulated sugar, then beat on high speed until soft peaks form.

6. Gently fold the whites into the chocolate-yolk mixture, blending carefully but thoroughly. A rubber spatula works best for this.

7. Carefully transfer the mixture to the prepared springform pan and set in the center of the oven with a large pan of hot water on the rack below it.

8. Bake the soufflé for 45 to 50 minutes. The cake should be firm to the touch and the top covered with cracks. Let rest in the pan on a wire rack

for 10 to 20 minutes. The soufflé will deflate and drop below the rim of the pan as it cools.

9. Invert the cake onto a serving plate and release the rim, then carefully remove the pan bottom from the cake. Dust with powdered sugar, if desired, and serve warm or at room temperature.

Serves 16

APPLEBEE'S
Chimi Cheesecake

THIS IS A SWEET AND CRUNCHY VERSION OF TEX-MEX CHIMICHANGAS. FLOUR TORTI-
LLAS ARE FILLED WITH CREAM CHEESE, APPLES, AND TOFFEE, THEN FRIED AND TOPPED
WITH ICE CREAM WHILE STILL HOT.

Two 8-ounce packages cream cheese, softened
1 cup sugar
2 eggs
1 teaspoon vanilla extract
¼ cup plus 2 tablespoons all-purpose flour
½ cup coarsely chopped almond toffee candy

One 20-ounce can apple pie filling, well drained
Twelve 6½-inch flour tortillas
4 cups canola oil, for deep-frying
3 tablespoons ground cinnamon
Vanilla ice cream and caramel sauce, for serving

1. With an electric mixer, beat together the cream cheese and ½ cup of the sugar until fluffy. Add the eggs, one at a time, beating after each addition. Stir in the vanilla extract.

2. Gradually add the flour, mixing thoroughly to avoid lumps.

3. Add the chopped toffee candy and blend, then fold in the apples and stir until all the ingredients are well mixed.

4. To assemble the chimis, spoon a portion of the filling down each tortilla, a little off center. Fold over the side nearest the filling, then tuck in both ends and roll the tortilla up. Place it, seam side down, on a tray.

5. Continue making the chimis until all the tortillas and filling have been used up. Refrigerate the chimis for at least 30 minutes or up to 1 hour to let the cream cheese set.

6. Preheat the oven to 350°F.

7. Preheat the oil to 375°F in a deep-fryer or a medium saucepan with a heavy bottom. Fry each chimi cheesecake until golden on all sides. Drain on paper towels.

8. Place the fried chimis on a baking sheet, seam side down, and bake in the hot oven for 20 to 25 minutes.

9. Combine the remaining ½ cup sugar with the cinnamon and sprinkle the chimis with the mixture. Serve the chimis while still warm with a scoop of vanilla ice cream and some caramel sauce poured over or on the side.

Serves 12

The chimis can be prepared ahead of time and kept refrigerated and tightly sealed with plastic wrap until it's time to fry them.

APPLEBEE'S
Chocolate Sin Cake

YOU WILL NEVER GO BACK TO PACKAGED CAKE AGAIN. APPLEBEE'S DRAWS CUSTOM-
ERS FROM MILES AROUND FOR THIS FAMOUS FLOURLESS CHOCOLATE CONFECTION.

½ pound (2 sticks) unsalted
   butter, cut into pieces
6 ounces semisweet chocolate,
   chopped
2 ounces bittersweet chocolate,
   chopped
1 teaspoon vanilla extract
½ cup packed dark brown sugar
4 eggs, at room temperature

4 egg yolks, at room temperature
6 tablespoons cornstarch
One 10-ounce package frozen
   raspberries in heavy syrup,
   thawed
12 triangle-shaped thin cookies
   or chocolate wafers
12 sprigs fresh mint
1 pint fresh raspberries

1. Preheat the oven to 375°F. Butter the sides and bottoms of twelve
   4-ounce ramekins.

2. Combine the butter in a medium mixing bowl with the semisweet and
   bittersweet chocolates. Set the bowl over a pan of simmering water
   and add the vanilla extract. Stir until the ingredients are well blended.
   Remove the bowl from the pan and keep warm.

3. In a separate bowl, combine the brown sugar with the eggs and egg
   yolks. Beat on high speed with an electric mixer until the mixture is
   thick and the volume has more than tripled.

4. Reduce the speed to low and add the cornstarch, 1 tablespoon at a time,
   beating after each addition.

5. Increase the speed again to high, and whip the mixture for about 5 minutes, or until soft peaks form.

6. Using a rubber spatula, fold the chocolate mixture into the egg mixture.
   This has to be done gently to avoid deflating the egg batter.

7. When the chocolate mixture and the egg batter are well combined,
   gently spoon a portion of the batter into each prepared ramekin. Bake in
   the hot oven for 10 minutes, or until each cake is lightly crusted.

8. Remove the cakes from the oven and let them cool completely before covering them with plastic wrap and refrigerating.

9. When ready to serve, run a thin knife around the edges of each cake to loosen it from the ramekin. Invert each ramekin into the center of a dessert plate.

10. Puree the frozen raspberries and strain them to remove the seeds. Pour a little of the sauce around each cake and garnish the plate with either a cookie or a chocolate wafer and a sprig of mint. Arrange a few of the fresh raspberries on the top of the cake and place a few in the sauce as well.

Serves 12

The raspberry puree can be made well ahead of time.
Once the cakes are baked and cooled, they can stay refrigerated,
well wrapped in plastic, for up to 3 days.

APPLEBEE'S
Cinnamon-Apple Turnover

THESE FRESH APPLE TURNOVERS CAN BE MADE AHEAD AND POPPED IN THE OVEN FOR A JUST-BAKED TREAT.

One 12 by 12-inch frozen puff pastry sheet
1 large Granny Smith apple, peeled, cored, and cut into small dice
½ cup unsweetened applesauce
¼ cup packed light brown sugar

1 teaspoon ground cinnamon
1 teaspoon vanilla extract
½ teaspoon ground nutmeg
1 tablespoon cornstarch
2 tablespoons unsalted butter, melted

1. Preheat the oven to 400°F.

2. Thaw the puff pastry sheet at room temperature and unfold it.

3. Cut the pastry into nine 4 by 4-inch squares and lay the squares on a sheet pan coated with cooking spray.

4. Combine the diced apple, applesauce, brown sugar, cinnamon, vanilla extract, nutmeg, and cornstarch in a bowl and stir to blend thoroughly.

5. Spoon an equal amount of the apple mixture onto the center of each pastry square. Fold one corner over to the other to make a triangle. Seal the edges with your fingers or use the tines of a fork.

6. Arrange the turnovers so that there is about 1 inch between them on the sheet pan, and brush them with the melted butter.

7. Bake for 20 to 25 minutes, until golden brown. Serve warm.

Makes 9 turnovers

A light dusting of powdered sugar makes a nice finishing touch.

APPLEBEE'S
Maple Butter Blondies

WHITE CHOCOLATE AND PECANS ARE BLENDED IN A BUTTERY BLONDIE, THEN SERVED UNDER A SCOOP OF BUTTER PECAN ICE CREAM AND A RICH SAUCE OF SOUR CREAM AND PURE MAPLE SYRUP.

Blondies

- ¾ pound (3 sticks) unsalted butter, softened
- 1½ cups packed golden brown sugar
- 2 eggs
- 2 teaspoons vanilla extract
- 1½ cups all-purpose flour
- 1 teaspoon baking powder
- ½ teaspoon kosher salt
- 1 cup chopped pecans
- 1 cup white chocolate chips

Maple Butter Sauce

- 1½ cups granulated sugar
- ½ cup pure maple syrup
- 12 tablespoons (1½ sticks) unsalted butter, softened
- ½ cup sour cream, at room temperature
- ½ teaspoon vanilla extract

Butter pecan ice cream, for serving

1. Preheat the oven to 350°F. Grease a 9 by 9-inch baking dish and set it aside.

2. To make the blondies, beat the butter and brown sugar with an electric mixer until light and fluffy. Add the eggs, one at a time, beating after each addition. Add the vanilla extract and blend it in.

3. Sift together the flour, baking powder, and salt. Gradually stir the dry ingredients into the butter mixture. Stir in the chopped pecans and white chocolate chips.

4. Pour the batter into the prepared baking dish and bake for 30 minutes, or until a knife inserted in the center comes out clean. Let the blondie cool while preparing the sauce.

5. To make the maple butter sauce, whisk together the granulated sugar, maple syrup, and butter in a small saucepan over medium heat. Let the sauce simmer for 2 minutes. Remove the pan from the heat and let it cool for a minute or two. Whisk in the sour cream and vanilla extract.

6. Cut the blondie into 9 large squares. Serve with a scoop of butter pecan ice cream and a drizzle of the maple butter sauce.

Serves 9

The blondies can be stored at room temperature, wrapped in plastic, for up to 5 days, and can be served chilled or at room temperature. Try the blondies with vanilla or toffee ice cream in place of the butter pecan and top them with a few more chopped pecans.

APPLEBEE'S

Strawberry Cheesecake Dessert Shooter

DESSERT SHOOTERS ARE A POPULAR RESTAURANT TREND EASY TO DUPLICATE AT HOME. USE 6-OUNCE HIGHBALL OR ROCKS BARWARE GLASSES FOR AN ELEGANT PRESENTATION.

Cheesecake Filling
1½ (8-ounce) packages cream cheese, softened
½ cup granulated sugar
2 eggs
¼ cup sour cream
1 teaspoon vanilla extract

Toppings
1 cup sliced strawberries, fresh or frozen and thawed
2 tablespoons granulated sugar
½ cup heavy cream
2 tablespoons powdered sugar
1 teaspoon vanilla extract

4 tablespoons (½ stick) unsalted butter, melted
½ cup graham cracker crumbs

1. To make the cheesecake filling, beat the cream cheese and granulated sugar with an electric mixer until light and fluffy. Add the eggs, one at a time, beating well after each addition. Stir in the sour cream and vanilla extract and blend well.

2. Set the bowl with the cream cheese mixture over a pan of simmering water and cook until thickened, about 8 minutes, stirring frequently. Pour the thickened mixture into a container and let cool before refrigerating, covered, for at least 4 hours.

3. To make the toppings, toss the strawberries with the granulated sugar and let them marinate while the cheesecake mixture is chilling.

4. Meanwhile, beat the heavy cream to soft peaks, add the powdered sugar and vanilla extract, then beat to stiff peaks. Refrigerate the whipped cream until ready to use.

5. To assemble the shooters, when the cheesecake is chilled, combine the melted butter with the graham cracker crumbs, and spoon 2 tablespoons into each 6-ounce glass.

6. Spoon equal amounts of the cheesecake filling over the crumbs, then top with the strawberries and any juice that has collected in the container.

7. Finish each shooter with a dollop of whipped cream. Serve immediately or refrigerate for up to 1 hour.

Serves 6

APPLEBEE'S
Triple-Chocolate Meltdown

TWO CHOCOLATE SAUCES AND A MOLTEN CHOCOLATE CAKE MAKE A SURPRISINGLY SIMPLE BUT STUNNING DESSERT.

2 cups heavy cream
1 cup white chocolate chips
1 cup semisweet chocolate chips
1 pound bittersweet chocolate chips

8 tablespoons (1 stick) unsalted butter, softened
1½ cups sugar
6 eggs
1½ cups all-purpose flour
Vanilla ice cream, for serving

1. In a small saucepan, bring 1 cup of the heavy cream to a simmer.

2. Remove the pan from the heat and whisk in the white chocolate chips. Whisk constantly until the chocolate is melted. Let the sauce cool, stirring occasionally, about 30 minutes.

3. Repeat the process with the semisweet chocolate chips—simmer the remaining 1 cup cream, whisk and melt the chips, and let cool.

4. Preheat the oven to 400°F. Butter six 6-ounce ramekins, thoroughly coating the bottom and sides.

5. Combine the bittersweet chocolate chips and softened butter in a medium bowl set over a pan of simmering water. Melt the butter and chocolate, stirring until well blended.

6. Remove the bowl from the pan and let the mixture cool for a few minutes.

7. In a separate bowl, beat the sugar and eggs with an electric mixer until foamy, about 2 minutes. Using a spatula, scrape in all of the chocolate-butter mixture and blend it into the egg mixture on medium speed.

8. Add the flour, ½ cup at a time, beating on medium speed after each addition, until it is completely incorporated. Do not overmix the ingredients.

9. Pour the batter into the prepared ramekins and place the ramekins on a sheet pan. Bake for about 18 minutes. The cakes should be slightly crusty on top and still liquid in the center when pierced with a clean knife. Let the ramekins rest on the sheet pan for 2 to 3 minutes. Don't let them cool too much before serving, as the butter that coats the ramekins will not release the cakes if it is allowed to start hardening.

10. Invert each cake onto a dessert plate. Spoon some of each sauce around the cake, and drizzle a little more of each over the top. Serve with a scoop of ice cream on the side.

Serves 6

ARBY'S
Apple Turnovers

THESE FLAKY TURNOVERS HAVE BEEN A HIT AT ARBY'S SINCE THEY FIRST APPEARED ON THE MENU. USING FROZEN PUFF PASTRY MAKES PERFECT TURNOVERS EVERY TIME.

Turnovers
One 17.25-ounce package frozen
  puff pastry sheets
2 tablespoons fresh lemon juice
4 cups plus 1 tablespoon water
4 Granny Smith apples, peeled,
  cored, and sliced ⅛-inch thick
2 tablespoons unsalted butter

1 cup packed golden brown sugar
2 teaspoons ground cinnamon
1 teaspoon vanilla extract
1 tablespoon cornstarch

Glaze
1 cup powdered sugar
2 tablespoons milk

1. To make the turnovers, thaw the puff pastry sheets in the refrigerator and keep them chilled until ready to use.

2. Combine the lemon juice with 4 cups of the water in a large bowl. Once the apples are peeled and sliced, keep them in the water so they won't discolor.

3. Preheat the oven to 400°F.

4. Melt the butter over medium heat in a large skillet. Drain the apples thoroughly and add them to the pan.

5. Add the brown sugar, cinnamon, and vanilla extract and cook the apples, stirring frequently with a wooden spoon, until they are softened. Mix in the remaining 1 tablespoon water and the cornstarch.

6. Trim each puff pastry sheet into a square, then cut each square into 4 equal quarters.

7. Spoon a portion of the sautéed apples onto the center of each pastry and fold one corner over the other to form a triangle. Pinch the sides of the dough together to seal the turnovers.

8. Place the turnovers on an ungreased baking sheet about 1 inch apart, and bake until puffed and golden brown, about 25 minutes. Let them cool before glazing.

9. To make the glaze, combine the powdered sugar and milk, then drizzle in a zigzag pattern over the tops of the turnovers.

Serves 8

The turnovers can also be finished with a simple sprinkling of powdered sugar. To give them extra color, brush each pastry with beaten egg and a sprinkling of granulated sugar before baking.

BABBO RISTORANTE E ENOTECA
Fregolotta

A SEASONAL SPECIALTY OF MARIO BATALI'S SIGNATURE RESTAURANT IN MANHATTAN, THIS CRUMBLY CAKE CAN BE SERVED WITH A GLASS OF GRAPPA OR A TOPPING OF FRESH FRUIT.

1 cup all-purpose flour	2 teaspoons olive oil
¾ cup finely ground almonds	1 tablespoon finely grated
¼ cup sugar	lemon zest
1 tablespoon fine cornmeal	½ teaspoon vanilla extract
½ teaspoon kosher salt	1 tablespoon grappa, or other
4 tablespoons (½ stick) unsalted	liqueur such as brandy, sherry,
butter, cut into pieces	or port
2 egg yolks	

1. Preheat the oven to 350°F. Coat a 9-inch cake pan with vegetable shortening or cooking spray.

2. Combine the flour, ground almonds, sugar, cornmeal, and salt in the bowl of a food processor and pulse just until the mixture is blended.

3. Add the pieces of butter and pulse until they are thoroughly blended and the ground mixture is the texture of fine meal.

4. Whisk together the egg yolks, olive oil, lemon zest, vanilla extract, and the grappa. Gradually stir the dry ingredients into the egg mixture and mix well.

5. Press the dough onto the bottom of the prepared cake pan, pressing evenly.

6. Bake in the hot oven for 15 to 20 minutes, until the cake is golden brown and springs back when touched in the center.

7. Let the cake cool completely in the pan, then unmold it. *Fregolotta* is traditionally broken into crumbly chunks and served with a glass of grappa, which is sometimes poured over the cake. A sprinkling of powdered sugar would do just as well.

Serves 10 to 12

Grappa is a traditional Italian after-dinner drink made from the discarded products of the wine-making process. The flavor depends on the grapes used in the wine—the stronger and drier types are preferred in Italy, while the sweeter varieties have gained popularity in the United States.

BABBO RISTORANTE E ENOTECA
Saffron Panna Cotta with Rhubarb Marmellata

PANNA COTTA MEANS "COOKED CREAM" IN ITALIAN. THIS VERSION IS SILKY SMOOTH, BRIGHTLY COLORED FROM THE SAFFRON, AND RICHLY FLAVORED WITH VANILLA AND THE RHUBARB MARMALADE.

Panna Cotta
5 sheets gelatin
3¼ cups heavy cream
¾ cups sugar
1 tablespoon finely grated
   lemon zest
½ teaspoon saffron threads
1 cup milk

Rhubarb Marmellata
3 stalks rhubarb, thinly sliced
½ cup sugar
1 vanilla bean, split lengthwise

1. Chill four 6-ounce ramekins or ceramic tart molds.
2. To make the panna cotta, soften the gelatin sheets in cold water.
3. Meanwhile, combine the heavy cream, sugar, lemon zest, and saffron in a medium saucepan and bring to a boil, whisking frequently, then remove the pan from the heat. Let the cream mixture sit for about 10 minutes.
4. Squeeze the excess water from the gelatin sheets and stir them into the cream mixture until completely dissolved.
5. Strain the mixture through a fine-mesh strainer into a bowl and whisk in the milk.
6. Pour the mixture into the chilled ramekins or ceramic tart molds, and refrigerate until firm.

7. Make the rhubarb *marmellata* while the panna cotta is chilling. Combine the sliced rhubarb and the sugar in a small saucepan. Scrape out the seeds of the vanilla bean using a small paring knife and add the seeds to the rhubarb mixture. Simmer the mixture over medium heat, stirring frequently, until the rhubarb is soft, about 15 minutes. Remove from the heat and let the sauce cool completely. Strain the *marmellata* into a bowl through a fine-mesh strainer.

8. Unmold the panna cotta onto dessert plates and spoon the *marmellata* over the top and around each portion.

Serves 4

BABBO RISTORANTE E ENOTECA
Sachertorte

THIS VIENNESE CLASSIC IS UPDATED AND GIVEN A NEW TWIST WITH AN APRICOT-BRANDY MARMALADE SET BETWEEN LAYERS OF CHOCOLATE SPONGE CAKE, AND DRIZZLED WITH A WARM CHOCOLATE GLAZE.

Note: You will need a 9-inch cardboard cake round and a candy thermometer for this recipe.

Cake
8 tablespoons (1 stick) unsalted butter, softened
½ cup powdered sugar
6 eggs, separated
½ cup bittersweet chocolate chips, melted
¼ teaspoon kosher salt
¼ cup granulated sugar
1 cup all-purpose flour

Marmellata
1 cup apricot preserves
3 tablespoons granulated sugar
3 tablespoons brandy

Chocolate Glaze
¾ cup granulated sugar
½ cup water
1 teaspoon vanilla extract
½ cup bittersweet chocolate chips

1. Preheat the oven to 350°F. Coat a 9-inch springform pan with vegetable shortening or cooking spray. Place a circle of parchment paper on the bottom.
2. To make the cake, cream the butter and powdered sugar with an electric mixer until light and fluffy. Add the egg yolks, one at a time, beating well after each addition. Stir in the melted chocolate.
3. In a separate bowl, with an electric mixer, beat the egg whites with the kosher salt until foamy. Gradually add the granulated sugar and beat until soft peaks form.
4. Gently fold half of the beaten egg whites into the chocolate mixture.

5. Sift the flour over the top of the chocolate mixture, then fold in the remaining egg whites. Fold gently but thoroughly, until no streaks show from the flour or the egg whites.

6. Spoon the batter into the prepared springform pan and bake in the center of the oven for 35 to 40 minutes. It should be firm to the touch in the center.

7. Let the cake cool completely on a wire rack, at least 15 minutes. Release the sides of the pan from around the cake, then remove the rim, using the tip of a sharp knife around the edges if it appears to be sticking.

8. Make the *marmellata* while the cake is cooling. Combine the apricot preserves, granulated sugar, and brandy in a small saucepan. Bring the mixture to a boil and cook until thickened. Remove any lumps by passing the mixture through a fine-mesh strainer or pulsing it a few times in a food processor. Set the *marmellata* aside.

9. To make the chocolate glaze, combine the sugar, water, and vanilla extract in a small saucepan and bring to a boil. When the syrup reaches 220°F on a candy thermometer, stir in the bittersweet chocolate chips and continue to cook until the mixture reaches 230°F, or the thread stage (dip a whisk in the syrup and look for thin threads of the syrup to drop off the wires).

10. To assemble the torte, use a long serrated knife to carefully slice the cooled cake horizontally into 2 layers. Put the bottom layer on a cardboard cake round and place it on a wire rack with paper towels underneath it to catch the drips while glazing.

11. Brush the apricot *marmellata* evenly over the top of the first layer. Place the second layer on top and brush it with the *marmellata*. Using a spatula, coat the sides of the torte with the remaining *marmellata*. Let the torte sit on the rack for an hour or so while the *marmellata* sets.

12. Pour the chocolate glaze evenly over the top and sides of the torte and let it set, or refrigerate it for a few minutes, before serving.

Serves 10 to 12

BAHAMA BREEZE
Banana Supreme with Butterscotch

IF YOU EVER FIND YOURSELF WITH A LOAF OF BANANA BREAD AND NEED AN IDEA FOR
DESSERT, TRY THIS TRULY LUSCIOUS CONCOCTION OF ALMONDS, BUTTERSCOTCH,
BANANA, AND WHIPPED CREAM.

Butterscotch Sauce
4 tablespoons (½ stick) unsalted
   butter
½ cup packed light brown sugar
½ cup heavy cream
1 tablespoon Grand Marnier

1 loaf banana bread
1 ripe banana
Vanilla ice cream, for serving
Whipped cream, for serving
4 ounces slivered almonds
Fresh mint sprigs, for garnish

1. To make the butterscotch sauce, in a medium saucepan, melt the butter over medium heat. Whisk in the brown sugar, whisking until it dissolves. Pour in the heavy cream and bring the mixture to a boil, whisking constantly. Remove the pan from the heat and add the Grand Marnier. Set the sauce aside.

2. To assemble the banana supreme, slice the banana bread into ½-inch-thick pieces and layer 3 slices on each plate.

3. Slice the banana into ¼-inch-thick pieces and put the slices in the pan with the butterscotch sauce. Heat gently over medium heat, just until the banana slices are heated through.

4. Spoon some of the heated banana slices around the stacked bread on each plate and pour some of the butterscotch sauce over the bread and banana.

5. Put a scoop of vanilla ice cream on top of the bread and dollops of whipped cream around the ice cream.

6. Sprinkle the slivered almonds over the ice cream, whipped cream, and banana slices. Garnish each serving with a sprig of fresh mint.

Serves 4 to 6

BAHAMA BREEZE
Piña Colada Bread Pudding

THE CARIBBEAN IS CALLING WITH THIS EXOTIC COMBINATION OF RUM, COCONUT, AND PINEAPPLE BAKED WITH CHUNKS OF BREAD AND SMOTHERED IN A CREAMY RUM SAUCE. IT'S EVEN BETTER THE NEXT DAY.

Bread Pudding
3 loaves French bread, crusts trimmed, cut into 1-inch cubes
4 tablespoons (½ stick) unsalted butter, melted
10 eggs, beaten
1¼ cups sugar
5 cups milk
1 tablespoon vanilla extract
½ cup coconut rum
½ cup shredded coconut
½ cup pineapple chunks, drained

Coconut Crème Anglaise
5 egg yolks
½ cup sugar
1½ cups heavy cream
¼ cup coconut rum

1. Preheat the oven to 350°F.

2. To make the bread pudding, toss the bread cubes with 3 tablespoons of the melted butter. Spread the cubes on a sheet pan and toast in the hot oven until golden.

3. With the remaining 1 tablespoon melted butter, coat the bottom and sides of a 9 by 13-inch baking dish. Remove the toasted bread to the prepared baking dish.

4. In a large bowl, whisk together the eggs, sugar, milk, vanilla extract, coconut rum, shredded coconut, and pineapple chunks. When the mixture is well combined, pour it over the toasted bread cubes.

5. Press the bread under the liquid, making sure that all the pieces are well soaked.

6. Lower the oven temperature to 300°F.

7. When the bread has absorbed the custard mixture, cover the dish with foil and bake for 1 hour. Remove the foil and bake for another 15 min-

utes, or until the pudding feels firm to the touch in the center and has a light golden crust.

8. While the pudding is baking, make the coconut crème anglaise. In a medium bowl, whip the egg yolks and sugar together with an electric mixer until the sugar is incorporated and the yolks have thickened.

9. Heat the heavy cream in a medium saucepan and bring to a boil, then remove the pan from the heat and let cool.

10. Put the bowl with the yolks over a pot of barely simmering water and slowly add the cream, whisking constantly. Make sure the water does not heat the eggs, or they will start to cook.

11. When the cream has been whisked in, stir in the coconut rum and set the bowl in a large pan of ice and cold water.

12. Stir the sauce occasionally until the mixture has thickened and cooled.

13. Serve the bread pudding warm or at room temperature with the coconut crème anglaise poured over it and with some on the plate.

Serves 10 to 12

If coconut rum is not available, you can use a spiced rum such as Captain Morgan or an equal amount of regular dark rum.

BAKERS SQUARE
French Silk Pie

AN EXTREMELY RICH CHOCOLATE-AND-CREAM DECADENCE, THIS FABULOUS DESSERT IS EASILY MADE WITH A PURCHASED PIE CRUST OR COOKIE CRUST. KEEP THE NO-BAKE RECIPE ON HAND FOR SPECIAL EVENTS OR HOLIDAY PARTIES, WHEN TIME MIGHT BE IN SHORT SUPPLY. IT IS EVEN BETTER AFTER CHILLING OVERNIGHT.

½ pound (2 sticks) unsalted
  butter, softened
1½ cups sugar
4 eggs
2 ounces unsweetened chocolate,
  melted
2 teaspoons vanilla extract

1 cup heavy cream
1 prebaked 8-inch piecrust,
  homemade (see page 47)
  or purchased
1 tablespoon unsweetened
  cocoa powder

1. Cream the butter and sugar, with an electric mixer until the sugar is incorporated.

2. Add the eggs, one at a time, beating well after each addition.

3. When the mixture is fluffy and smooth, stir in the melted chocolate and the vanilla extract.

4. Pour the mixture into the baked piecrust and refrigerate for at least 2 hours.

5. Whip the heavy cream to stiff peaks and either spoon it over the pie or put a dollop on each slice. Sprinkle a little cocoa powder over the whipped cream.

Serves 6 to 8

You can make this pie into individual desserts by using single-serving piecrusts or tart crusts. A few slivered almonds on top of the whipped cream make a memorable final touch.

BASKIN-ROBBINS
Turtle Pie

EVERYONE MAKES THEIR TURTLE PIE DIFFERENTLY—SOME PUT PECAN TURTLES ON THE BOTTOM, SOME PUT TURTLES ON THE TOP. ALL CAN AGREE THAT THE ICE CREAM VERSION FROM BASKIN-ROBBINS IS ONE OF THE BEST.

I quart Baskin-Robbins
   Pralines 'n Cream ice cream
½ cup hot fudge sauce
One 9-inch chocolate cookie
   crumb piecrust, homemade or
   purchased

I cup caramel sauce
I cup pecan halves

1. Let the ice cream soften in the refrigerator until it is spreadable, not melted.
2. Spread the hot fudge sauce over the bottom of the cookie crust.
3. Spread the softened ice cream over the fudge, then top with the caramel sauce.
4. Arrange the pecan halves all over the top of the pie and freeze for 30 minutes before serving.

Serves 6 to 8

THE BAZAAR
Traditional Spanish Flan

CHEF JOSÉ ANDRÉS IS WORLD FAMOUS FOR HIS IMAGINATION AND INFLUENTIAL STYLE
OF GASTRONOMIC COOKING, BUT IT IS HIS MOTHER'S FLAN THAT HE MAKES FOR HIS
FAMILY.

Caramel
½ cup sugar
½ cup water

Flan
½ cup heavy cream
½ cup half-and-half

Peel from 1 lemon, removed in
    strips with a vegetable peeler
1 cinnamon stick
¾ cup sugar
1 vanilla bean, split
3 eggs
2 egg yolks

1. To make the caramel (you will need four 3-ounce ramekins or tart dishes), put the sugar in a small saucepan over low heat for 5 to 6 minutes—it should start turning light brown. Continue cooking for another 7 to 8 minutes, until the sugar becomes a dark brown.

2. Remove the pan from the heat and carefully add the water. The caramel will crackle and release steam as it hardens.

3. Return the pan to low heat and after about 5 minutes, the caramel should become a thick syrup. Divide the syrup among the ramekins and spread it evenly over the bottom and sides, using a spatula. Set the ramekins aside. DO NOT use fingers to spread the caramel—it will be at about 230°F and burn like napalm!

4. Preheat the oven to 275°F.

5. To make the flan, combine the heavy cream and half-and-half in a saucepan over medium-high heat. Stir in the lemon peel, cinnamon stick, and the sugar. Scrape the seeds from the split vanilla bean and add them to the mixture.

6. Remove the pan from the heat just as the mixture comes to a boil.

7. Whisk together the eggs and the egg yolks. Pour in ½ cup of the hot cream mixture, whisking constantly, until well blended. Slowly pour in the remaining cream mixture, whisking constantly.

8. Strain the custard into another bowl through a fine-mesh strainer. Pour the custard into each of the caramel-coated ramekins.

9. Set the ramekins in a baking pan and fill it with enough hot water to come halfway up the sides of the ramekins.

10. Bake the custards in the hot oven for 45 minutes, then remove them and let cool.

11. Cover them with plastic wrap and refrigerate until chilled. Serve cold.

12. To serve, run a knife around the inside edge of each ramekin. Place a serving dish upside down on top of a ramekin, then flip the whole assembly. Wait a few moments for the flan to loosen and the caramel to run. Carefully lift off the ramekin. Spoon any caramel still in the ramekin over the flan.

Serves 4

BENIHANA
Azuki Red Bean Ice Cream

AZUKI BEANS ARE A SMALL RED BEAN USED FREQUENTLY IN JAPANESE SWEETS, USU-
ALLY AS A PASTE. NOTHING COMPARES TO THE TASTE OF HOMEMADE ICE CREAM FROM
FRESH INGREDIENTS. YOU'LL NEED AN ICE CREAM MAKER FOR THIS RECIPE, AND IT
WILL BE WELL WORTH THE INVESTMENT.

Bean Paste
1 cup dried azuki beans, rinsed
  under cold water
⅓ cup sugar
2 teaspoons fresh lemon juice
3½ cups cold water

Custard Base
1 cup milk
1 cup heavy cream
4 egg yolks
⅔ cup sugar
1 teaspoon vanilla extract

1. To make the bean paste, combine the beans, sugar, lemon juice, and water in a medium saucepan. Bring the mixture to a boil and cook, uncovered, for 3 minutes.

2. Reduce the heat to low and cook the beans, covered, until they are very tender, 2½ to 3 hours. Add a little warm water if needed to keep the beans from burning.

3. Measure the beans and liquid when the beans have finished cooking. You should have a total of 3 cups of the mixture. Add more water or pour off the excess to make 3 cups.

4. Strain the mixture through a fine-mesh strainer, pressing the beans through until there is nothing left in the strainer but the skins. Discard the skins.

5. Refrigerate the bean paste until it is completely chilled, 2 to 3 hours.

6. Make the custard base when the bean paste is almost completely chilled. In a small saucepan, bring the milk and heavy cream to a simmer. Remove from the heat.

7. In a heatproof bowl, whisk together the egg yolks and sugar.

8. Briskly stir ¼ cup of the heated milk mixture into the egg yolks. When it is well incorporated, gradually whisk in the remaining milk mixture. Be careful not to add it too fast, as the yolks may cook.

9. Transfer the milk-and-egg mixture back into the saucepan over very low heat. Stir constantly until thickened, about 5 minutes.

10. Remove the pan from the heat and add the vanilla extract. Pour the custard into a shallow pan and refrigerate it until it is completely cold, 1 to 2 hours.

11. Thoroughly mix together the azuki bean paste and the prepared custard, then follow the manufacturer's directions for making ice cream.

Serves 8

BIERGARTEN RESTAURANT

Apple Strudel

GOLDEN BROWN AND FLAKY, THIS APPLE STRUDEL IS EASIER TO MAKE THAN THOSE USING PUFF PASTRY. THE APPLE FILLING IS SPICED WITH CINNAMON AND STUDDED WITH RAISINS, A CLASSIC STRUDEL MADE EVEN MORE INVITING WHEN SERVED WARM WITH A SCOOP OF ICE CREAM ON THE SIDE.

½ cup bread flour

I cup all-purpose flour

½ teaspoon kosher salt

I egg yolk

2 teaspoons canola oil or other
vegetable oil

¼ cup warm water

Apple Filling

¼ cup unseasoned bread crumbs,
toasted

2 pounds Granny Smith
apples, peeled, cored, and sliced

½ cup raisins

¼ cup sugar

½ teaspoon ground cinnamon

8 tablespoons (I stick) unsalted
butter, melted

1. In the bowl of an electric mixer, combine the bread flour and all-purpose flour with the salt and mix with the dough hook attachment.

2. Slowly add the egg yolk, oil, and the warm water at medium speed until the dough is well mixed and is pulling away from the sides of the bowl.

3. Turn the dough out into a bowl coated with a little vegetable oil or melted butter. Turn the dough over once to equally coat all sides.

4. Cover the bowl tightly with plastic wrap and refrigerate overnight.

5. Remove the dough the next day and blot the excess oil with paper towels.

6. Preheat the oven to 400°F.

7. On a work surface, lay the dough on a clean, lint-free kitchen towel and use your hands to pull the dough into a paper-thin rectangle.

8. Fill and roll the strudel. With 3 tablespoons of the bread crumbs, make a 3-inch-wide stripe down one of the long sides of the dough rectangle.

9. Combine the sliced apples with the raisins and spoon them onto the bread crumbs.

10. Combine the sugar and cinnamon and sprinkle over the apples. Top with the remaining 1 tablespoon bread crumbs.

11. Brush the uncovered portion of the dough with some of the melted butter.

12. Roll the strudel into a cylinder by using the towel on the same side as the apple filling to roll the dough to the other side, being careful to keep the apple filling even.

13. Brush the outside of the strudel with the remaining melted butter and transfer the strudel to a baking sheet. Bake for 25 to 30 minutes, until golden brown. Let cool before cutting into portions with a serrated knife.

Serves 8 to 10

BIERGARTEN
RESTAURANT
Black Forest Cake

IT'S HARD TO BEAT A TRIPLE-DECKER CHOCOLATE CAKE LAYERED WITH CHERRY FILLING AND CROWNED WITH WHIPPED CREAM AND MORE CHOCOLATE. THIS IS A GREAT BIRTHDAY CAKE FOR SOMEONE SPECIAL IN YOUR LIFE.

Cake
5 eggs
3 egg yolks
⅔ cup sugar
1½ teaspoons vanilla extract
¾ cup cake flour
¼ teaspoon baking powder
¼ teaspoon baking soda
¼ cup plus 2 tablespoons
   unsweetened cocoa powder

Syrup
⅓ cup water
½ cup sugar
3 tablespoons kirsch or other
   cherry liqueur

Filling
1½ cups cherry pie filling
3 tablespoons kirsch or other
   cherry liqueur

Frosting and Garnish
2½ cups heavy cream, whipped
12 ounces dark chocolate, shaved

1. Preheat the oven to 350°F. Grease three 8-inch cake pans and line the bottoms of each with a circle of waxed paper.

2. To make the cake, combine the eggs, egg yolks, and sugar in a medium mixing bowl and beat with an electric mixer until the mixture is light and thickened. Stir in the vanilla extract.

3. Sift together the flour, baking powder, baking soda, and the cocoa powder. Gradually stir the dry ingredients into the egg mixture. Mix until well blended.

4. Pour equal amounts of the batter into each of the cake pans and bake in the center of the hot oven for 18 to 20 minutes, until the cake springs back when touched in the middle.

5. Let the cake layers cool for at least 10 minutes before removing them from the pans.

6. Make the syrup and filling while the cakes are baking: For the syrup, combine the water and sugar in a small saucepan and bring the mixture to a boil. Remove the pan from the heat immediately and let the syrup cool. Stir in the kirsch and set aside. For the filling, mix the cherry pie filling and the kirsch in a small bowl and set aside.

7. To assemble and frost the cake, put one of the cake layers on a cake plate. Brush the surface with some of the syrup, then spoon on some of the cherry pie filling in an even layer.

8. Repeat with the second layer of cake, then top with the final cake layer and brush it with the syrup.

9. Frost the top of the cake with a thick layer of the whipped cream, leaving the sides plain.

10. Sprinkle the entire top of the cake with the shaved chocolate and refrigerate for at least 1 hour.

Serves 8 to 10

BIG BOY RESTAURANT
Strawberry Pie

THIS IS A GREAT CHOICE FOR DESSERT DURING STRAWBERRY SEASON. MAKE THE PIECRUST EARLY IN THE MORNING, THEN ALL YOU HAVE TO DO IS MAKE THE SYRUP AND PILE EVERYTHING INTO THE CRUST. A TOPPING OF WHIPPED CREAM MAKES IT FESTIVE.

Piecrust
- 1 cup all-purpose flour
- 3 tablespoons sugar
- ¼ teaspoon kosher salt
- 8 tablespoons (1 stick) cold unsalted butter, cut into small pieces
- 1 teaspoon vanilla extract

Syrup
- 1 cup water
- ¾ cup sugar
- ¼ teaspoon kosher salt
- 4 drops red food coloring
- 2 tablespoons cornstarch

Pie Filling
- 2 cups strawberries, hulled and sliced
- ⅓ cup sugar

1. Preheat the oven to 350°F.

2. To make the piecrust, whisk together the flour, sugar, and salt. Cut in the butter with a pastry cutter, or use your hands and mix, until the mixture resembles small peas.

3. Stir in the vanilla extract with a fork and blend well.

4. Roll out the dough on a floured surface and fit it into a 9-inch pie pan. Trim the excess pastry and flute the edges on the rim.

5. Prick the dough all over with the tines of a fork and bake in the hot oven until golden brown, 15 to 20 minutes. Set the crust aside to cool.

6. To make the syrup, whisk together the water, sugar, and salt in a small saucepan over medium heat. Stir until the sugar is dissolved. Stir in the red food coloring.

7. Bring the mixture to a simmer and whisk in the cornstarch. Stir the mixture until thickened. Set aside to cool.

8. To make the pie filling and assemble, toss the strawberries with the sugar and refrigerate, covered, for about 1 hour.

9. Drain the berries and pile them into the prepared pie shell. Mix the collected juices in with the syrup and pour over the filling.

10. Refrigerate until ready to serve.

Serves 8

BISTRO DE PARIS
Crème Brûlée

A RICH VANILLA CUSTARD WITH A CARAMELIZED SUGAR CRUST IS AN IMPRESSIVE DESSERT FOR GUESTS OR FAMILY. THIS TIMELESS CLASSIC CAN BE PREPARED AHEAD AND REFRIGERATED UNTIL YOU'RE READY FOR THE PRESENTATION.

12 egg yolks
1 cup granulated sugar
3 cups heavy cream
1 cup half-and-half

1 vanilla bean, split
½ cup packed light brown sugar
Fresh raspberries, for garnish
8 fresh mint leaves

1. Using an electric mixer, beat the egg yolks with the granulated sugar until light and foamy.

2. Whisk in the heavy cream and half-and-half.

3. Scrape the seeds out of the vanilla bean with the tip of a small, sharp knife. Stir them into the cream mixture. Add the vanilla pod as well. Refrigerate the mixture, covered, for 1 hour.

4. Preheat the oven to 250°F.

5. Remove the vanilla pod and strain the custard into another bowl through a fine-mesh strainer. Stir the mixture, and pour the custard into eight 6-ounce ramekins. Set the ramekins in a high-sided baking dish and fill with enough hot water to reach a third of the way up the sides of the ramekins.

6. Set the baking dish in the center of the oven and bake for 1 hour and 30 minutes. The custards should be set and just slightly wiggly in the center. Remove the ramekins from the water bath and let them cool at room temperature.

7. Wrap each custard in plastic and refrigerate until you are ready to finish the crème brûlée and serve.

8. Preheat the broiler and place the broiler pan as far from the heat source as possible.

9. Evenly sprinkle a tablespoon of brown sugar over each custard. Broil the desserts, one or two at a time, until the sugar caramelizes. Be careful not to burn the sugar—if you do, just lift it off and start over.

10. The sugar will harden as it cools. Garnish each crème brûlée with a couple of raspberries and a mint leaf.

Serves 8

BOARDWALK BAKERY
Brownie Cheesecake

A FULL BAKING DISH OF DENSE, CHOCOLATY BROWNIE IS TOPPED WITH CREAMY CHEESECAKE AND BAKED AGAIN. THIS KNOCKOUT DESSERT IS ACTUALLY EASY TO PREPARE AND TASTES EVEN BETTER THE NEXT DAY.

Brownie
- 1¼ cups all-purpose flour
- ⅔ cup unsweetened cocoa powder
- 1½ teaspoons salt
- ½ teaspoon baking powder
- 2 cups sugar
- 5 eggs
- ½ pound (2 sticks) unsalted butter, melted
- ½ cup semisweet chocolate chips

Cheesecake
- ¾ cup sugar
- Four 8-ounce packages cream cheese, softened
- 3 tablespoons cornstarch
- 2 eggs
- 2 teaspoons vanilla extract
- 1 tablespoons fresh lemon juice
- 2 tablespoons heavy cream
- 2 tablespoons sour cream

1. Preheat the oven to 350°F. Coat a 9 by 13-inch baking dish with vegetable shortening or cooking spray.

2. To make the brownie, whisk together the flour, cocoa powder, salt, and baking powder in a medium bowl.

3. In a large bowl, using an electric mixer, beat the sugar and eggs until light and foamy. Slowly beat in the melted butter.

4. Gradually stir the dry ingredients into the egg mixture. When the ingredients are just combined, add the chocolate chips and blend them in. Do not overmix the dough.

5. Spread the brownie dough in the prepared baking dish and smooth it out evenly.

6. Bake in the hot oven until a toothpick inserted in the center comes out clean, about 30 minutes.

7. Reduce the oven temperature to 325°F.

8. Let the brownie cool while you prepare the cheesecake. Cream the sugar and cream cheese in a large bowl with an electric mixer. Add the cornstarch and blend it in.

9. Add the eggs, one at a time, beating well after each addition. Add the vanilla extract and lemon juice and blend well.

10. Pour in the heavy cream, add the sour cream, and stir until the ingredients are well blended.

11. Spread the mixture over the cooled brownie and bake until the cheesecake is lightly browned on top and firm to the touch, 55 to 60 minutes.

12. Let the brownie cheesecake cool completely, then refrigerate for at least 1 hour. If you are going to keep it until the next day, cover it in plastic wrap after it is completely chilled.

Serves 12

BOARDWALK BAKERY
Chocolate Chip Crumb Cakes

BOARDWALK BAKERY IS PART OF THE WALT DISNEY WORLD RESORT IN LAKE BUENA VISTA, FLORIDA. THESE MINI LOAF CRUMB CAKES ARE A VISITOR FAVORITE. AN INDIVIDUALLY WRAPPED LOAF MAKES A PERFECT HOSTESS GIFT.

Cakes
½ pound (2 sticks) unsalted
   butter, softened
I cup sugar
4 eggs
I teaspoon vanilla extract
½ teaspoon lemon extract
I cup cake flour
I cup cornstarch
½ teaspoon baking powder
I cup semisweet chocolate chips

Crumb Topping
½ cup cake flour
¼ cup sugar
½ teaspoon vanilla extract
2 tablespoons unsalted butter,
   cut into pieces

1. Preheat the oven to 350°F. Lightly grease and flour three 3 by 5-inch mini loaf pans.

2. To make the cakes, cream the butter with the sugar with an electric mixer until light and fluffy.

3. Add the eggs, one at a time, beating well after each addition. Stir in the vanilla extract and lemon extract.

4. Whisk together the flour, cornstarch, and baking powder. Gradually add the dry ingredients to the butter-and-sugar mixture. When the flour has been thoroughly blended in, fold in the chocolate chips.

5. Spoon equal portions of the batter into the prepared loaf pans.

6. To make the crumb topping, whisk together the flour, sugar, and vanilla extract. Use a fork to cut in the pieces of butter. Mix until the mixture resembles coarse meal.

7. Sprinkle equal portions of the crumb topping over each cake and bake the cakes for 35 to 40 minutes, until a toothpick inserted in the center of the cake comes out clean.

8. Let the cakes cool in the pans before unmolding.

Makes 3 mini loaves

BOATWRIGHT'S DINING HALL
Sweet Potato Pancakes

BOATWRIGHT'S DINING HALL IS A SOUTHERN-STYLE RESTAURANT AT DISNEY WORLD IN FLORIDA. THESE PANCAKES, A SIGNATURE ITEM AT BREAKFAST, COME WITH HONEY-PECAN BUTTER AND A CHOICE OF BACON, HAM, OR SAUSAGE.

I cup cooked cubed sweet potato

I¼ cups packed golden brown sugar

3 eggs

I½ cups nonfat milk

I teaspoon vanilla extract

3 tablespoons canola oil

I¼ cups all-purpose flour

I cup whole wheat flour

¼ teaspoon ground cinnamon

¼ teaspoon ground nutmeg

2 teaspoons baking powder

1. Combine the sweet potato and brown sugar in a bowl and beat with an electric mixer until well blended.

2. Add the eggs, one at a time, beating well after each addition. Stir in the milk, vanilla extract, and canola oil. Mix until well blended.

3. In a separate bowl, combine the all-purpose and whole wheat flours. Whisk together with the cinnamon, nutmeg, and baking powder.

4. Gradually stir the dry ingredients into the sweet potato mixture, mixing well. The batter may still be a bit lumpy.

5. Coat a nonstick skillet with cooking spray. Pour 3 ladles of batter for 3 pancakes. Cook until bubbles form on the top of each pancake, and the bottom is golden brown. Flip the pancake and cook until the bottom is golden brown. Hold in a warm oven while you repeat the process and all the batter is used up.

6. This recipe makes about 36 regular-sized pancakes. You can adjust the size of the pancakes to suit your needs.

Serves 6 to 8

BOMA—FLAVORS OF AFRICA
Cocomisù

THIS IS A TROPICAL VERSION OF TIRAMISÙ. THE LADYFINGERS ARE SOAKED IN A KAHLÚA SYRUP AND THEN LAYERED WITH A MASCARPONE FILLING LACED WITH JUST THE RIGHT AMOUNT OF COCO LÓPEZ. YOUR GUESTS WILL SIMPLY BE AMAZED.

Syrup
1 cup granulated sugar
2 cups water
1¼ cups coconut puree
1 cup Kahlúa coffee liqueur

Tiramisù
30 ladyfingers
7 sheets gelatin
1¼ cups coconut puree

3 pounds mascarpone cheese, softened
1 pound powdered sugar
8 egg yolks
1 cup Coco López cream of coconut
4 cups heavy cream
1 cup unsweetened shredded coconut, toasted

1. To make the syrup, combine the sugar and water in a medium saucepan. Bring to a boil, then remove the pan from the heat and transfer the syrup to a bowl. When it cools off just a little, stir in the coconut puree and Kahlúa.

2. To make the cocomisù, soak each ladyfinger in the syrup, then set it on a sheet pan lined with waxed paper.

3. Soak the sheets of gelatin in cold water until they are soft. Squeeze out the excess water, then combine the gelatin with the coconut puree in a bowl. Set the bowl in a larger bowl filled with hot water so that the gelatin will dissolve.

4. Beat the mascarpone and powdered sugar with an electric mixer until fluffy and smooth. Add the egg yolks, one at a time, beating well after each addition. Stir in the Coco López and the heavy cream. Beat on high speed until the mixture is thick.

5. Add 1 cup of the mascarpone mixture to the coconut-gelatin mixture and stir it in. When the coconut gelatin–mascarpone mixture is well blended, return it to the mascarpone mixture.

6. Beat on medium speed until the mascarpone-gelatin mixture has doubled in volume. Be careful not to overwhip the mixture, as the cheese may break.

7. To assemble the cocomisù, layer a high-sided 9 by 13-inch baking dish with the soaked ladyfingers, about 4 inches deep. Ladle about 1½ inches of the filling over the cookies. Place another layer of ladyfingers on top, then ladle another layer of the filling.

8. Smooth the top of the cocomisù, then sprinkle with the toasted coconut.

9. Refrigerate until the mixture firms up, and then cut into squares to serve.

Serves 15

Coconut puree is used most often in Caribbean cooking.
Look in Latin American markets or online
if you can't find it in your local market.

BOMA—FLAVORS OF AFRICA

Passion Fruit Meringue Tart

THE BOMA—FLAVORS OF AFRICA RESTAURANT IS A BUFFET-STYLE DINING EXPERI-
ENCE AT DISNEY'S ANIMAL KINGDOM LODGE AT WALT DISNEY WORLD IN FLORIDA.
IT FOCUSES ON FRESH INGREDIENTS THAT REPRESENT THE CUISINES OF OVER FIFTY
AFRICAN COUNTRIES. THIS DENSELY FLAVORFUL PASSION FRUIT TART CAN ALSO BE
PREPARED AS A SINGLE LARGE DESSERT.

3 egg yolks
2½ cups sweetened condensed
  milk
3 ounces passion fruit puree

2 tablespoons fresh lemon juice
Eight 2½-inch tart shells, baked
5 egg whites
¼ cup sugar

1. Preheat the oven to 375°F.

2. Whisk together the egg yolks, sweetened condensed milk, passion fruit
    puree, and lemon juice until the ingredients are thoroughly combined.

3. Pour the mixture into the individual tart shells. Set the tarts on a sheet
    pan and bake in the hot oven until the fillings are set, 15 to 18 minutes.
    Remove the tarts from the oven and let them cool for a few minutes
    before topping them with the meringue.

4. Beat the egg whites to soft peaks. Gradually add the sugar and continue
    beating to firm peaks.

5. Transfer the whipped whites to a star-tipped pastry bag and pipe the
    meringue in a decorative pattern over each tart. You can also just spoon
    the meringue onto each tart.

6. Bake in the hot oven just until the egg whites begin to brown. Remove
    and let cool before serving.

Serves 8

BOMA—FLAVORS OF AFRICA

Pineapple Upside-Down Cheesecake

CREAM CHEESE AND FRESH PINEAPPLE DOMINATE THE RICH TEXTURE OF THESE MINI CHEESECAKES. THE CRUST OF WHITE CHOCOLATE AND GRAHAM CRACKERS THAT STARTS ON THE TOP BECOMES THE BOTTOM WHEN THE MINI CHEESECAKES ARE UNMOLDED.

Topping
¼ fresh pineapple, chopped
¾ cup packed light brown sugar

Cheesecake
2 pounds cream cheese, softened
1 cup granulated sugar
5 eggs
½ teaspoon vanilla extract

½ teaspoon fresh lemon juice
¼ cup heavy cream
½ cup sour cream

Crust
1 cup white chocolate chips, melted
½ cup graham cracker crumbs

1. Preheat the oven to 300°F.

2. To make the topping, combine the pineapple and ¼ cup of the brown sugar in a small saucepan and cook over medium-low heat for about 5 minutes, or until the sugar has melted and the pineapple is translucent. Set aside to cool.

3. Spray a 12-cup mini muffin pan with cooking spray. Portion out the remaining ½ cup brown sugar into each of the cups, smoothing it over the bottom.

4. Spoon the pineapple into the prepared cups in equal amounts.

5. To make the cheesecake, cream the cream cheese and granulated sugar with an electric mixer.

6. Add the eggs, one at a time, beating well after each addition. When the eggs are incorporated, add the vanilla extract.

7. Beat in the lemon juice, heavy cream, and sour cream. When thoroughly blended, spoon the mixture into the mini muffin cups, filling them almost to the top.

8. Put the muffin pan in a shallow baking dish and fill the dish with enough hot water to come halfway up the sides of the pan. Bake the mini cheesecakes for 30 to 40 minutes, until they are set; remove the pan from the water bath and set aside to cool.

9. To make the crust, blend the melted white chocolate with the graham cracker crumbs. Spoon an equal portion of the crust mixture on top of each cheesecake. Cover the pan with plastic wrap and refrigerate the cheesecakes overnight.

10. Invert the pan on a large platter to release the chilled cheesecakes—the white chocolate–graham cracker topping is now the bottom crust and the sautéed pineapple is on top.

Serves 8

BOSTON MARKET
Cinnamon Apples

USE THIS EASY RECIPE FOR MAKING APPLE FILLINGS FOR PIES AND TARTS, OR FOR SERVING OVER ICE CREAM, OR EVEN FOR ENJOYING BY ITSELF.

3 Granny Smith apples, peeled, cored, and cut into 16 slices
¾ cup water
1 tablespoon all-purpose flour
1 tablespoon cornstarch

1 tablespoon unsalted butter, melted
½ cup packed light brown sugar
1 teaspoon ground cinnamon
¼ teaspoon kosher salt

1. Preheat the oven to 350°F.

2. Arrange the apple slices in an 8 by 8-inch baking dish.

3. Whisk together the water, flour, and cornstarch, then stir in the butter, brown sugar, cinnamon, and salt. Stir until the mixture has no lumps and is smooth.

4. Pour the mixture over the apples, cover the dish with foil, and bake for 40 minutes, until the apples are tender, stirring every 10 to 15 minutes.

Serves 4 to 8

BOSTON MARKET
Sweet Potato Casserole

THOUGH NOT STRICTLY A DESSERT, THIS SWEET POTATO CASSEROLE CAN DOUBLE AS A SIDE DISH OR A REPLACEMENT FOR SWEET POTATO PIE. EITHER WAY IS DELICIOUS.

Filling

5 pounds sweet potatoes or yams, peeled and cut into chunks

¼ cup water

8 tablespoons (1 stick) unsalted butter, melted

2 eggs, well beaten

1 teaspoon kosher salt

1 teaspoon vanilla extract

1 teaspoon ground cinnamon

½ teaspoon ground nutmeg

½ teaspoon ground cloves

½ cup packed dark brown sugar

½ cup heavy cream

Oatmeal Cookie Crumble

½ cup all-purpose flour

1 cup packed dark brown sugar

1 cup quick-cooking oats

1 teaspoon ground cinnamon

¼ teaspoon kosher salt

8 tablespoons (1 stick) cold unsalted butter, cut into small pieces

2 cups miniature marshmallows

1. To make the filling, put the sweet potato chunks in a microwave-safe covered dish with the water. Microwave on high for 12 to 15 minutes, until soft. Drain, transfer to a large bowl, and mash with a fork.

2. Combine the mashed sweet potatoes with the melted butter, beaten eggs, salt, vanilla extract, cinnamon, nutmeg, cloves, and brown sugar. Stir in the heavy cream and whip the mixture with an electric mixer or a hand masher.

3. Spoon the mixture into a 9 by 13-inch baking dish.

4. Preheat the oven to 350°F.

5. To make the oatmeal cookie crumble, combine the flour, brown sugar, oats, cinnamon, and salt in a medium bowl. Cut in the butter with a pastry cutter or use your hands, and mix until it resembles small peas.

6. To assemble, scatter the mini marshmallows over the whipped sweet potatoes in an even layer, then sprinkle the crumble topping over the marshmallows.

7. Bake in the hot oven for 45 minutes, or until the marshmallows are melted and the sweet potatoes are hot.

Serves 10 to 12

BOUCHON BAKERY
Chocolate Bouchon

A *BOUCHON* IS A BOTTLE STOPPER, AND THESE CHOCOLATE TREASURES RESEMBLE THE CORK OF A WINE BOTTLE. USE FLEXIBLE *BOUCHON*-SHAPED BAKING MOLDS, IF YOU LIKE, OR INDIVIDUAL TIMBALE MOLDS IN A 2- OR 3-OUNCE SIZE. EITHER WAY, YOU WILL HAVE DENSE, FUDGE-LIKE BITES SIMPLY DUSTED WITH POWDERED SUGAR.

1½ cups granulated sugar

3 eggs

½ teaspoon vanilla extract

2 tablespoons chocolate liqueur, such as Godiva or Cadbury cream

¾ cup all-purpose flour

1 cup unsweetened cocoa powder

1 tablespoon ground espresso

1 teaspoon kosher salt

12 tablespoons (1½ sticks) unsalted butter, melted

1¼ cups semisweet chocolate chips

½ cup powdered sugar

1. Preheat the oven to 350°F. Coat a flexible *bouchon* mold with cooking spray, or butter and flour twelve 2- or 3-ounce timbale molds.

2. Combine the granulated sugar and the eggs in a medium bowl, and with an electric mixer, beat until the mixture is light and fluffy. It should be pale yellow in color, and the sugar must be completely incorporated.

3. Beat in the vanilla extract and the chocolate liqueur.

4. Sift together the flour, cocoa powder, espresso, and salt.

5. Add the dry ingredients and the melted butter to the beaten egg mixture in three alternating additions, starting with the dry ingredients. Blend thoroughly after each addition.

6. Fold in the chocolate chips.

7. Fit a pastry bag with a large plain tip and fill the bag with the batter. Pipe the batter into the prepared molds, filling the cups about three quarters of the way full. Put the timbale molds, if using, on a baking sheet before putting them in the oven.

8. Bake the *bouchons* for 18 to 20 minutes. *Bouchons* should be brownie-like when done. Test with a toothpick; it should be clean, not dry. Let them cool in the molds, then turn them upside down on a clean work surface and pull off the molds. Set the *bouchons* upright on a platter and dust lightly with the powdered sugar.

Serves 12

BOUCHON BAKERY
Hot Chocolate

THIS HOMEMADE HOT CHOCOLATE WILL MAKE YOU FORGET ANYTHING YOU'VE EVER HAD FROM A PACKET. IT USES BOTH MILK CHOCOLATE AND DARK CHOCOLATE PLUS COCOA POWDER AND IS LIGHTLY SCENTED WITH TOASTED CORIANDER.

1 cup plus 1 tablespoon milk
2 tablespoons heavy cream
½ cinnamon stick
½ teaspoon coriander seeds, crushed
½ vanilla bean, split

1 tablespoon unsweetened cocoa powder
3 tablespoons milk chocolate chips
3 tablespoons dark chocolate chips

1. Combine the milk and heavy cream in a small saucepan and bring to a boil. Reduce the heat to low.

2. Put the cinnamon stick half and the crushed coriander seeds in a small skillet and toast until fragrant.

3. With the tip of a small knife, scrape out the seeds from the vanilla bean and add them to the milk along with the toasted coriander and cinnamon.

4. Stir in the cocoa powder and whisk until well blended.

5. Put the milk chocolate chips and dark chocolate chips in a mug and pour the hot milk mixture through a fine-mesh strainer into the mug. Stir until the chocolate chips are melted. Strain one more time for an extra-smooth drink.

Serves 1

This chocolate drink can also be served cold or at room temperature. Make a large batch and keep it refrigerated in a tightly covered container and gently heat however many portions you would like.

BOULANGERIE PATISSERIE
Chocolate Mousse

MOUSSE IS A LIGHT WAY TO END A MEAL. IT'S EASY TO PREPARE AND CAN BE MADE WELL AHEAD OF TIME.

⅔ cup semisweet chocolate chips
2 egg yolks, lightly beaten
¼ cup cold heavy cream

1 teaspoon vanilla extract
3 egg whites
¼ cup sugar

1. Melt the chocolate chips in a bowl set over a pan of simmering water, then set aside.

2. In a medium bowl, whisk together the beaten egg yolks and the heavy cream, blending thoroughly.

3. Scrape the melted chocolate into the cream mixture, whisking to blend it in well. Add the vanilla extract and blend.

4. Beat the egg whites to stiff peaks, gradually adding the sugar 1 tablespoon at a time. Using a rubber spatula, fold the whites into the chocolate mixture.

5. Refrigerate until very firm and serve cold.

Serves 4 to 6

For a decorative touch, pour the mousse into a fancy mold or soufflé dish before refrigerating, and sprinkle with bits of shaved chocolate when ready to serve. This mousse can also be served in individual ramekins.

BRENNAN'S
Bananas Foster

THIS INTERNATIONAL FAVORITE WAS INVENTED AT BRENNAN'S IN NEW ORLEANS IN THE EARLY FIFTIES AND NAMED FOR A LOCAL PUBLIC OFFICIAL. MAKE SURE THE BANANAS ARE RIPE, AND DON'T SKIMP ON THE RUM, EVEN IF YOU'RE NOT GOING TO FLAME THE DISH.

I cup packed golden brown sugar
8 tablespoons (I stick) unsalted butter, softened
½ teaspoon ground cinnamon

¼ cup banana liqueur, such as DeKuyper or Hiram Walker
4 bananas, split lengthwise
¼ cup dark rum
Vanilla ice cream

1. Heat a large skillet over low heat and whisk together the brown sugar, butter, and cinnamon. Stir until the sugar dissolves.

2. Stir in the banana liqueur and let it cook for a minute or two.

3. Cut the split bananas in half, so you have 16 pieces the same size. Add them to the skillet

4. When the pieces of banana begin to soften and brown, carefully add the rum and let the sauce simmer until the rum is hot. Ignite the rum with a long matchstick. Shake the pan to distribute the flaming rum and let the flames subside.

5. Put a scoop of the ice cream on each of four plates. Carefully lift 4 banana pieces out of the skillet and lay them over the ice cream.

6. Spoon the sauce over each portion of bananas and ice cream, and serve while still warm

Serves 4

BURTON'S SUNNYBROOK RESTAURANT

Apple Dapple Cake

THIS OLD-FASHIONED APPLE CAKE IS FILLED WITH FRESH APPLES AND CHOPPED NUTS AND SCENTED WITH CINNAMON AND VANILLA. THE TOPPING SOAKS INTO THE CAKE, GIVING IT EXTRA MOISTURE AND A RICHER TEXTURE.

Cake
2 cups granulated sugar
1½ cups canola oil
3 eggs
2 teaspoons vanilla extract
3 cups all-purpose flour
1 teaspoon baking soda
1 teaspoon baking powder
1 teaspoon kosher salt
1 teaspoon ground cinnamon

3 Granny Smith apples, peeled, cored, and chopped
1 cup chopped walnuts

Topping
8 tablespoons (1 stick) unsalted butter
1 cup packed light brown sugar
¼ cup half-and-half

1. Preheat the oven to 350°F. Grease and flour, or use cooking spray to coat, a 9 by 13-inch baking pan.

2. To make the cake, beat the granulated sugar and oil with an electric mixer until the mixture is well combined. Add the eggs, one at a time, beating well after each addition. Stir in the vanilla extract and beat until the mixture is light and creamy.

3. Whisk together the flour, baking soda, baking powder, salt, and cinnamon. Gradually stir the dry ingredients into the egg mixture. Stir in the chopped apples and walnuts. Stir the batter until all the ingredients are well combined.

4. Pour the batter into the prepared pan and give the pan a couple of strong taps on the counter to settle the batter.

5. Bake for 1 hour and 15 minutes, or until the cake springs back when touched in the center. Let the cake cool before inverting it to remove the pan. Set it upright on a large plate.

6. Make the topping while the cake is baking. Melt the butter in a medium saucepan. Whisk in the brown sugar and stir until it is dissolved.

7. Whisk in the half-and-half and bring the mixture to a boil.

8. Boil for 3 minutes, stirring occasionally. Let the mixture cool for a couple of minutes.

9. Pierce the cooled cake in several places with a long skewer. Spread the topping over the cake, allowing it to sink in where pierced.

Serves 12

CALIFORNIA PIZZA KITCHEN
Butter Cake

THIS IS A GREAT ALL-AROUND BASIC CAKE RECIPE. THE BUTTERMILK GIVES IT EXTRA
MOISTURE AND A DELICATE TEXTURE. USE THE ORIGINAL TOPPING BELOW OR ONE OF
YOUR OWN.

Cake
½ pound (2 sticks) unsalted
  butter, softened
2 cups sugar
4 eggs
2 teaspoons vanilla extract
1 cup buttermilk
3 cups all-purpose flour
1 teaspoon kosher salt
1 teaspoon baking powder
½ teaspoon baking soda

Butter Topping
6 tablespoons (¾ stick) unsalted
  butter
¾ cup sugar
2 teaspoons vanilla extract

1. Preheat the oven to 325°F. Grease and flour a 10-inch Bundt pan or
   other tube pan.

2. To make the cake, cream the butter and sugar with an electric mixer
   until light and fluffy. Beat in the eggs, one at a time, beating well after
   each addition. Stir in the vanilla extract. Add the buttermilk and beat on
   medium speed until the ingredients are well combined.

3. Whisk together the flour, salt, baking powder, and baking soda. Gradually stir the dry ingredients into the egg mixture and blend thoroughly.

4. Pour the batter into the prepared pan and bake in the hot oven for
   1 hour, or until a toothpick inserted in the center comes out clean.

5. When the cake is finished baking, use a skewer to make several holes all
   over the surface of the cake.

6. Make the topping just before the cake is ready to come out of the oven. Melt the butter in a small saucepan and whisk in the sugar. Whisk until the sugar dissolves, being careful not to let the mixture boil.

7. Stir in the vanilla extract and let the mixture cool for a few minutes while the cake finishes baking.

8. Pour the topping over the warm cake, making sure it goes over the pierced holes. Let the cake cool completely before removing it from the pan.

Serves 8

CALIFORNIA PIZZA KITCHEN
Pumpkin Cheesecake

SOUR CREAM GIVES THIS RICH CHEESECAKE A CREAMY TEXTURE, AND EXOTIC SPICES CREATE QUITE A HEADY SCENT WHILE BAKING.

Graham Cracker Crust

1 sleeve graham crackers

3 tablespoons granulated sugar

6 tablespoons (¾ stick) unsalted butter, melted

Cheesecake

Three 8-ounce packages cream cheese, softened

1½ cups packed dark brown sugar

3 eggs

¼ teaspoon ground cardamom

¼ teaspoon ground cloves

¼ teaspoon ground ginger

¼ teaspoon ground nutmeg

1 teaspoon ground cinnamon

1 cup sour cream

2 teaspoons vanilla extract

1½ cups canned pumpkin puree

1. To make the crust, grind the graham crackers in a food processor to the texture of fine meal. You should have about 1½ cups of crumbs.

2. Add the granulated sugar and pulse to combine, then pour in the melted butter with the motor running. The butter should moisten all the crumbs.

3. Press the mixture evenly on the bottom and halfway up the sides of a 9-inch springform pan.

4. Preheat the oven to 350°F.

5. To make the cheesecake, beat the cream cheese and brown sugar with an electric mixer until light and fluffy. Add the eggs, one at a time, beating well after each addition.

6. Whisk together the cardamom, cloves, ginger, nutmeg, and cinnamon, and stir into the mixture. Beat in the sour cream, vanilla extract, and pumpkin puree.

7. Pour the cheesecake mixture into the prepared crust and bake in the center of the oven for 1 hour, or until firm in the center. Bake longer if it still seems too wet.

8. Let the cheesecake cool on a wire rack, then refrigerate it for at least 1 hour, or overnight if possible.

9. When it has been thoroughly chilled, loosen the crust from the sides of the pan with a knife, then release the ring.

Serves 12 to 16

Serve with a dollop of cinnamon whipped cream, if desired.

CARNIVAL CRUISE LINES
Chocolate Melting Cake

THIS IS THE PERFECT CHOICE FOR OCCASIONS WHEN YOU NEED INDIVIDUAL DESSERTS—BUFFETS, PARTIES, AND HOLIDAY CELEBRATIONS. EACH CAKE IS BAKED IN ITS OWN RAMEKIN AND SERVED WITH A SPOON TO SCOOP UP EVERY DROP OF MOLTEN CHOCOLATE.

1 pound dark chocolate chips
1 pound (4 sticks) unsalted butter, softened
2½ cups pasteurized egg product, or 8 large eggs, well beaten

½ cup granulated sugar
⅔ cup all-purpose flour
¾ cup powdered sugar

1. Preheat the oven to 300°F. Spray eight 6-ounce ramekins with cooking spray.

2. Combine the chocolate chips and butter in a medium saucepan and stir over low heat until completely melted and the mixture is smooth.

3. With an electric mixer, beat the egg product and granulated sugar until light and foamy.

4. Whisk the flour into the egg mixture and blend until smooth.

5. Stir the melted chocolate mixture into the batter and blend thoroughly.

6. Set the ramekins on a sheet pan and fill with the batter. Put the pan with the ramekins in the hot oven and bake for 12 to 15 minutes. Just the edges of each cake should be firm—the centers should still be jiggly.

7. Put the powdered sugar in a small fine-mesh strainer and dust the tops of the cakes. Serve warm.

Serves 8

For an elegant touch, make a small stencil in a shape you prefer, such as a heart or a star, and lay it on each cake before dusting with the powdered sugar. The outline of the stencil will contrast the brown of the cake with the white of the powdered sugar.

CARRABBA'S ITALIAN GRILL
Chocolate Dream

THIS EASY-TO-MAKE DESSERT IS TRULY A DREAM. CHOCOLATE MOUSSE AND WHIPPED CREAM ARE SANDWICHED BETWEEN TWO LAYERS OF FUDGE-LIKE BROWNIES THAT HAVE BEEN SOAKED IN KAHLÚA. A SPRINKLING OF SHAVED CHOCOLATE COMPLETES THE PICTURE.

4 eggs
½ cup milk
Vegetable oil
Two 21.25-ounce boxes fudge
   brownie mix
½ cup Kahlúa coffee liqueur

4 cups chocolate mousse,
   homemade (recipe follows)
   or purchased
4 cups whipped cream
2 ounces semisweet
   chocolate bar

1. Preheat the oven to 350°F. Grease or spray the bottoms of two 9 by 13-inch baking pans and line them with parchment or waxed paper.

2. Prepare one brownie layer at a time. Whisk together 2 of the eggs and ¼ cup of the milk, and add the amount of oil specified in the brownie-mix instructions. Pour 1 box of the brownie mix into a medium bowl and stir in the egg mixture. With an electric mixer, beat until well combined and smooth.

3. Pour the batter into one of the prepared pans.

4. Repeat the procedure with the other box of brownie mix.

5. Bake the brownies for 25 to 30 minutes, until a toothpick inserted in the center comes out clean. Let cool completely while still in the baking pans.

6. Loosen the sides with a knife, then turn the brownies, upside down and in one piece, onto a clean work surface and remove the paper.

7. Brush each brownie with ¼ cup of the Kahlúa, brushing from the edges toward the center.

8. Put one of the brownies back in its baking pan, Kahlúa side up, and spread with 2 cups of the chocolate mousse. Spread 2 cups of the whipped cream over the mousse.

9. Using a vegetable peeler, shave curls of chocolate from the bar. Sprinkle half of them over the top of the whipped cream.

10. Place the remaining brownie, Kahlúa side up, on top of the one in the pan and layer with the remaining 2 cups chocolate mousse and 2 cups whipped cream. Sprinkle with the remaining chocolate curls. Refrigerate for at least 1 hour before cutting into portions.

Serves 10 to 20

Chocolate Mousse

I teaspoon vanilla extract
8 ounces dark chocolate chips,
  melted and slightly cooled

1 ½ cups heavy cream

1. Stir the vanilla extract into the melted chocolate.
2. Beat the heavy cream to soft peaks with an electric mixer. Fold gently but thoroughly into the melted chocolate with a rubber spatula.
3. Refrigerate for at least 30 minutes before using.

Makes 4 cups

CHART HOUSE
Mud Pie

THIS FAVORITE HAS BEEN AROUND FOR YEARS. IT COMES TOGETHER WITH PUR-
CHASED ITEMS, MAKING IT IDEAL FOR THOSE TIMES YOU NEED A DESSERT THAT CAN
BE MOSTLY MADE AHEAD AND FINISHED AT THE LAST MINUTE.

I quart coffee-flavored ice cream
I Oreo cookie piecrust,
  homemade (recipe follows)
  or purchased

I cup hot fudge sauce
I ½ cups heavy cream

1. Let the ice cream come to room temperature to soften enough for spreading.
2. Spoon the ice cream into the piecrust and freeze for at least 4 hours.
3. When ready to serve, warm the hot fudge sauce and pour it over the frozen pie. Whip the heavy cream to stiff peaks and spoon it on top of the chocolate sauce. Serve the pie whole or cut it into wedges.

Serves 8

Oreo Piecrust

24 Oreo cookies (filling, too)

8 tablespoons (I stick) unsalted
butter, melted

1. Put the cookies in a resealable plastic bag and break them up with a rolling pin. Transfer them to the bowl of a food processor and pulse until they resemble coarse meal.
2. Add the melted butter and process until well combined.
3. Press the mixture evenly on the bottom and up the sides of a 9- or 10-inch pie plate. Freeze the piecrust for at least 1 hour before filling.

Makes one 9- or 10-inch piecrust

THE CHEESECAKE FACTORY

French Toast Napoleon

IF YOU CAN'T GET TO THE CHEESECAKE FACTORY FOR SUNDAY BRUNCH, TRY THIS ELABORATE PREPARATION AT HOME.

French Toast

4 eggs
1 cup half-and-half
1 tablespoon vanilla extract
2 tablespoons packed light brown sugar
1 teaspoon ground cinnamon
Six ¾-inch-thick slices brioche
12 tablespoons (1½ sticks) unsalted butter

Sweetened Whipped Cream

1 cup heavy cream
1 teaspoon vanilla extract
3 tablespoons powdered sugar

Toppings

3 cups ripe strawberries, hulled and sliced
1 tablespoon granulated sugar
½ cup glazed pecans
1 tablespoon melted butter
1 cup maple syrup, warmed
1 tablespoon powdered sugar

1. Preheat the oven to 200°F.

2. To make the French toast, combine the eggs, half-and-half, vanilla extract, brown sugar, and cinnamon in a blender and puree until smooth.

3. Lay the slices of brioche in a 9 by 13-inch baking dish and pour the batter over them. Turn the slices over to make sure both sides are coated, and gently press down on the bread to submerge it. Let the bread sit in the batter for about 10 minutes.

4. Heat a griddle or cast-iron skillet over medium-high heat and melt the butter, figuring 2 tablespoons per slice. If your griddle can hold all the bread at once, use more butter at one time. Coat the skillet all over and fry the brioche until golden brown and crispy, about 4 minutes per side. Keep the bread warm in the oven.

5. To make the sweetened whipped cream, beat the heavy cream to soft peaks. Add the vanilla extract and powdered sugar and beat to stiff peaks. Refrigerate until ready to use.

6. To prepare the toppings, toss the sliced strawberries with the granulated sugar and let them marinate until ready to use.

7. Swirl the glazed pecans in the melted butter to warm them up.

8. Warm a small pitcher under hot water, then fill it with the warm maple syrup.

9. Put the powdered sugar in a sugar shaker to make dusting easy and to eliminate clumps.

10. To assemble the napoleon, warm two large plates. Put 1 slice of the toasted bread on each plate and spoon ½ cup of the sliced strawberries over the toast. Repeat the procedure with the remaining brioche and most of the strawberries. Scatter the remaining berries on the plates.

11. Put 1 cup of the whipped cream on top of the final slice of toast on each plate. Spoon the pecans evenly between the two plates on top of the whipped cream. Dust each napoleon with the powdered sugar and serve immediately with the pitcher of warm maple syrup.

Serves 2 to 4

THE CHEESECAKE FACTORY

Carrot Cake Cheesecake

THIS DESSERT HAS BECOME A CHEESECAKE FACTORY ALL-TIME FAVORITE. MAKE SURE THE CARROTS ARE GRATED, NOT JULIENNED OR GROUND.

Cheesecake

Two 8-ounce packages cream cheese, softened

¼ cup granulated sugar

3 eggs

2 teaspoons vanilla extract

1 tablespoon all-purpose flour

Carrot Cake

2 eggs

1 cup granulated sugar

1 teaspoon vanilla extract

1 cup all-purpose flour

¼ teaspoon kosher salt

1 teaspoon ground cinnamon

1 teaspoon baking soda

One 8½-ounce can crushed pineapple, drained and juice reserved

1 cup grated carrots

½ cup sweetened shredded coconut

½ cup chopped walnuts

Cream Cheese Frosting

1 tablespoon unsalted butter, softened

2 ounces cream cheese, softened

1¾ cups powdered sugar

1 teaspoon vanilla extract

1 tablespoon reserved pineapple juice

Pinch of kosher salt

1. Preheat the oven to 350°F. Use butter or cooking spray to coat the bottom of a 9-inch springform pan.

2. To make the cheesecake batter, combine the cream cheese, the granulated sugar, and eggs. Beat with an electric mixer until smooth and creamy. Add the vanilla extract and flour, then beat until well mixed.

3. Set the cheesecake batter aside while you make the carrot cake batter. Using an electric mixer, beat the eggs and granulated sugar until light and smooth. Add the vanilla extract and mix well.

4. Whisk together the flour, salt, cinnamon, and baking soda. Gradually stir the dry ingredients into the egg mixture, blending well.

5. Fold in the crushed pineapple, grated carrots, coconut, and walnuts.

6. Pour 1½ cups of the carrot cake batter into the prepared springform pan.

7. Drop large spoonfuls of the cheesecake batter over the carrot cake batter.

8. Top with the remaining carrot cake batter.

9. Drop large spoonfuls of the remaining cheesecake batter over the cake and smooth it over with a metal spatula or a dinner knife. Be careful not to disturb the layers underneath.

10. Bake the cake in the hot oven for 50 to 60 minutes, until the cake is set. Let the cake cool to room temperature, then refrigerate it until you're ready to frost it.

11. To make the frosting, cream the butter and cream cheese with an electric mixer. Beat in the powdered sugar, vanilla extract, 1 tablespoon reserved pineapple juice, and salt. The mixture should be smooth and spreadable.

12. Spread the frosting evenly over the top of the cake and refrigerate the cake for 3 to 4 hours until chilled. Release the rim of the pan and cut the cake into serving portions.

Serves 12

THE CHEESECAKE FACTORY

Hershey's Chocolate Bar Cheesecake

Cheesecake

Two 8-ounce packages cream
  cheese, softened
½ cup granulated sugar
1 teaspoon vanilla extract
3 eggs
¼ cup sour cream
½ cup chopped Hershey's
  chocolate bar, melted and
  cooled

Chocolate Cake

2 cups granulated sugar
1¾ cups all-purpose flour
¾ cup Hershey's cocoa
1½ teaspoons baking powder
1½ teaspoons baking soda

1 teaspoon kosher salt
2 eggs
1 cup milk
½ cup vegetable oil
2 teaspoons vanilla extract
1 cup boiling water

Chocolate Frosting

8 tablespoons (1 stick) unsalted
  butter
⅔ cup Hershey's cocoa
3 cups powdered sugar
⅓ cup milk
1 teaspoon vanilla extract

2 cups Hershey's milk chocolate
  chips

1. Preheat the oven to 325°F. Line a 10-inch cake pan with foil, letting the edges of the foil extend over the sides of the pan. Spray the foil with nonstick cooking spray.

2. To make the cheesecake, in a large bowl, beat the cream cheese, granulated sugar, and vanilla extract with an electric mixer until creamy and smooth. Whisk the eggs in a bowl, then add to the cream cheese mixture. Blend just until the eggs are incorporated. Stir in the sour cream and melted chocolate.

3. Pour the batter into the prepared pan. Bake for 45 minutes, or until the top just starts to turn golden.

4. Let the cheesecake cool completely in its pan on a wire rack, then cover and refrigerate for at least 4 hours.

5. When the cheesecake is done and cooling, increase the oven temperature to 350°F. Grease and flour two 10-inch cake pans.

6. To make the chocolate cake, stir together the granulated sugar, flour, cocoa, baking powder, baking soda, and salt in large bowl. Add the eggs, milk, oil, and vanilla extract. Beat with an electric mixer for 2 minutes. Stir in the boiling water (the batter will be thin). Pour the batter into the prepared pans.

7. Bake for 30 to 35 minutes, until a toothpick inserted in the center comes out clean. Let cool for 10 minutes, then remove from the pans to wire racks. Let cool completely.

8. To make the chocolate frosting, melt the butter and stir in the cocoa.

9. Alternately add the powdered sugar and the milk, beating to a spreading consistency with a wooden spoon.

10. Add a small amount of additional milk, if needed. Stir in the vanilla extract.

11. To assemble, spread some of the frosting on top of one of the chocolate cake layers.

12. Using the edges of foil as handles, remove the cheesecake from the pan and peel away the foil. Carefully place the cheesecake on top of the frosted layer. If the cheesecake becomes hard to work with, you can put it in the freezer for 20 to 30 minutes.

13. Spread some of the chocolate frosting on top of the cheesecake layer.

14. Place the remaining chocolate cake layer on top and ice with the frosting on top and on the sides of all the layers. Decorate the sides of the cake with the Hershey's chocolate chips.

Makes one 10-inch cake

THE CHEESECAKE FACTORY

White Chocolate–Raspberry Truffle Cheesecake

THIS RECIPE IS A BIT TIME CONSUMING, BUT THE DECADENCE IS WELL WORTH THE EFFORT. THE CRUST OF THIS TRUFFLE CHEESECAKE IS MADE WITH OREO COOKIE CRUMBS—IT JUST GETS BETTER FROM THERE!

Crust
1½ cups Oreo cookie crumbs, (made from 24 wafers, without the filling)
5 tablespoons unsalted butter, melted

Filling
½ cup seedless raspberry preserves
¼ cup water
Four 8-ounce packages cream cheese, softened
1¼ cups sugar
½ cup sour cream
2 teaspoons vanilla extract
5 eggs
½ cup white chocolate chips

1. Preheat the oven to 475°F. Line a 9-inch springform pan with parchment paper on the bottom and sides.

2. To make the crust, combine the cookie crumbs with the melted butter and mix thoroughly.

3. Press the crumb mixture evenly on the bottom and about two thirds of the way up the sides of the prepared pan. Put the crust in the freezer while you make the filling.

4. To make the filling, combine the raspberry preserves with the water in a small saucepan over low heat. Stir until the preserves are melted and well blended with the water. Set aside to cool.

5. Using an electric mixer, beat the cream cheese with the sugar and sour cream until creamy and smooth. Stir in the vanilla extract.

6. Add the eggs, one at a time, beating well after each addition.

7. Remove the crust from the freezer and sprinkle the bottom with the white chocolate chips. Pour half of the cream cheese mixture over the chocolate chips.

8. Drizzle the entire surface of the cheesecake filling with the cooled raspberry preserves. Use a metal spatula or dinner knife to swirl the raspberry preserves into the cheesecake filling. Pour the remaining cream cheese mixture over the filling.

9. Wrap a large piece of foil around the bottom of the springform pan and place the pan in a large baking dish. Fill the dish with enough hot water to come halfway up the sides of the pan.

10. Bake the cheesecake in the hot oven for 12 minutes, then reduce the heat to 350°F and bake for another 50 to 60 minutes. The top of the cheesecake should just be turning a light golden brown.

11. Remove the cheesecake from the water bath and let cool in the pan at room temperature, then wrap lightly in the same foil and refrigerate for at least 4 hours.

12. Remove the sides of the pan and the parchment paper before serving.

Serves 12

For an optional garnish, melt about 2 ounces of white chocolate chips and pour into a small cup. When the chocolate hardens, use a vegetable peeler to make shavings from the solid chocolate. Sprinkle the shavings over the top of the cheesecake before serving.

CHERYL'S
Buttery Sugar Cookies

FROSTED BUTTER COOKIES ARE PERFECT FOR HOLIDAY CELEBRATIONS, PARTIES, OR ANY TIME YOU WANT SOMETHING JUST A LITTLE SPECIAL. TINT THE FROSTING FOR SEASONAL COLOR.

Cookies
½ pound (2 sticks) unsalted butter, softened
¾ cup granulated sugar
I egg
I teaspoon vanilla extract
2½ cups all-purpose flour
I teaspoon baking powder
¼ teaspoon kosher salt
½ teaspoon ground cinnamon

Frosting
8 tablespoons (I stick) unsalted butter, softened
3½ cups powdered sugar
I teaspoon vanilla extract
¼ cup milk
Food coloring (optional)

1. Preheat the oven to 375°F.

2. To make the cookies, cream the butter and granulated sugar with an electric mixer until light and fluffy. Add the egg and vanilla extract and beat them in.

3. Whisk together the flour, baking powder, salt, and cinnamon. Gradually stir the dry ingredients into the creamed mixture. Mix until all the ingredients are thoroughly blended.

4. Load the dough into a cookie press with your favorite design plate and press the cookies onto an ungreased baking sheet, spacing them about 2 inches apart. If you aren't using a cookie press, roll walnut-sized pieces of the dough between your palms and place them on the baking sheet. Flatten them with the bottom of a drinking glass.

5. Bake the cookies for 6 to 8 minutes, until the edges are firm and the bottoms are lightly browned, being careful not to overbake them. Remove the cookies from the baking sheet and let them cool on wire racks while you make the frosting.

6. To make the frosting, combine the butter and 2 cups of the powdered sugar in a medium bowl. Using an electric mixer, begin beating on medium speed until the mixture is smooth, then add the remaining 1½ cups powdered sugar in ½-cup increments.

7. Stir in the vanilla extract and a few drops of food coloring, if using, and slowly add the milk. Beat until the mixture reaches a spreading consistency.

8. Frost the warm cookies using a small metal spatula or a butter knife. Let them cool completely if you are going to store them in an airtight container.

Makes 42 cookies

CHILI'S
Apple and Raisin Cobbler

COBBLERS ARE EASY TO MAKE AND CAN BE SEASONALLY ADJUSTED. THIS FAVORITE FROM CHILI'S HAS ALL THE FLAVOR OF A GOOD APPLE PIE WITHOUT THE CRUST.

Topping
1 cup all-purpose flour
3 tablespoons granulated sugar
1 ½ teaspoons baking powder
¼ teaspoon kosher salt
4 tablespoons (½ stick) cold unsalted butter, cut into small pieces
1 egg, well beaten
¼ cup milk

Apple and Raisin Filling
½ cup packed light brown sugar
2 tablespoons cornstarch
¼ teaspoon ground ginger
1 cup water
¼ cup seedless raisins
1 tablespoon fresh lemon juice
1 tablespoon unsalted butter
6 Granny Smith apples, peeled, cored, and sliced ¼-inch thick

Ice cream, for serving (optional)

1. To make the topping, whisk together the flour, 2 tablespoons of the granulated sugar, the baking powder, and salt.

2. Cut in the pieces of butter using a pastry cutter or fork. Blend until the mixture resembles coarse meal.

3. Whisk together the beaten egg and the milk. Stir the mixture into the dough, mixing just until all the dry ingredients are moistened. Set the topping aside.

4. Preheat the oven to 425°F.

5. To make the apple and raisin filling, combine the brown sugar, cornstarch, ginger, and water in a large saucepan. Bring the mixture to a simmer over medium heat and stir until it is blended and thickened.

6. Stir in the raisins, lemon juice, and butter. Let the mixture simmer, stirring frequently.

7. Fold in the sliced apples, gently turning them in the mixture to make sure they are well coated. Cook until the apples are heated through and softened, about 5 minutes.

8. Pour the cooked apples into a 2-quart casserole or 9 by 9-inch baking dish.

9. Place 8 to 12 mounds of the topping on the cobbler and sprinkle with the remaining 1 tablespoon granulated sugar.

10. Bake the cobbler for 20 minutes, or until the topping is lightly golden brown. Serve with a scoop of vanilla ice cream on the side, if you wish.

Serves 8 to 12

CHILI'S
Chocolate Brownie Sundae

THIS IS ONE DESSERT YOU CAN ALWAYS HAVE READY TO MAKE. IT RELIES ON PURCHASED ITEMS THAT ARE PANTRY STAPLES. PERFECT FOR A KIDS' PARTY, OR WHEN A GREAT, GOOEY, CHOCOLATY CONCOCTION IS THE ONLY THING TO MEET AN URGENT NEED!

One 19.8-ounce box premium brownie mix
1½ cups coarsely chopped walnuts
One 16-ounce jar hot fudge sauce, warmed

1 quart vanilla ice cream
One 14-ounce jar maraschino cherries

1. Prepare the brownie mix according to the package directions. Stir ½ cup of the chopped walnuts into the batter before baking.

2. Pour the batter into a greased 9 by 13-inch baking dish and smooth it evenly.

3. Note the amount of time as directed on the box, but remove the pan 5 minutes before it reaches the time listed.

4. Remove the pan from the oven and let the brownie cool for a few minutes, then slice the brownie into 12 portions.

5. To assemble the dessert, drizzle each of twelve dessert plates with some of the fudge sauce. Place a brownie on top of the sauce and put a scoop of ice cream on the brownie.

6. Drizzle more of the fudge sauce over the ice cream and sprinkle each dessert with some of the remaining 1 cup chopped walnuts.

7. Top each dessert with a maraschino cherry and serve while the brownies are still warm.

Serves 12

If you have whipped cream on hand, drop a spoonful on each dessert before topping it with the cherry.

CHILI'S
Mighty Ice Cream Pie

THE PERFECT RECIPE FOR A FAMILY THAT DEVOURS DESSERT IN 10 SECONDS FLAT
IS THE ONE THAT YOU DON'T HAVE TO SPEND A LOT OF TIME PREPARING. KEEP THIS
NO-BAKE PIE RECIPE HANDY.

2 quarts vanilla ice cream
One 6-ounce package Heath
 toffee bits
1 cup semisweet chocolate chips
One 9-inch Oreo cookie crust
 (see page 86)

One 16-ounce jar hot fudge
 sauce
One 12-ounce jar caramel sauce

1. Soften the ice cream in the refrigerator, but do not let it melt.

2. Put the Heath toffee bits, the chocolate chips, and the cookie crust in
   the freezer. Make sure the Heath bits are not wrapped, and put the toffee
   and chocolate chips in a large metal bowl.

3. When frozen, put the bits and chips in the bowl of a food processor and
   grind until they are the texture of fine meal.

4. When the ice cream is soft enough, turn it out into the bowl that held
   the candy in the freezer. Stir in the ground toffee and chocolate chips.

5. Spread the ice cream in the frozen cookie crust and put the pie in the
   freezer until it is frozen hard.

6. Warm the fudge sauce and caramel sauce enough so that they can be
   drizzled. When the pie is frozen, pour the sauces in zigzag drizzles all
   over the top of the pie, then put it back in the freezer. Once the sauces
   on top are frozen, the pie can be tightly wrapped in plastic and stored in
   the freezer for up to 2 weeks.

Serves 8 to 12

CICI'S PIZZA
Cherry Pizza

ALTHOUGH THEY USED TO BE UNUSUAL, DESSERT PIZZAS ARE GAINING IN POPULARITY. THIS ONE WITH CHERRY PIE FILLING AND A BUTTER CRUMB TOPPING IS A FAVORITE AT CICI'S PIZZA. USE YOUR OWN PIZZA DOUGH RECIPE OR BUY PLAIN DOUGH.

Crumb Topping
½ cup all-purpose flour
3 tablespoons granulated sugar
1 tablespoon dark brown sugar
¼ teaspoon kosher salt
4 tablespoons (½ stick) cold
   unsalted butter, cut into small
   pieces

1 fresh or thawed frozen package
   pizza dough (about 1 pound)
One 20-ounce can cherry pie
   filling

1. Preheat the oven to 450°F.

2. To make the crumb topping, whisk together the flour, granulated sugar, brown sugar, and salt. Cut in the butter using a pastry cutter and blend until the mixture resembles coarse meal, then set the topping mixture aside.

3. Spread the pizza dough into an 8- to 10-inch circle and place on a sheet pan or pizza pan. Pierce the dough all over with the tines of a fork and put it in the hot oven for 5 minutes.

4. Remove the dough from the oven and spread it with the cherry pie filling. Sprinkle with the crumb topping and bake for another 20 minutes, or until the topping is golden brown.

Serves 4 to 6

CINDERELLA'S ROYAL TABLE
Blueberry-Cheese Buckle

THIS DESSERT, SERVED AT CINDERELLA'S ROYAL TABLE AT DISNEY'S MAGIC KINGDOM, WILL BE A DELIGHT FOR ALL THE LITTLE PRINCESSES IN YOUR LIFE—AND THE BIG ONES, TOO!

Muffins

6 tablespoons (¾ stick) unsalted butter, melted

⅓ cup milk

1 egg

1 egg yolk

1 teaspoon vanilla extract

1½ cups all-purpose flour

1½ teaspoons baking powder

¾ cup sugar

2 cups fresh blueberries

¾ cup cream cheese, softened

Topping

3 tablespoons cold unsalted butter, cut into pieces

½ cup all-purpose flour

3 tablespoons sugar

½ teaspoon ground cinnamon

1. Preheat the oven to 375°F. Coat a 12-cup muffin pan with butter or cooking spray.

2. To make the muffins, combine the melted butter, milk, egg, and egg yolk. Beat with an electric mixer until smooth. Stir in the vanilla extract.

3. Whisk together the flour, baking powder, and sugar. Gradually add the dry ingredients to the egg mixture, beating well after each addition. Fold in the blueberries with a wooden spoon and mix until just combined.

4. Spoon the batter into each of the prepared muffin cups. Insert 1 tablespoon of the softened cream cheese in the center of each muffin.

5. To make the topping, rub the pieces of butter together with the flour, sugar, and cinnamon until the mixture resembles large crumbs.

6. Sprinkle some of the topping over each muffin and bake for 18 to 20 minutes. A toothpick inserted in the center of the muffin should come out clean.

7. Let the muffins rest in the pan for 10 to 15 minutes before removing them.

Serves 12

Cinderella's Royal Table serves these with a scoop of lemon ice cream on the side. If you like the idea of lemon but don't want the ice cream, mix 1 tablespoon of grated lemon zest into the cream cheese before filling the unbaked muffins.

CINNABON
Cinnamon Roll

THESE ROLLS HAVE ALL THE GOODNESS OF THE ORIGINAL STICKY, CREAMY, SOFT HUNK OF PUFFY SWEET DOUGH AND BUTTERY CINNAMON THAT WOULD STOP YOU IN YOUR TRACKS JUST WALKING BY THE FRONT OF THE STORE. A BREAD MACHINE MAKES QUICK WORK OF THE PREPARATION.

Dough
¼ cup warm water
1 cup milk, at room temperature
1 egg, well beaten
4 tablespoons (½ stick) unsalted butter, softened
1 tablespoon granulated sugar
½ teaspoon kosher salt
4 cups all-purpose flour
Half a 3.4-ounce package instant vanilla pudding mix
1 tablespoon yeast for bread machines

Filling
1 cup packed light brown sugar
1 tablespoon ground cinnamon
4 tablespoons (½ stick) unsalted butter, softened

Frosting
8 tablespoons (½ stick) unsalted butter, softened
4 ounces cream cheese, softened
½ teaspoon vanilla extract
½ teaspoon ground cinnamon
1½ cups powdered sugar
1 tablespoon milk

1. To make the dough, follow the instructions for your bread machine on the "dough" setting. Add the water, milk, egg, butter, granulated sugar, salt, flour, pudding mix, and yeast, in the order listed, to the machine and process the ingredients.

2. Lightly flour a work surface and roll the dough out to a rectangle approximately 18 by 30 inches.

3. To make the filling and assemble, whisk together the brown sugar and cinnamon. Spread the softened butter over the dough, making sure it is soft enough to be spread evenly. Sprinkle the sugar and cinnamon mixture over the butter.

4. Starting with one of the long ends, roll the dough up into a log. Using regular sewing thread, cut pieces off the log at 2½-inch intervals by slipping the thread under the log as it lies on the work surface, then pulling the two ends of the thread together so that it cuts through the dough. You should have 12 rolls.

5. Grease two 9 by 9-inch baking pans and place the rolls 2 inches apart. Cover each pan with a clean kitchen towel and let the rolls rise until almost doubled in size, about 1 hour. The edges of the rolls should stick to one another and the sides of the pans.

6. Preheat the oven to 350°F.

7. Bake the rolls in the hot oven for 15 to 20 minutes, until golden brown.

8. While the rolls are baking, make the frosting. Cream the butter and cream cheese until well blended. Add the vanilla extract and cinnamon.

9. Stir in ½ cup of the powdered sugar and blend it in well. Continue to add the remaining 1 cup sugar in ½-cup intervals.

10. Add the milk to adjust the consistency. You may need to add more if the mixture is too thick to spread.

11. Spread a portion of the frosting on each cinnamon roll as it comes out of the oven.

Serves 12

If you are not using a bread machine, dissolve 2¼ teaspoons (1 envelope) active dry yeast in ½ cup warm water. After it activates, stir in the remaining ingredients, then cover the bowl and let the dough rise, covered, for about 45 minutes or until almost doubled in volume. Follow the instructions above to finish the cinnamon rolls.

CITRICOS
Gingerbread Ice Cream with Chocolate Soup

HERE IS A NOVEL WAY TO ENJOY YOUR COOKIES AND ICE CREAM. THE "SOUP" IS A MIXTURE OF CHOCOLATE AND CREAM, HOLDING A SCOOP OF VANILLA ICE CREAM BLENDED WITH GINGERBREAD COOKIES. THE FLAVOR AND TEXTURE ARE LIKE NO OTHER DESSERT.

Gingerbread Ice Cream
1 pint vanilla ice cream, softened
2 tablespoons molasses
2 teaspoons ground ginger
16 Pepperidge Farm Gingerman cookies

Chocolate Soup
1 cup bittersweet chocolate chips
1 cup boiling water
¼ cup fresh orange juice
¼ cup heavy cream
1 teaspoon vanilla extract

1. To make the gingerbread ice cream, combine the ice cream, molasses, and ginger in a bowl and whisk vigorously until well blended.
2. Crush 8 of the cookies and stir them in.
3. Refreeze the ice cream for 4 hours.
4. To make the chocolate soup, place the chocolate chips in a bowl and pour in the boiling water; stir until the chocolate melts. Let cool to room temperature.
5. Stir in the orange juice, heavy cream, and vanilla extract and mix well.
6. Ladle the chocolate soup into 8 bowls and serve with a scoop of the ice cream and a Gingerman cookie, for garnish.

Serves 8

CLINKERDAGGER
Burnt Crème

CLINKERDAGGER IS FAMOUS IN SPOKANE FOR ITS VERSION OF CRÈME BRÛLÉE, THE VANILLA-SCENTED CUSTARD UNDER A THIN SURFACE OF CARAMELIZED SUGAR. IF YOU HAVE A VERY SMALL BUTANE TORCH, YOU CAN WATCH THE SUGAR BUBBLE AND TURN COLOR WHEN YOU APPLY THE DIRECT FLAME.

2 cups heavy cream	1 cup sugar
4 egg yolks	1 tablespoon vanilla extract

1. Preheat the oven to 350°F.

2. Heat the heavy cream over low heat, just until bubbles begin to form around the edges.

3. With an electric mixer, beat the egg yolks and ½ cup of the sugar until thick and smooth, about 3 minutes.

4. Very gradually whisk the heated cream into the yolk mixture. Stir in the vanilla extract.

5. Pour the custard into six 6-ounce ramekins and fill them almost to the top. Set the ramekins in a large baking dish and fill the dish with enough hot water to come almost halfway up the sides of the ramekins.

6. Bake in the hot oven until the custard is set, 40 to 45 minutes.

7. Let the custards cool, then wrap them in plastic and refrigerate them until ready to serve.

8. Preheat the broiler and place the rack close to the heat source.

9. Sprinkle the remaining ½ cup sugar in an even layer over the entire surface of each custard. Place the custards on the boiler rack and brown them under the flame. When the sugar has evenly caramelized, set the ramekins aside to cool, then refrigerate until ready to serve.

Serves 6

A simple garnish of fresh berries and a mint leaf turns this dessert into something special.

COCO'S
Harvest Pie

THIS IS A TERRIFIC AUTUMN DESSERT THAT IS AN IDEAL ALTERNATIVE TO THE TRA-
DITIONAL PUMPKIN PIE AND WHIPPED CREAM. EVEN IF PUMPKIN IS NOT IN SEASON,
YOU CAN EASILY SUBSTITUTE MASHED YAMS OR SWEET POTATOES. SINCE THIS RECIPE
MAKES TWO PIES, YOU SHOULD BE READY FOR LOTS OF HOLIDAY ENTERTAINING.

Pumpkin Mousse
- 1 tablespoon (1 envelope) unflavored powdered gelatin
- 3 tablespoons cold water
- 6 egg yolks
- 1½ cups sugar
- One 30-ounce can pumpkin, or 3 cups roasted and mashed fresh pumpkin
- 2 teaspoons ground cinnamon
- ½ teaspoon ground ginger
- ¼ teaspoon ground cloves
- ¼ teaspoon ground nutmeg
- 3 cups heavy cream
- 2 teaspoons vanilla extract

Pumpkin Pies
- 1½ cups sugar
- 2 teaspoons ground cinnamon
- ½ teaspoon kosher salt
- 1 teaspoon ground ginger
- ½ teaspoon ground cloves
- ¼ teaspoon ground nutmeg
- One 30-ounce can pumpkin, or 3 cups roasted and mashed fresh pumpkin
- 4 egg yolks
- Two 12-ounce cans evaporated milk
- Two 9-inch deep-dish piecrusts, homemade (see page 149) or purchased
- Whipped cream (optional)

1. To make the pumpkin mousse, sprinkle the gelatin powder over the water and let it soften, about 1 minute.

2. Combine the egg yolks and the sugar in a bowl and place it over a pan of simmering water. Using an electric mixer, beat the mixture until it has started to thicken and the sugar has dissolved.

3. Remove the bowl from the pan and whisk in the softened gelatin. Place the bowl back on the pan of water and whisk the mixture until it is thick and smooth.

4. Whisk together the pumpkin, cinnamon, ginger, cloves, and nutmeg. Fold the pumpkin into the thickened egg mixture and blend well. Cover with plastic wrap and refrigerate for 1 hour.

5. Combine the heavy cream and vanilla extract and beat to stiff peaks. Fold the whipped cream into the pumpkin mixture and blend gently but thoroughly. Keep refrigerated.

6. Preheat the oven to 425°F.

7. Once the mousse is set, you can make the pumpkin pies. Whisk together the sugar, cinnamon, salt, ginger, cloves, and nutmeg in a large bowl. Stir in the pumpkin and mix until well blended.

8. Whisk the egg yolks until light and foamy. Gradually whisk in the evaporated milk.

9. Add the pumpkin mixture to the egg mixture and whisk vigorously until thoroughly combined.

10. Pour the mixture in even amounts into the 2 pie shells. Bake in the hot oven for 15 minutes, then reduce the heat to 350°F and bake for another 40 to 45 minutes. A toothpick inserted in the center should come out clean.

11. When the pies have cooled, top them with large spoonfuls of the pumpkin mousse. Serve warm or cold. Garnish with a dollop of whipped cream, if desired.

Each pie serves 8

COCO'S
Nutella Crepes

NUTELLA, MADE FROM HAZELNUTS, SKIM MILK, AND COCOA POWDER, IS A SPREAD
THAT ORIGINATED IN ITALY. BECAUSE OF THE CHOCOLATE, IT IS OFTEN CONSIDERED
A DESSERT, BUT IT GOES ON EVERYTHING FROM TOAST TO BAGELS. THESE TENDER
CREPES SPREAD WITH NUTELLA AND A LITTLE POWDERED SUGAR ARE PERFECT FOR
AN EASY BRUNCH.

2 cups all-purpose flour	2 cups milk
1 teaspoon kosher salt	1 teaspoon vanilla extract
2 eggs, beaten	One 13-ounce jar Nutella
2 tablespoons melted butter	½ cup powdered sugar

1. In a large bowl, whisk together the flour and salt. Make a well in the center of the dry ingredients and pour in the beaten eggs, 1 tablespoon of the melted butter, and ½ cup of the milk. Whisk thoroughly until well blended.

2. Gradually whisk in the remaining 1½ cups milk and the vanilla extract. Refrigerate the batter until ready to use.

3. Use a well-seasoned medium skillet or one with a nonstick surface to make the crepes. Put the skillet over medium heat and brush a thin film of the remaining 1 tablespoon melted butter over the bottom of the pan.

4. Pour ½ cup of the batter into the skillet and swirl it around to form a thin crepe. When the bottom is golden brown, flip the crepe over and cook for about 1 minute. Repeat with the remaining butter and batter, for a total of 30 crepes.

5. Keep the crepes warm while you finish making them. Spread each one with 2 or 3 teaspoons of Nutella and roll it up. Dust the crepes with a little powdered sugar before serving warm.

Makes 30 crepes

COLD STONE CREAMERY
Slab Cake Batter Ice Cream

THIS VERSION OF THE COLD STONE CREAMERY CLASSIC HAS ALL THE CREAMINESS OF THE ORIGINAL, BUT YOU DON'T NEED AN ICE CREAM MAKER. JUST FREEZE SCOOPS OF THE CHILLED BATTER UNTIL THEY'RE HARD, AND SERVE AS MANY OR AS FEW AS YOU WANT AT ANY TIME.

3 cups heavy cream
¼ teaspoon kosher salt
¾ cup sugar

½ cup Duncan Hines Moist Deluxe Butter Recipe Fudge Cake Mix
1 cup milk

1. Combine 1 cup of the heavy cream with the salt and sugar in a large saucepan over medium heat.

2. Stir until the sugar has dissolved. Once the sugar is dissolved, take the pan off the heat.

3. Whisk in the ½ cup cake mix. Stir in the remaining 2 cups heavy cream and the 1 cup milk. Whisk the mixture until it is completely smooth and free of lumps.

4. Pour the mixture into a bowl or tray and refrigerate for at least 4 hours. To make sure the scoops will stay together when served, portion out as many scoops as you want and put them either on a parchment paper–lined tray or on individual dessert plates. Put them in the freezer for 1 to 2 hours to harden, then serve.

Makes 1 quart

COMMANDER'S PALACE
Bread Pudding Soufflé with Whiskey Sauce

THIS LEGENDARY RESTAURANT, LOCATED IN THE NEW ORLEANS GARDEN DISTRICT, HAS BEEN GIVING ITS PATRONS EXCEPTIONAL FOOD AND SERVICE SINCE 1880. TRY THIS RICH DESSERT, CALLED A CREOLE SOUFFLÉ BY THE CHEF, FOR AN AUTHENTIC TASTE OF ONE OF THE CITY'S FINEST RESTAURANTS. AND DON'T SKIMP ON THE WHISKEY!

Bread Pudding
¾ cup sugar
1 teaspoon ground cinnamon
¼ teaspoon ground nutmeg
3 eggs
1 cup heavy cream
1 teaspoon vanilla extract
5 cups New Orleans–style French bread, trimmed and cut into 1-inch cubes
½ cup seedless raisins, soaked

Whiskey Sauce
1½ teaspoons cornstarch
1 tablespoon cold water
1 cup heavy cream
3 tablespoons sugar
¼ cup bourbon or other whiskey

Meringue
9 egg whites
¼ teaspoon cream of tartar
¾ cup sugar

1. Preheat the oven to 350°F. Butter an 8 by 8-inch baking pan.

2. To make the bread pudding, combine the sugar, cinnamon, and nutmeg in a large bowl with the eggs. Beat with an electric mixer until the eggs are smooth and light. Slowly add the heavy cream and mix until well combined.

3. Stir in the vanilla extract, then fold in the bread cubes. Let the bread sit until the egg mixture has been soaked up.

4. Sprinkle the raisins over the bottom of the prepared baking pan and spoon in the bread mixture.

5. Bake in the hot oven for 25 to 30 minutes, until the top is golden brown and the pudding is firm to the touch. A toothpick inserted in the center should come out clean. Let the pudding cool. Keep the oven turned on to the same temperature.

6. To make the whiskey sauce, whisk together the cornstarch and water to make a paste.

7. Pour the heavy cream into a small saucepan and bring it to a boil. Whisk in the cornstarch paste and reduce the heat.

8. Stir the cream until it has thickened.

9. Whisk in the sugar and simmer the sauce, stirring frequently, until the sugar is incorporated.

10. Take the sauce off the heat and stir in the bourbon. Let cool to room temperature.

11. Butter six 6-ounce ramekins and set them on a sheet pan.

12. To make the meringue, whip the egg whites with the cream of tartar until they form soft peaks.

13. Gradually add the sugar with the mixer running and beat the whites until they are thick and shiny.

14. To assemble the soufflés, remove the bread pudding from the baking pan and divide it in half. Break up one of the halves with your hands, making chunky pieces, and set the pieces in a medium bowl.

15. Fold in one quarter of the meringue, being careful not to break down the whites. Put a portion of this mixture into each of the prepared ramekins.

16. Break up the remaining bread pudding, set the pieces in the bowl, and fold in the remaining meringue.

17. Top the ramekins with this mixture, forming a smooth dome over each individual pudding.

18. Bake for about 20 minutes, or until the domes are golden brown.

19. To serve, use a large spoon to open a hole in the top of each soufflé. Pour a little of the whiskey sauce into the hole and serve immediately.

Serves 6

New Orleans–style French bread is very light and soft. Using a dense bread will keep the soufflé from being tender. Use regular French or Italian bread if you can't find the New Orleans style.

CORAL REEF RESTAURANT

Baileys and Jack Daniel's Mousse

ANOTHER OVER-THE-TOP DESSERT FROM WALT DISNEY WORLD IN FLORIDA, THIS COMBINATION OF WHITE CHOCOLATE MOUSSE WITH BAILEYS ORIGINAL IRISH CREAM AND DARK CHOCOLATE MOUSSE WITH JACK DANIEL'S IS DEFINITELY FOR GROWN-UPS. KEEP IT IN MIND WHEN YOU NEED A SPECTACULAR ENDING TO A FABULOUS MEAL.

Baileys Mousse
2 cups white chocolate chips
2 ounces (2 envelopes) unflavored powdered gelatin
2 cups hot water
¼ cup Baileys Original Irish Cream liqueur
5 egg yolks
I cup heavy cream

Jack Daniel's Mousse
2 cups dark chocolate chips
2 ounces (2 envelopes) unflavored powdered gelatin
2 cups hot water
¼ cup Jack Daniel's whiskey
5 egg yolks
I cup heavy cream

Garnishes
Fresh blueberries
Rolled chocolate wafers
Chocolate shavings
Raspberry sauce
Whipped cream
Hot fudge sauce

1. Prepare each mousse separately, but use the same method: Melt the chocolate chips in a medium bowl over a saucepan of simmering water. Stir frequently until the chocolate is smooth.

2. Dissolve the gelatin in the 2 cups hot water. When it has cooled a bit, whisk it into the melted chocolate. Stir in the Baileys with the white chocolate and the Jack Daniel's with the dark chocolate.

3. Beat the egg yolks with an electric mixer until light and foamy. Fold the yolks into the chocolate mixture.

4. Whip the cream to soft peaks. Stir 2 tablespoons of the whipped cream into the chocolate mixture, then fold in the remaining whipped cream using a rubber spatula, folding gently but thoroughly.

5. Coat twelve 6-ounce ramekins with cooking spray. Spoon the white mousse into six of them and the dark mousse into the other six. Put the ramekins in the freezer until set.

6. To serve, unmold the mousse and serve one of each flavor on a dessert plate. Garnish with fresh berries, rolled chocolate wafers, or chocolate shavings. You can also make a sauce with seedless raspberry preserves simmered with a little water. Whipped cream and hot fudge topping blended together make a quick and easy ganache and would go well with any of the other garnishes.

Serves 6

CORAL REEF RESTAURANT
Chocolate Wave Cake

THE "WAVE" IN THIS DESSERT COMES FROM A SWIRL OF WHITE CHOCOLATE TRUFFLE BAKED INTO A FLOURLESS CHOCOLATE CAKE. BOTH ARE FLAVORED WITH GRAND MARNIER AND MAKE A BEAUTIFUL PRESENTATION.

Cake Batter
12 tablespoons (1½ sticks) unsalted butter, softened
1 cup semisweet chocolate chips
1 cup sugar
2½ teaspoons cornstarch
4 eggs
4 egg yolks
1 tablespoon Grand Marnier

White Chocolate Truffle
¾ cup white chocolate chips
3 tablespoons heavy cream
3 tablespoons unsalted butter, softened
2 tablespoons Grand Marnier

Fresh berries (optional)
Warm chocolate sauce (optional)
Ice cream (optional)

1. To make the cake batter, melt the butter and chocolate chips in a medium bowl set over a saucepan of simmering water. Stir frequently until the mixture is smooth.

2. Combine the sugar and cornstarch in a separate bowl. Stir in the melted chocolate mixture and beat until well combined.

3. Beat the eggs and egg yolks with an electric mixer until light and foamy. Stir in the Grand Marnier, then gradually whisk the egg mixture into the chocolate mixture, blending well.

4. Cover the bowl and refrigerate for at least 8 hours.

5. To make the white chocolate truffle, combine the white chocolate chips and heavy cream in a medium bowl over a saucepan of simmering water.

6. Whisk in the softened butter. When it has melted, add the Grand Marnier and blend it in.

7. Cover the bowl and refrigerate for at least 8 hours.

8. Preheat the oven to 400°F. Coat six 5-ounce ramekins with butter or cooking spray.

9. To assemble the dessert for baking, fill each ramekin less than half full with the dark chocolate cake batter and smooth the top.

10. Put a rounded tablespoon of the white truffle mixture in the center, then fill the ramekin with more of the dark chocolate cake batter, so that the white truffle is completely enclosed.

11. Put the ramekins on a sheet pan and bake in the hot oven for 15 minutes. Remove from the oven and let cool for 15 to 20 minutes. Loosen the edges if necessary by running a knife around them.

12. Invert each cake onto a dessert plate and unmold it. Serve with fresh berries, warm chocolate sauce, or ice cream, if desired.

Serves 6

CORAL REEF RESTAURANT
Key Lime Parfait

LIKE KEY LIME PIE WITHOUT THE CRUST, THIS REFRESHING CUSTARD SITS ON A SLICE OF POUND CAKE IN A LARGE BALLOON GLASS. TOPPED OFF WITH WHIPPED CREAM AND A SLICE OF KIWIFRUIT, THIS DESSERT IS THE PERFECT WAY TO END A SUMMER DAY.

One 14-ounce can sweetened condensed milk
4 egg yolks
¼ cup fresh Key lime juice
One 8-ounce pound cake
½ cup heavy cream

2 tablespoons powdered sugar
½ teaspoon vanilla extract
1 kiwifruit, peeled and cut into 6 slices
6 strawberries

1. Beat the sweetened condensed milk and egg yolks with an electric mixer at low speed until thoroughly combined. Slowly pour in the lime juice while still beating and mix until well blended.

2. Cut the pound cake into six 1-inch-thick slices, then trim each slice to fit inside of a balloon wineglass or other large enough glass such as a parfait glass or brandy snifter.

3. Put a slice of pound cake inside each glass, then spoon the Key lime filling over it, leaving room for the whipped cream.

4. Refrigerate the filled glasses for at least 2 hours. The recipe can be made ahead up to this point.

5. In a small bowl, whip the heavy cream with the powdered sugar until soft peaks form. Add the vanilla extract and continue whipping until the cream is stiff.

6. Spoon a portion of the whipped cream into each glass and garnish with a slice of kiwifruit and a whole strawberry.

Serves 6

CRACKER BARREL
Pumpkin Custard n' Ginger Snaps

FOR A LIGHTER SEASONAL DESSERT THAN PUMPKIN PIE, TRY INDIVIDUAL PUMPKIN
DESSERTS WITH NO CRUST, GARNISHED WITH JUST A CRUMBLING OF GINGER SNAPS.
THE WHIPPED CREAM ON TOP IS A REFRESHING TOUCH.

Custards
8 egg yolks
One 15-ounce can pumpkin puree
1½ cups heavy cream
½ cup granulated sugar
2 teaspoons pumpkin pie spice
1 teaspoon vanilla extract
1 cup ginger snap crumbs (about
   15 cookies)

1 tablespoon unsalted butter,
   melted

Pumpkin Whipped Cream
1 cup heavy cream
1 tablespoon powdered sugar
1 teaspoon pumpkin pie spice

1. Preheat the oven to 350°F.

2. To make the custards, beat the yolks with an electric mixer until pale
   yellow and creamy. Beat in the pumpkin puree, heavy cream, granulated
   sugar, pumpkin pie spice, and vanilla extract. Beat the mixture until
   smooth.

3. Put the bowl with the yolk mixture over a saucepan of simmering water
   and stir until the mixture is thickened enough to coat the back of a
   spoon.

4. Pour the custard into eight custard cups and set the cups on a sheet pan.
   Place on the top rack in the hot oven and bake the custards for 20 to
   25 minutes. Test for doneness with a thin-bladed knife. Insert the knife
   midway between the center and edge of the cups. (If making a family-
   sized custard—see the tip opposite—insert the knife about 1 inch from
   the center of the dish.) If the knife is clean when pulled out, the custard
   is done. If any custard clings to the blade, bake a few minutes longer and
   test again.

5. Halfway through the baking time, combine the ginger snap crumbs and the melted butter. Sprinkle the crumb mixture over the custards and continue baking. When finished baking, let the custards cool to room temperature.

6. To make the pumpkin whipped cream, whip the heavy cream to soft peaks. Add the powdered sugar and pumpkin pie spice, then whip to stiff peaks. Keep refrigerated until ready to use.

7. To finish the custards, spoon on the whipped cream or fill a pastry bag and pipe the whipped cream onto each of the custards. Serve chilled or at room temperature.

Serves 8

You can also make just one family-sized custard by making it in an 8 by 8-inch baking dish. Increase the baking time to 30 to 35 minutes.

CRACKER BARREL
Baked Apple Dumplings

IF YOU LIKE APPLE STRUDEL AND BAKED APPLES, YOU'LL LOVE THIS COMBINATION OF THE TWO. FLAKY PUFF PASTRY IS FILLED WITH HALF AN APPLE AND SPICED FILLING, THEN BAKED WITH A PECAN-STREUSEL TOPPING AND FINISHED WITH A DRIZZLE OF VANILLA ICING.

Pecan Streusel
¾ cup chopped pecans
¾ cup packed light brown sugar
¾ cup all-purpose flour
4 tablespoons (½ stick) unsalted
    butter, melted

Filling
1 cup granulated sugar
½ cup bread crumbs
3 tablespoons ground cinnamon
¼ teaspoon ground nutmeg

Dumplings
One 17.25-ounce package frozen
    puff pastry, thawed
1 egg, beaten
4 Granny Smith apples, peeled,
    cored, and halved

Icing
1 cup powdered sugar
1 teaspoon vanilla extract
2 to 3 tablespoons milk

1. To make the pecan streusel, combine the chopped pecans, brown sugar, and flour in a medium bowl. Stir the ingredients to blend them, then, using a fork to keep the mixture like crumbs, stir in the melted butter. Mix to make sure all the dry ingredients are moistened.

2. To make the filling for the baked apples, in a small bowl, combine the sugar, bread crumbs, cinnamon, and nutmeg.

3. To make the dumplings, preheat the oven to 425°F. Lightly grease a baking sheet.

4. Roll out each sheet of puff pastry to measure 12 by 12 inches. Cut each square into quarters, so you have a total of eight 6-inch squares.

5. Brush each square with some of the beaten egg.

6. Put a tablespoon of the filling in the center of each piece of pastry. Lay half an apple, core side down, on top of the filling.

7. Top with another tablespoon of the filling, then pull up the corners of the pastry and pinch the sides together to seal the seams over the apple.

8. Brush the top of each dumpling with the beaten egg.

9. Lay the dumplings on the prepared baking sheet and top each one with some of the pecan streusel.

10. Bake in the hot oven for 15 minutes, then reduce the heat to 350°F and bake for another 25 minutes, or until the tops are lightly browned.

11. While the pastries are baking, make the icing: Combine the powdered sugar and vanilla extract. Stir in just enough of the milk so that it can be drizzled from the tip of a spoon.

12. Remove the dumplings from the oven and let them cool at room temperature.

13. Drizzle some of the icing over each dumpling before serving.

Serves 4 to 8

CRACKER BARREL
Chocolate Pecan Pie

A PECAN PIE WITH A TWIST—THE CHOCOLATE CHIPS WILL MAKE THIS A NEW FAMILY
FAVORITE. THE FILLING CAN BE USED TO MAKE INDIVIDUAL TARTS, BAR COOKIES, OR
DROP COOKIES. THINK OF IT AS FOUR DELICIOUS DESSERTS IN ONE RECIPE.

3 eggs
½ cup sugar
I cup light corn syrup
½ teaspoon kosher salt
I ½ teaspoons vanilla extract
½ teaspoon ground cinnamon
4 tablespoons (½ stick) unsalted
   butter, melted

I ¾ cups coarsely chopped
   pecans
One 9-inch piecrust, homemade
   (see page xxii) or purchased
½ cup semisweet chocolate chips

1. Preheat the oven to 350°F.

2. Beat the eggs with an electric mixer until light and foamy. Gradually
   pour in the sugar and beat until it is incorporated.

3. Stir in the corn syrup, salt, vanilla extract, cinnamon, and melted butter.

4. Layer the pecans on the bottom of the piecrust and sprinkle the chocolate chips over them.

5. Scrape the batter into the crust and bake in the hot oven for 50 to 60
   minutes, until the filling has set. Remove the pie from the oven and let it
   cool almost to room temperature before serving.

Serves 8

*A scoop of ice cream, either vanilla or butter pecan,
can be placed next to the slice of pie before serving.
You can also finish it with a dollop of whipped cream on top.*

CRACKER BARREL

Double Fudge Coca-Cola Cake

THIS GUEST FAVORITE WAS ADDED TO THE DESSERT MENU TO CELEBRATE THE CRACKER BARREL'S FORTIETH ANNIVERSARY. SERVE THE CAKE WARM WITH VANILLA ICE CREAM AND HOT FUDGE SAUCE.

Cake

1 cup Coca-Cola

8 tablespoons (1 stick) unsalted butter, cut into pieces

¼ cup unsweetened cocoa powder

½ cup vegetable oil

1 cup mini marshmallows

2 cups all-purpose flour

2 cups granulated sugar

½ teaspoon kosher salt

1 teaspoon baking soda

2 eggs

½ cup buttermilk

1 teaspoon vanilla extract

Frosting

8 tablespoons (1 stick) unsalted butter

¼ cup unsweetened cocoa powder

¼ cup heavy cream

1 teaspoon vanilla extract

2½ cups powdered sugar

½ cup chopped pecans

1. Preheat the oven to 350°F. Grease and flour a 9 by 13-inch baking pan.

2. To make the cake, combine the Coca-Cola, butter, and the cocoa powder in a medium saucepan. Bring to a boil, then stir in the vegetable oil. Add the marshmallows and stir until they are all well coated.

3. Whisk together the flour, sugar, salt, and baking soda. Gradually add the dry ingredients to the marshmallow mixture and beat until well blended.

4. In a medium bowl, beat the eggs and buttermilk with an electric mixer until light and foamy. Stir in the vanilla extract.

5. Add the egg mixture to the marshmallow batter and blend well with a wooden spoon.

6. Pour the batter into the prepared baking pan and bake in the hot oven for 20 to 25 minutes. The cake is done when a toothpick inserted in the center comes out clean.

7. Make the frosting while the cake is baking. Melt the butter with the cocoa powder in a large saucepan. Whisk in the heavy cream and stir until smooth.

8. Stir in the vanilla extract and the powdered sugar. Beat with a spoon until the mixture is smooth, then stir in the chopped pecans. Add a little extra cream or milk if the frosting is too stiff.

9. Invert the cake onto a large platter and allow to cool completely before frosting. Top with the frosting, including the sides. Cut into squares for serving.

Serves 10

DAIRY QUEEN
Ice Cream

THE FIRST DAIRY QUEEN CLAIM TO FAME WAS ITS ICE CREAM. YOU CAN RE-CREATE IT
HERE IF YOU HAVE AN ICE CREAM MAKER.

Two .25-ounce envelopes
   unflavored powdered gelatin
½ cup cold water
4 cups milk

2 cups sugar
1 tablespoon vanilla extract
½ teaspoon kosher salt
3 cups heavy cream

1. Sprinkle the gelatin powder over the water to dissolve.

2. Heat the milk in a medium saucepan over medium heat, but do not let
   it boil. Remove it from the heat and add the gelatin and water, sugar,
   vanilla extract, and salt.

3. Let the mixture cool, then whisk in the heavy cream and refrigerate the
   mixture for 5 to 6 hours.

4. Pour the mixture into a 1.5-quart ice cream maker and process according
   to the manufacturer's directions.

Serves 16

DENNY'S
Maple Bacon Sundae

IF THIS SOUNDS TOO STRANGE, YOU'LL JUST HAVE TO TRY IT. ALL YOU NEED IS ICE CREAM, COOKED BACON, AND MAPLE SYRUP—AND THREE VERY GOOD FRIENDS!

8 strips thick-cut bacon
8 scoops vanilla ice cream

I cup maple syrup, slightly warmed

1. Line a sheet pan with foil and arrange the bacon in a single layer.

2. Put the pan in a cold oven and set the oven to 400°F.

3. Bake for 20 to 25 minutes. The bacon is done when it is golden brown, not crispy. Drain the bacon on paper towels and let cool.

4. Place 2 scoops of ice cream in each of four dessert glasses. Pour ½ cup of the maple syrup over the servings.

5. Top each portion with 2 strips of the bacon, either left whole or chopped up. Drizzle the remaining ½ cup maple syrup over the bacon in each glass and serve.

Serves 4

DUNKIN' DONUTS
Pumpkin-Spice Muffins

COMBINE THE BEST OF TRADITIONAL HOLIDAY FLAVORS WITH MUFFINS MADE FROM
SPICE CAKE MIX AND PUMPKIN PUREE. PERFECT FOR BREAKFAST OR AFTER DINNER.

One 18.25-ounce box spice cake
  mix
One 3.4-ounce package instant
  vanilla pudding mix
One 30-ounce can pumpkin
  puree
2 eggs

1 teaspoon vanilla extract
1 tablespoon plain yogurt
½ cup canola oil
2 teaspoons pumpkin pie spice
½ cup packed golden brown
  sugar

1. Preheat the oven to 350°F. Line a 12-cup muffin pan with paper liners.

2. Whisk together the box of spice cake mix and the instant vanilla pudding. Stir in the pumpkin puree and blend well.

3. Using an electric mixer, beat in the eggs, one at a time, beating well after each addition. Add the vanilla extract, yogurt, canola oil, and pumpkin pie spice. Beat until the ingredients are well incorporated.

4. Fill the muffin cups three-quarters full with the muffin batter. Sprinkle with the brown sugar and bake for 30 minutes, or until a toothpick inserted in the center comes out clean.

Makes 12 muffins

DUNKIN' DONUTS
Vanilla-Filled Doughnuts

MAKE YOUR OWN DOUGHNUTS AND STUFF THEM WITH A CREAMY VANILLA FILLING.
DUST THEM WITH POWDERED SUGAR AND SERVE WARM.

Doughnuts

1 envelope (2¼ teaspoons) active
dry yeast
2 tablespoons very warm water
(about 100°F)
¾ cup scalded milk, cooled
¼ cup granulated sugar
½ teaspoon kosher salt
1 egg
¼ cup vegetable shortening
2½ cups all-purpose flour

Vanilla Filling

4 tablespoons (½ stick) unsalted
butter, softened
¼ cup vegetable shortening
2 cups powdered sugar
1 to 2 tablespoons milk
1 teaspoon vanilla extract

4 to 6 cups canola oil, for
deep-frying
Powdered sugar, for dusting

1. To make the doughnuts, dissolve the yeast in the warm water in a large
   bowl and let it sit for about 5 minutes to activate.

2. Stir in the milk, granulated sugar, salt, egg, vegetable shortening, and
   1 cup of the flour. Using an electric mixer, beat the ingredients on low
   speed for 30 seconds. Increase the speed to medium and beat for another
   2 minutes.

3. Add the remaining 1½ cups flour and beat until smooth. Cover the
   bowl and set the dough in a warm place to rise until doubled in volume,
   about 1 hour.

4. Flour a work surface and knead the dough for a few seconds. Roll it out
   to about ½ inch thick, and cut the doughnuts with a floured 2-inch
   cookie cutter. Flour a baking sheet and put the doughnuts on it to rise,
   covered, for about 30 minutes.

5. Make the vanilla filling while the doughnuts are rising. Using an electric mixer, cream the butter and vegetable shortening until well blended. Stir in the powdered sugar ½ cup at a time and beat well after each addition. Beat in the milk until the mixture is light and fluffy, then add the vanilla extract and blend. Transfer the filling to a pastry bag fitted with a small plain tip.

6. Heat the oil in a deep-fryer or heavy-bottomed saucepan. Keep the temperature between 350° and 375°F. Slide the doughnuts, 2 or 3 at a time, into the oil and fry until golden brown, then flip them over and fry until golden on the other side. Remove them from the oil and drain on paper towels.

7. When the doughnuts are cool enough to handle, insert a thin knife from the side of each doughnut into the center and carefully make a cavity inside for the filling.

8. Pipe the vanilla filling into each doughnut, then dust with powdered sugar.

Serves 8 to 12

DUQUESNE CLUB
Macaroons

LIGHT AND AIRY, THESE BITE-SIZED MACAROONS ARE THE PERFECT ACCOMPANIMENT
TO A MIDMORNING CUP OF COFFEE OR A LATE-NIGHT HOT COCOA.

1 pound almond paste	¾ cup granulated sugar
1½ cups powdered sugar	6 egg whites

1. Preheat the oven to 325°F. Line a sheet pan with parchment paper.

2. Using an electric mixer, break up the almond paste, then add the powdered sugar and the granulated sugar and mix until the ingredients are finely blended.

3. Add the egg whites in increments, beating well after each addition. Mix until the ingredients form a paste.

4. Fit a pastry bag with a round tip and fill it with the macaroon mixture. Pipe evenly sized balls onto the parchment paper, spacing them about 1 inch apart.

5. Bake in the hot oven for 15 to 20 minutes. The macaroons should be golden on the outside and moist in the center.

Makes 24 macaroons

Add a little extra flavor with a teaspoon of vanilla or almond extract beaten in with the egg whites. You could also add a tablespoon of finely grated orange or lemon zest.

EAT'N PARK
Strawberry n' Crème Muffins

THESE GORGEOUS MUFFINS ARE GOING TO MAKE YOUR STRAWBERRY LOVERS VERY HAPPY. THE CREAM IN THE BATTER GIVES THEM A SMOOTH TEXTURE, JUST BEGGING TO BE TOPPED OFF WITH STRAWBERRY JAM.

8 tablespoons (1 stick) unsalted butter, softened
1¼ cups sugar
2 eggs
1 teaspoon vanilla extract
2 cups all-purpose flour

2 teaspoons baking powder
¼ teaspoon kosher salt
½ cup heavy cream
20 strawberries, hulled and chopped

1. Preheat the oven to 375°F. Coat 18 fairly shallow muffin cups, less than 3 inches wide and just over 1 inch deep, with butter or cooking spray.

2. Using an electric mixer, cream the butter and sugar until light and fluffy.

3. Add the eggs, one at a time, beating well after each addition. Stir in the vanilla extract.

4. Whisk together the flour, baking powder, and the salt.

5. Alternately add the flour mixture and the heavy cream to the creamed mixture, beating until well combined. Fold in the chopped strawberries.

6. Fill the muffin cups three-quarters full with the batter. Sprinkle a little extra sugar on top.

7. Bake for 30 minutes in the hot oven. Let the muffins cool for 10 to 15 minutes before removing them from the muffin pans.

Makes 18 muffins

EDY'S
Girl Scout Thin Mint Cookie Ice Cream

YOU WILL NEED A SLEEVE OF GIRL SCOUT THIN MINTS FOR THIS ICE CREAM, SO WHEN THAT TIME OF YEAR ROLLS AROUND, BE SURE TO BUY EXTRA. YOU'LL ALSO NEED AN ICE CREAM MAKER.

2 eggs
¾ cup sugar
2 cups heavy cream
1½ cups milk
1 teaspoon vanilla extract

1 teaspoon mint extract
2 to 3 drops green food coloring
One 15-count sleeve Girl Scout Thin Mints cookies, coarsely crushed

1. Beat the eggs with an electric mixer until pale yellow. Slowly add the sugar while mixing and beat until fluffy.

2. Combine the heavy cream and the milk in a saucepan over medium-low heat, stirring frequently until the mixture is warm.

3. Whisk ½ cup of the cream mixture into the egg mixture, stirring constantly. When well blended, whisk in the remaining warm cream mixture. When well mixed, return the mixture to the saucepan and heat, stirring constantly, until the mixture thickens enough to coat the back of a spoon.

4. Stir in the vanilla and mint extracts, then add the green food coloring and blend well.

5. Remove the pan from the heat and let the cream mixture cool to room temperature. When it is no longer warm, cover the mixture and refrigerate for at least 4 hours.

6. Transfer the cream mixture to an ice cream maker and follow the manufacturer's directions. When the ice cream is almost ready, pour in the crushed Thin Mints and stir well.

Makes about 1 quart

EL CHICO
Fried Ice Cream

GIVE YOURSELF PLENTY OF TIME TO PREPARE THESE HOT AND COLD TREATS: THE ICE
CREAM NEEDS TIME TO FIRM UP AFTER BEING SOFTENED. USE A CANDY THERMOMETER
TO CHECK THE TEMPERATURE OF THE FRYING OIL IF YOU DO NOT HAVE A DEEP-FRYER.

1 cup crushed cornflakes
½ cup sugar
1 teaspoon ground cinnamon
1 quart vanilla ice cream,
   softened in the refrigerator

4 cups vegetable oil, for frying
Favorite toppings

1. Combine the cornflakes with the sugar and cinnamon and place in a shallow bowl.
2. Make 6 large balls of ice cream and roll them in the cornflake mixture. Make sure the mixture is pressed into the ice cream to make a solid crust.
3. Wrap the balls in foil and freeze them for at least 5 hours. They will last for up to 2 weeks in the freezer.
4. Heat the oil in an electric deep-fryer to 450°F. If you don't have a deep-fryer, use a heavy-bottomed saucepan and heat the oil to 450°F.
5. When ready to serve, unwrap each ball and submerge it in the hot oil very briefly, about 2 or 3 seconds. Drain on paper towels.
6. Place the fried ice cream in dessert bowls and serve immediately with your favorite toppings.

Serves 6

You may only be able to fry two balls at a time, so just take out however many you need from the freezer. Once you get started, you have to move quickly. Have your toppings ready—try chopped nuts, hot fudge, whipped cream, cherries, and honey.

EL TORITO
Kahlúa Mousse

HAVING A QUICK WAY TO MAKE MOUSSE USING COOL WHIP MEANS YOU WILL AL-
WAYS BE ABLE TO WHIP UP THIS COFFEE-FLAVORED DESSERT WITHOUT A LOT OF
TIME OR EFFORT.

2½ cups Cool Whip
½ cup heavy cream
1 tablespoon unsweetened cocoa
powder
2 teaspoons instant coffee
powder

3 tablespoons sugar
¼ cup Kahlúa coffee liqueur
Chocolate sprinkles, for garnish
Wafer cookies (optional)

1. Using an electric mixer, whip 2 cups of the Cool Whip with the heavy cream until stiff peaks form.

2. Combine the cocoa powder, instant coffee, and sugar. Using a rubber spatula, gently fold the sugar mixture into the Cool Whip mixture. Add the Kahlúa and carefully mix it in.

3. Spoon the mousse into six 6-ounce ramekins, and refrigerate until set, at least 1 hour.

4. When ready to serve, whip the remaining ½ cup Cool Whip to stiff peaks.

5. Top each mousse with a dollop of the whipped topping and some chocolate sprinkles. Serve with wafer cookies, if desired.

Serves 6

EL TORITO
Sweet Corn Cake

THIS CRUMBLY CORN BREAD IS THE PERFECT DESSERT FOR THOSE WHO DON'T REALLY LIKE DESSERTS—IT'S VERY RICH AND SWEET WITH THE FLAVOR OF CORN. SPREAD WITH SOME WHIPPED HONEY-BUTTER WHILE STILL WARM, OR TOAST IT ON A GRIDDLE THE NEXT DAY AND SERVE IT WITH MAPLE SYRUP.

One 7½-ounce package sweet
  corn bread mix
4 tablespoons (½ stick) unsalted
  butter, melted

¼ cup milk
One 15-ounce can cream-style
  corn

1. Preheat the oven to 350°F.
2. Follow the package directions for making the corn bread.
3. Stir in the melted butter, milk, and corn.
4. Pour the batter into a 5 by 9-inch loaf pan and bake in the hot oven for 40 to 45 minutes, until all the liquid has been absorbed.
5. Scoop out the warm corn bread and serve it for dessert or as a side dish.

Serves 8

If you would prefer the corn bread a little drier, bake it in a 9 by 9-inch baking dish for the same amount of time.

FANNIE MAY CANDY
Trinidads

FANNIE MAY HAS BEEN PRODUCING FINE CHOCOLATES AND CANDIES IN CHICAGO FOR OVER NINETY YEARS. BE SURE TO USE BEST-QUALITY INGREDIENTS FOR THESE CHOCOLATE AND COCONUT CONFECTIONS.

½ cup unsweetened flaked coconut
1 cup heavy cream
1 pound dark chocolate, chopped
1 pound white chocolate, chopped
1 tablespoon vegetable oil

1. Heat a small skillet over medium-low heat and toast the coconut, stirring frequently, until it is lightly golden brown. Set the coconut aside.

2. Bring the heavy cream to a boil in a medium saucepan. Remove it from the heat as soon as it boils and stir in the chopped dark chocolate. Let the chocolate melt in the hot cream, stirring occasionally.

3. Once the chocolate has melted, use a wire whisk and stir the mixture until it is smooth and creamy. Transfer to a small bowl and refrigerate for at least 2 hours.

4. Once the chocolate mixture is chilled, line a sheet pan with waxed paper and drop the chocolate by the teaspoonful. Put the whole tray in the freezer for 15 minutes.

5. Pull the drops of chocolate off the waxed paper, one at a time, rolling each drop into a ball between your palms. Stick a toothpick into the top of each ball and return to the tray and then to the freezer.

6. Melt the white chocolate in a medium bowl set over a saucepan of simmering water. Remove it from the heat and stir in the toasted coconut and the vegetable oil. Let this mixture cool at room temperature for about 10 minutes.

7. Take the dark chocolate balls out of the freezer and dip each one into the white chocolate mixture, using the toothpick. Swirl the ball around to make sure it is evenly coated, then give it a very easy shake to let the excess white chocolate drip off. Replace the coated ball on the waxed paper.

8. When all the balls are coated, return the tray to the freezer and let the candies harden completely. When they are completely frozen, you can easily remove the toothpicks without leaving any fingerprints or disturbing any of the chocolate.

9. Let the candies come to room temperature before serving.

Makes 36 pieces

Quality chocolate is easy to find these days in specialty shops and online. Look for Ghirardelli, Callebaut, Valrhona, Guittard, or Lindt. Do not use chocolate chips for this recipe, as they have additional ingredients that will affect the candies.

FLEMING'S STEAKHOUSE
Chocolate Lava Cake

MANY RESTAURANTS HAVE A LIQUID CHOCOLATE CAKE LISTED ON THE DESSERT MENU. THIS VERSION FROM FLEMING'S HAS SO LITTLE FLOUR THAT IT TAKES ON THE TEXTURE OF A CUSTARD. GARNISH THE FINISHED CAKE WITH FRESH BERRIES, CHOPPED NUTS, OR WHIPPED CREAM.

1 pound (4 sticks) lightly salted butter	8 egg yolks
1 pound semisweet chocolate chips	1 cup sugar
8 eggs	1 teaspoon vanilla extract
	2 tablespoons all-purpose flour
	¼ teaspoon kosher salt

1. Preheat the oven to 400°F. Grease and flour a 2-quart soufflé dish.

2. Cut the sticks of butter into pieces and combine with the chocolate chips in a medium bowl. Set the bowl over a saucepan of simmering water and stir until the butter and chocolate are both melted.

3. Using an electric mixer, beat the eggs and egg yolks in a medium bowl for about 5 minutes. The mixture should be slightly thickened.

4. Add the sugar and vanilla extract to the eggs and beat for another minute.

5. Whisk the melted butter and chocolate until they are well blended and smooth. Gradually whisk the chocolate mixture into the egg mixture, stirring to blend thoroughly.

6. Whisk together the flour and salt, then whisk into the chocolate mixture. Blend well.

7. Pour the chocolate mixture into the prepared dish and bake in the hot oven for 12 to 15 minutes. The cake should puff up initially and sink down a bit as it cools.

8. Let the cake cool for a few minutes, then invert it onto a serving platter and unmold it. Serve with ice cream or other garnishes.

Serves 8

FURR'S FRESH BUFFET
Fruit Punch Jell-O Salad

HERE'S A CLASSIC THAT DOESN'T FIND ITS WAY INTO TOO MANY CONTEMPORARY COOKBOOKS. USE A VARIETY OF JELL-O FRUIT FLAVORS TO CHANGE THE DESSERT EACH TIME YOU MAKE IT.

3 cups boiling water
Three 3-ounce packages fruit-
    flavored Jell-O
2½ cups cold water

One 14.5-ounce can fruit
    cocktail, drained
1 cup sweetened flaked coconut
1 cup miniature marshmallows

1. Pour the boiling water over the Jell-O in a medium bowl and whisk until the dry gelatin mix dissolves.

2. Stir in the cold water. Pour 1 cup of the gelatin into a small bowl and reserve at room temperature.

3. Pour the remaining gelatin into a decorative mold or a 9 by 13-inch baking dish and refrigerate until partially set.

4. Remove the partially set gelatin from the refrigerator and scatter the drained fruit cocktail on top.

5. Toss the coconut and marshmallows together and scatter them over the fruit. Gently press the toppings into the gelatin.

6. Pour the reserved gelatin over the top, covering the fruit and marshmallows evenly, and refrigerate until set.

Serves 8

FURR'S FRESH BUFFET
Pineapple Millionaire Pie

FURR'S IS A SIXTY-YEAR-OLD TRADITION IN TEXAS AND NEIGHBORING SOUTHERN AND MIDWESTERN STATES. IT PRIDES ITSELF ON FRESHLY PREPARED FOOD AND CUSTOMER SATISFACTION. THIS LIGHT PINEAPPLE PIE IS A GOOD EXAMPLE OF HOW REFRESHING WELL-PREPARED, HOME-STYLE FOOD CAN BE.

Pie Filling

2 cups powdered sugar

8 tablespoons (1 stick) unsalted
   butter, softened

2 eggs

¼ teaspoon kosher salt

1 teaspoon vanilla extract

2 prebaked 9-inch piecrusts,
   homemade (see page 47)
   or purchased

Pineapple Topping

1 cup heavy cream

½ cup powdered sugar

One 20-ounce can crushed
   pineapple, drained

½ cup chopped pecans

1. To make the pie filling, combine the powdered sugar and the butter and beat with an electric mixer until light and fluffy.

2. Add the eggs, one at a time, beating well after each addition. Stir in the salt and vanilla extract and blend well.

3. Pour half of the filling mixture into each of the pie shells and refrigerate for at least 30 minutes.

4. To make the pineapple topping, whip the heavy cream to soft peaks. Gradually add the powdered sugar and continue beating until stiff peaks form.

5. Using a rubber spatula, fold in the crushed pineapple and the pecans.

6. Pour half of the topping mixture over each of the chilled pies and spread it evenly. Refrigerate until ready to serve.

Each pie serves 8

GHIRARDELLI SODA FOUNTAIN AND CHOCOLATE SHOP
Chocolate Chip–Pecan Cookies

SAN FRANCISCO'S FAVORITE CHOCOLATIER HAS FOUND A HOME AT DISNEY WORLD. VISITORS TO DOWNTOWN DISNEY CAN STOP IN FOR A MALT, A SHAKE, OR MAYBE THESE ADDICTIVE COOKIES.

10 ounces Ghirardelli bittersweet baking chocolate, chopped

8 tablespoons (1 stick) unsalted butter, softened

1 cup packed golden brown sugar

½ cup granulated sugar

4 eggs

1 teaspoon vanilla extract

2¼ cups all-purpose flour

1 teaspoon baking powder

½ teaspoon baking soda

½ teaspoon kosher salt

1 teaspoon espresso powder (optional)

1½ cups Ghirardelli milk chocolate chips

1 cup chopped pecans

1. Place the chopped chocolate in a bowl and set over a saucepan of simmering water. Stir until melted.

2. In a large bowl, cream the butter with the brown and granulated sugars with an electric mixer until light and fluffy. Add the eggs, one at a time, beating well after each addition. Stir in the vanilla extract and blend well.

3. Whisk together the flour, baking powder, baking soda, and salt. Add the espresso powder, if using. Gradually stir the dry ingredients into the egg and butter mixture alternately with the melted chocolate until all the ingredients are well combined.

4. Fold in the chocolate chips and chopped pecans. Blend thoroughly with a spatula.

5. Cover the bowl with plastic wrap and refrigerate for 1 hour.

6. Preheat the oven to 350°F.

7. Drop tablespoonfuls of the cookie dough onto an ungreased baking sheet, spacing them about 2 inches apart, and bake for 15 minutes, until the edges are lightly browned.

8. Transfer the cookies to wire racks to cool completely before storing.

Makes about 24 cookies

HARDEE'S
Peach Cobbler

WHEN IT WAS BEGUN IN NORTH CAROLINA IN THE 1960S BY WILBUR HARDEE, THE HARDEE'S CHAIN WAS WIDELY KNOWN FOR ITS BISCUITS AND BURGERS. THE RESTAU-RANTS TODAY ARE CLUSTERED THROUGHOUT THE MIDWEST AND SOUTHEAST AND ARE STILL SERVING A FULL MENU OF FAMILIAR FAVORITES.

One 21-ounce can peach pie filling
4 tablespoons (½ stick) cold unsalted butter, thinly sliced
1 frozen piecrust, thawed

2 tablespoons ground cinnamon
3 tablespoons sugar
Whipped cream or vanilla ice cream, for serving

1. Preheat the oven to 375°F.
2. Spread the peach filling on the bottom of an 8 by 8-inch baking dish. Layer the slices of butter on top of the peaches as evenly as you can.
3. Flatten out the thawed piecrust and cut it to fit the baking dish. Carefully lay the crust on top of the peaches and sprinkle with the cinnamon and sugar.
4. Bake for 20 to 25 minutes, until the crust is lightly browned.
5. Serve hot, with whipped cream or vanilla ice cream.

Serves 8

HOUSE OF PLENTY
Turtle Pie

THE OWNERS OF HOUSE OF PLENTY IN HIGHLAND, ILLINOIS, BELIEVE IT'S HAUNTED BY FOUR SPIRITS. THEY MUST ALL BE AFTER THE TURTLE PIE!

Pie
¾ cup semisweet chocolate chips
¼ cup pecan halves
I prebaked 9-inch piecrust, homemade (see page 47) or purchased
¼ cup caramel sauce
Two 8-ounce packages cream cheese, softened
¾ cup powdered sugar
¼ cup heavy cream

Toppings
½ cup heavy cream
2 tablespoons powdered sugar
½ teaspoon vanilla extract
¼ cup semisweet chocolate chips
¼ cup pecan halves
¼ cup caramel sauce

1. Scatter ¼ cup of the chocolate chips and the pecan halves over the bottom of the piecrust. Cover with the caramel sauce.

2. Beat together the cream cheese and powdered sugar with an electric mixer until creamy and smooth.

3. Melt the remaining ½ cup chocolate chips in the heavy cream and blend well.

4. Whisk the melted chocolate mixture into the cream cheese mixture and mix thoroughly.

5. Spoon the filling into the pie shell and spread it carefully to avoid disturbing the caramel.

6. Finish the pie with the toppings: Whip the heavy cream to soft peaks. Add the powdered sugar and vanilla extract, then whip to stiff peaks.

7. Spoon big dollops of the whipped cream over the top of the pie. Sprinkle with the chocolate chips. Arrange the pecan halves around the rim of the pie and drizzle with the caramel sauce.

8. Refrigerate the pie for 1 hour before serving.

Serves 8

IHOP
Cheesecake Pancakes

THESE PANCAKES DESERVE AN AWARD FOR ORIGINALITY. ALL THE COMPONENTS OF A CHEESECAKE ARE HERE, JUST NOT WHERE YOU WOULD EXPECT TO FIND THEM!

Pancakes

One 8-ounce package cream cheese

1¼ cups all-purpose flour

1¼ cups buttermilk

1 egg

¼ cup canola oil

¼ cup granulated sugar

1 teaspoon baking powder

1 teaspoon baking soda

½ cup graham cracker crumbs

Toppings

¼ cup seedless strawberry jam

2 cups strawberries, hulled and sliced

½ cup heavy cream

2 tablespoons powdered sugar

1 teaspoon vanilla extract

1. Quarter the cream cheese lengthwise, wrap each quarter in plastic, and freeze until very hard, at least 4 hours.

2. To make the pancake batter, combine the flour, buttermilk, egg, canola oil, sugar, baking powder, and baking soda in a blender and process until smooth and creamy.

3. Remove the frozen sticks of cream cheese and cut them into small dice.

4. Put the diced cream cheese and the graham cracker crumbs in a large bowl and pour the pancake batter over them. Stir just to evenly distribute the crumbs and cheese cubes.

5. To make the toppings, melt the strawberry jam and stir it into the sliced strawberries.

6. Whip the heavy cream to soft peaks. Add the powdered sugar and vanilla extract, then whip to stiff peaks. Refrigerate until ready to use.

7. To cook the pancakes, coat a griddle or cast-iron skillet with cooking spray and place it over medium heat.

8. Pour ¼ cup of batter for each pancake, making sure that you are getting some of the frozen cream cheese in every cupful. Cook until the batter starts to bubble on top and the bottom is golden brown. Flip the pancake over and cook the other side for a couple of minutes, until browned.

9. To serve, warm four ovenproof plates and stack the pancakes. Spoon the strawberry sauce over the top and finish with a dollop of whipped cream.

Serves 4

JACK IN THE BOX
Eggnog Milkshake

THIS IS EASY TO MAKE FROM STORE-BOUGHT EGGNOG, OR YOU CAN MAKE YOUR OWN.

I cup vanilla ice cream
⅓ cup eggnog (recipe follows)

Pinch of ground nutmeg

1. Put the ice cream and eggnog in a blender and process until smooth.
2. Pour into a tall glass and add the nutmeg.

Serves 1

Eggnog

TRY THIS RECIPE TO MAKE YOUR OWN EGGNOG WHEN THE COMMERCIAL PRODUCT IS NOT AVAILABLE.

2 eggs, separated
3 tablespoons sugar
1 cup milk

1 cup heavy cream
½ teaspoon ground nutmeg

1. Beat the egg yolks with an electric mixer until they are light yellow. Gradually pour in 2 tablespoons of the sugar, and beat until the sugar is dissolved.
2. Beat in the milk, heavy cream, and nutmeg.
3. Whip the whites to soft peaks. Add the remaining 1 tablespoon sugar and beat to stiff peaks.
4. Using a wire whisk, combine the beaten whites with the yolk mixture until well incorporated and smooth.

Makes about 3 cups

If you choose, you can add 2 to 3 tablespoons of bourbon, brandy, or rum to the eggnog.

JACK IN THE BOX
Marshmallow–Rice Krispies Shake

IF YOU LIKE HAVING DESSERT EARLY IN THE MORNING AND WANT AN EXCUSE TO CALL
IT BREAKFAST, THIS MAY BE AN EYE-OPENER FOR YOU.

1 cup vanilla ice cream
¼ cup milk
1 to 2 tablespoons marshmallow
  creme

¼ cup Rice Krispies

1. Whisk together the ice cream, milk, and marshmallow creme until smooth and creamy.
2. Stir in the Rice Krispies.

Serves 1

JAI BY WOLFGANG PUCK
Caramelized Lemon-Lime Tart

LOCATED NEXT TO THE LA JOLLA PLAYHOUSE AND OPEN ONLY WHEN A PRODUCTION IS IN PERFORMANCE, JAI BLENDS ASIAN AND WESTERN CUISINES. THIS CITRUS-INTENSE TART WITH A SWEET PASTRY CRUST *(PÂTE SUCRÉE)* IS AN EXCELLENT EXAMPLE.

Pâte Sucrée
¾ cup almonds, toasted
⅓ cup all-purpose flour
¾ pound (3 sticks) unsalted
  butter, softened
1 cup sugar
1 egg
Finely grated zest of 2 lemons

Filling
4 eggs
4 egg yolks
1 cup sugar, plus extra for
  sprinkling
⅔ cup fresh lemon juice
⅔ cup fresh lime juice
Finely grated zest of ½ lemon
Finely grated zest of 2 limes
12 tablespoons (1½ sticks) cold
  unsalted butter, cut into pieces

1. To make the *pâte sucrée,* put the toasted almonds in the bowl of a food processor and pulse until they are coarsely ground. Add the flour to the almonds and pulse for a few seconds, just until the ingredients are mixed.

2. Cream the butter and sugar with an electric mixer until light and fluffy. Add the egg and one fourth of the lemon zest and beat until well blended.

3. Stir in the nut mixture and mix just until well combined.

4. Knead the dough on a floured surface for a few seconds and form it into a ball. Flatten the ball into a disk and wrap it in plastic. Refrigerate the dough for at least 1 hour.

5. Preheat the oven to 375°F.

6. Roll out the tart dough on a floured surface to a ¼-inch thickness. It should be a circle big enough to fill a 9-inch tart pan with a removable

bottom. Fit the pastry into the pan and trim any excess dough that goes over the edges of the pan.

7. Lay a sheet of parchment paper over the dough and fill the pan with dried beans or rice—this will keep the crust from puffing up while it bakes.

8. Bake the shell in the hot oven for 20 to 25 minutes, or until golden brown. Carefully remove the paper liner and the beans. Return the tart shell to the oven and bake for another 5 to 10 minutes, until it is golden brown.

9. To make the filling, whisk together the eggs and egg yolks. Set the bowl over a saucepan of simmering water and add the 1 cup sugar, the lemon juice, lime juice, and lemon and lime zest.

10. Whisk continuously until the mixture is very thick and creamy, 10 to 12 minutes.

11. Take the bowl off the pan of simmering water and start whisking in the pieces of butter, a few pieces at a time. Strain the mixture through a fine-mesh strainer into a bowl.

12. Pour the filling into the baked tart shell and smooth the top with a metal spatula. Let the tart cool to room temperature, then refrigerate until firm, 3 to 4 hours, or up to overnight.

13. To finish the tart, sprinkle sugar over the chilled tart and caramelize it with a very small butane torch. You can also run the tart under the broiler, being very careful not to burn the crust or the sugar.

14. Refrigerate the tart for at least 30 minutes before removing the bottom of the tart pan and serving.

Serves 8 to 10

You can skip the final sugar step entirely, if you choose, and just garnish with a few fresh raspberries sprinkled with powdered sugar set in the center of the tart.

JOE'S CRAB SHACK
Crabby Apple Crumble

ALMOST EVERYTHING IN THIS RECIPE IS MADE FROM SCRATCH, JUST AS IT IS AT JOE'S CRAB SHACK. TO DO THE SAME, YOU WILL NEED AN ICE CREAM MAKER AND PLENTY OF TIME.

Cinnamon Ice Cream
1 cup milk
2 cups heavy cream
1 cup granulated sugar
1 tablespoon ground cinnamon
6 egg yolks, well beaten
1 teaspoon vanilla extract

Apple Pie
6 large Granny Smith apples, peeled, cored, and thinly sliced
One 9-inch piecrust, homemade (see page xxii) or purchased

¾ cup granulated sugar
2 tablespoons all-purpose flour
¼ teaspoon ground nutmeg
1 tablespoon ground cinnamon
1 tablespoon fresh lemon juice

Crumble Topping
½ cup packed light brown sugar
¾ cup all-purpose flour
6 tablespoons (¾ stick) cold unsalted butter, cut into small pieces

1. To make the cinnamon ice cream, whisk together the milk, 1 cup of the heavy cream, the granulated sugar, and cinnamon in a saucepan over medium heat and bring to a simmer. Remove from the heat.

2. Whisk ½ cup of the cream mixture into the beaten egg yolks, whisking constantly. When well blended, slowly whisk the remaining cream mixture into the egg mixture, stirring constantly, until all the cream has been incorporated.

3. Pour the mixture back into the saucepan over low heat and add the vanilla extract and the remaining 1 cup of heavy cream. Cook, stirring constantly, until the mixture has thickened enough to coat the back of a spoon.

4. Pour the mixture into an ice cream maker and follow the manufacturer's directions. Transfer to a covered container and store in the freezer until ready to serve.

5. Preheat the oven to 375°F.

6. To make the apple pie, layer the apple slices in the piecrust and sprinkle with the granulated sugar, flour, nutmeg, and cinnamon. Sprinkle with the lemon juice.

7. To make the crumble topping, put the brown sugar, flour, and butter pieces in the bowl of a food processor and pulse until the mixture resembles fine meal. Pack the mixture on top of the apples and cover the pie loosely with foil.

8. Bake in the hot oven for 25 minutes, then remove the foil and bake for 25 to 30 minutes more, until the topping is golden brown. Let the pie cool and serve with the cinnamon ice cream.

Serves 8 to 12

JOE'S CRAB SHACK
Strawberry Comfort

THIS IS NOT SO MUCH A DESSERT AS A SUBSTANTIAL COCKTAIL; THE RUM AND SOUTHERN COMFORT CAN BE OMITTED FOR THOSE WHO PREFER THEIR STRAWBERRY DRINKS NONALCOHOLIC.

2 cups strawberries, hulled and chopped
⅓ cup sugar
2 lemons

⅓ cup sweet-and-sour mix
⅓ cup lemon-lime soda
1 tablespoon light rum
3 tablespoons Southern Comfort

1. In the bowl of a food processor, combine the strawberries and sugar. Pulse until the mixture is well blended but not smooth.

2. Squeeze the juice of the lemons into a cocktail shaker and put the squeezed lemons in the bottom of a 1-quart mason jar. Fill the jar with ice.

3. Fill the cocktail shaker with the sweet-and-sour mix, lemon-lime soda, rum, and Southern Comfort. Add 1 cup of the strawberry puree and shake. Pour the mixture into the mason jar and stir, adding the remaining strawberry puree.

4. Serve in tall glasses.

Serves 2

JOE'S STONE CRAB RESTAURANT
Apple Pie

THE ORIGINAL JOE'S IN MIAMI HAS BEEN SERVING THE RICH AND FAMOUS—AND THE REST OF US—SINCE 1913. ONE OF THE TRUE DELIGHTS OF DINING AT JOE'S IS THE HOMEMADE DESSERTS. THIS APPLE PIE IS THE ONE TO BEAT ALL OTHERS.

Piecrust

2 cups all-purpose flour

1 tablespoon granulated sugar

½ teaspoon kosher salt

8 tablespoons (1 stick) cold unsalted butter, cut into pieces

⅓ cup vegetable shortening, such as Crisco

1 tablespoon white vinegar

2 tablespoons cold water

Apple Filling

8 red apples

1 tablespoon fresh lemon juice

½ cup granulated sugar

¼ cup all-purpose flour

1½ teaspoons ground cinnamon

½ teaspoon ground cloves

½ teaspoon ground nutmeg

½ teaspoon kosher salt

Topping

1¼ cups all-purpose flour

12 tablespoons (1½ sticks) unsalted butter, cut into pieces

⅔ cup packed dark brown sugar

½ cup coarsely chopped pecans

1. To make the piecrust, whisk together the flour, granulated sugar, and salt.

2. Cut in the butter and vegetable shortening with a pastry cutter or in a food processor until the mixture resembles coarse meal.

3. Combine the vinegar and water and add to the dough. Mix it in, and add just a little more cold water if needed to make the dough come together in a ball.

4. Wrap the ball of dough in plastic and refrigerate for at least 30 minutes.

5. Flour a clean work surface and roll the dough out into a circle. Fit it into a 9- or 10-inch deep-dish pie plate that has been lightly buttered. Flute

the top edge of the dough and refrigerate the pie shell while you make the filling.

6. To make the apple filling, peel and core the apples. Quarter them, then slice them into a bowl with the lemon juice, mixing them as you add them to coat them with the juice.

7. Combine the granulated sugar, flour, cinnamon, cloves, nutmeg, and salt in a separate bowl.

8. Sprinkle the spice mixture over the apples and toss them to coat them evenly.

9. Taste the apples and add more sugar if you would prefer more sweetness.

10. Refrigerate the apples while you prepare the topping.

11. To make the topping, combine the flour and butter. Cut the butter in with two knives or use your hands, but leave the pieces about the size of nickels.

12. In a separate bowl, combine the brown sugar and pecans. Mix in with the flour and butter, using your hands to just incorporate the ingredients.

13. Keep the topping refrigerated until you are ready to begin assembling the pie.

14. Preheat the oven to 375°F.

15. To assemble and bake the pie, fill the prepared pie shell with the apple mixture, mounding it in the center.

16. Put a sheet pan on the lower rack to catch the drips and bake the pie in the hot oven for 25 minutes.

17. Take the pie out of the oven and increase the temperature to 400°F.

18. Scatter the pecan topping over the pie, pressing it gently into the mounded apples.

19. Put the pie back into the oven and bake for another 25 to 30 minutes, until the fruit is tender and the filling is bubbly.

20. Set the finished pie on a wire rack to cool, and serve warm or at room temperature.

Serves 8

JOE'S STONE CRAB RESTAURANT
Key Lime Pie

JOE'S MAKES THEIR KEY LIME PIE VERY FRESH AND SERVES IT VERY COLD. IF YOU CAN'T FIND FRESH KEY LIMES, USE A GOOD-QUALITY BOTTLED KEY LIME JUICE, OR REGULAR LIMES.

Piecrust

1¼ cups graham cracker crumbs

6 tablespoons (¾ stick) unsalted butter, melted

⅓ cup granulated sugar

Key Lime Filling

3 egg yolks

2 teaspoons finely grated Key lime zest

One 14-ounce can sweetened condensed milk

⅔ cup fresh Key lime juice

Topping

1 cup heavy cream

1 tablespoon powdered sugar

1 teaspoon vanilla extract

1. Preheat the oven to 350°F.

2. To make the piecrust, put the graham cracker crumbs in the bowl of a food processor and add the melted butter and granulated sugar.

3. Pulse the mixture until it is just combined, then press it into a lightly buttered 9-inch pie pan. Bring the mixture all the way up the sides, and make the top edge neat and even.

4. Bake the crust in the hot oven for 8 to 10 minutes, until golden brown. Let it cool on a wire rack but leave the oven on.

5. To make the Key lime filling, combine the egg yolks and lime zest. With an electric mixer, beat until the mixture is light and foamy, about 5 minutes. Gradually beat in the condensed milk and whip until thickened. Reduce the speed of the mixer and gradually add the lime juice, mixing just until blended.

6. Pour the mixture into the prepared piecrust and bake in the hot oven for 10 minutes, or until the custard is just set.

7. Let cool at room temperature on a wire rack, then refrigerate. Freeze for 10 to 15 minutes just before serving.

8. To make the topping, whip the heavy cream until soft peaks form. Add the powdered sugar and vanilla extract. Beat until the peaks are stiff.

9. Top each slice of pie with a large dollop of the whipped cream and serve.

Serves 8

In a pinch, you can use a store-bought graham cracker crust.

KFC
Huckleberry Cake

THE COLONEL NOT ONLY KNEW HIS WAY AROUND A CHICKEN, HE MADE A PRETTY GOOD HUCKLEBERRY CAKE. HUCKLEBERRIES ARE SMALL AND ROUND, SOMEWHAT LIKE BLUEBERRIES, BUT SWEETER. USE FRESH OR FROZEN BLUEBERRIES IF YOU CAN'T FIND FRESH HUCKLEBERRIES IN SEASON.

4 tablespoons (½ stick) unsalted butter, softened
⅔ cup sugar
1 egg
1 teaspoon vanilla extract
1½ cups all-purpose flour

2 teaspoons baking powder
½ teaspoon kosher salt
¼ cup milk
2 cups huckleberries or blueberries

1. Preheat the oven to 350°F. Grease an 8 by 8-inch baking dish or an 8-inch cake pan.

2. Cream the butter and sugar with an electric mixer until light and fluffy. Add the egg and beat until incorporated. Stir in the vanilla extract.

3. Whisk together the flour, baking powder, and salt.

4. Gradually add the dry ingredients, alternately with the milk, to the butter-sugar mixture, beating until the mixture is well blended.

5. Fold in the huckleberries and pour the batter into the prepared pan.

6. Bake for 35 to 40 minutes in the hot oven. The cake is done when it springs back when lightly touched in the center. Let the cake cool on a wire rack before cutting.

Serves 8 to 10

Top the cake with a dollop of whipped cream or serve it with a scoop of vanilla ice cream on the side.

KFC
Pecan Pie

TRUE TO THE SOUTHERN ORIGINS OF THIS POPULAR CHAIN OF RESTAURANTS, PECAN PIE HAS BEEN ON THE MENU FOR GENERATIONS. THE DARK CORN SYRUP GIVES THE PIE A RICH, GLEAMING FINISH, AND IT IS EVEN BETTER THE NEXT DAY.

4 eggs, well beaten
⅓ cup sugar
1 cup dark corn syrup
¼ teaspoon kosher salt
1 tablespoon fresh lemon juice
4 tablespoons (½ stick) unsalted butter, melted

2 teaspoons vanilla extract
1½ cups pecan halves
1 prebaked 9-inch piecrust, homemade (see page 47) or purchased

1. Preheat the oven to 350°F.

2. Whisk together the eggs, sugar, corn syrup, salt, lemon juice, melted butter, and vanilla extract.

3. Add 1 cup of the pecan halves and stir well.

4. Pour the filling into the prepared pie shell.

5. Arrange the remaining ½ cup pecan halves around the rim of the pie—any extras can be pressed gently into the pie filling.

6. Gently press the pecans on the rim into the filling so they are moistened with the liquids.

7. Put a sheet pan on the bottom shelf of the oven to catch any drips, and bake the pie for 45 to 50 minutes. The tip of a small knife should come out clean when inserted in the center of the pie.

Serves 8 to 12

KRINGLA BAKERI OG KAFÉ

Rice Cream with Strawberry Sauce

KRINGLA BAKERI IS NORWAY'S CONTRIBUTION TO EPCOT THEME PARK IN FLORIDA. THIS CREAMY RICE DESSERT CAN BE COMPARED TO RICE PUDDING, BUT IS LIGHTER. SERVE IT WITH A SPOONFUL OR TWO OF STRAWBERRY SAUCE OR ANOTHER FAVORITE, SUCH AS HOT FUDGE OR SOFTENED VANILLA ICE CREAM.

1 pound short-grain rice
(about 2¼ cups)
3 cups water
1 teaspoon kosher salt
4 cups milk

2 cups heavy cream
¼ cup powdered sugar
2 teaspoons vanilla extract
Strawberry sauce, homemade
(recipe follows) or purchased

1. Combine the rice with the water and salt in a large saucepan and bring to a boil. Reduce the heat and simmer for 20 minutes. Most of the water should be absorbed.

2. Stir in the milk and cook for another 30 minutes, or until the rice is tender and the liquid has thickened.

3. Let the rice cool and continue to thicken, stirring occasionally.

4. Whip the heavy cream to soft peaks. Add the powdered sugar and vanilla extract, then whip the mixture to stiff peaks.

5. Fold the whipped cream into the rice mixture and blend well.

6. Fill glasses or mugs two-thirds full and top the rice cream with the strawberry sauce.

Serves 12 to 16

Strawberry Sauce

TRY THIS QUICK AND EASY RECIPE FOR A FRESH STRAWBERRY SAUCE.

1 pint strawberries, hulled and halved

⅓ cup granulated sugar

1 teaspoon vanilla extract

1. Put the strawberries, granulated sugar, and vanilla extract into a heavy-bottomed saucepan and simmer for 5 to 10 minutes until the berries are soft and the juice is slightly syrupy. Taste the sauce and add more sugar if it is not sweet enough for you.
2. Let the sauce cool, then transfer it to a blender. Pulse until all the large pieces of strawberry have been pureed. You can pass the sauce through a fine-mesh strainer to remove the seeds, if you wish.
3. Let the sauce cool and store it in a container with a tight-fitting lid in the refrigerator for up to 3 days.

Makes 1½ cups

KRISPY KREME
Glazed Doughnuts

WHO DOESN'T CRAVE WARM GLAZED DOUGHNUTS? MAKE THESE YOURSELF, AND YOU'LL GET THE EXTRA TREAT OF GLAZED DOUGHNUT HOLES. MAKE SURE YOU HAVE A DOUGHNUT CUTTER BEFORE YOU START.

Doughnuts

- 2 envelopes (4½ teaspoons) active dry yeast
- ¼ cup warm water (105° to 115°F)
- 1½ cups milk, scalded and cooled
- ½ cup granulated sugar
- 2 eggs, well beaten
- ⅓ cup vegetable shortening
- 5 cups all-purpose flour
- 1 teaspoon kosher salt
- ½ teaspoon ground nutmeg

Glaze

- 3 cups powdered sugar
- ½ teaspoon kosher salt
- ½ cup warm milk
- ½ teaspoon vanilla extract

- 5 cups canola oil, for deep-frying

1. Make the doughnuts: In a large bowl, dissolve the yeast in the warm water. Let it activate, about 5 minutes.

2. Add the cooled milk, the sugar, eggs, vegetable shortening, 2 cups of the flour, the salt, and the nutmeg.

3. Using an electric mixer with the paddle attachment or a hand mixer, beat on low speed just until the ingredients are combined, about 30 seconds.

4. Scrape the bowl, then beat on medium speed for 2 minutes, scraping the bowl occasionally.

5. Beat in the remaining 3 cups flour until the dough is smooth.

6. Cover the bowl with a clean kitchen towel and let the dough double in volume, about 1 hour.

7. Turn the dough out onto a floured surface and knead it for about 30 seconds.

8. Roll the dough out ½ inch thick and cut with a floured doughnut cutter.

9. Place the doughnuts and doughnut holes on sheet pans and cover them with clean kitchen towels. Let them rise until doubled in volume, 30 to 40 minutes.

10. Make the glaze while the doughnuts are rising the second time. Whisk together the powdered sugar and salt.

11. Slowly whisk in the warm milk, stirring constantly. When the glaze is smooth and creamy, stir in the vanilla extract. If the glaze is too thick, continue to add warm milk until it reaches the desired consistency. Keep the glaze warm while you finish the doughnuts.

12. Fill a deep-fryer or a heavy-bottomed saucepan with the oil and heat to between 355° and 375°F.

13. Deep-fry the doughnuts, one or two at a time, for about 1 minute and 15 seconds per side, or until evenly golden brown.

14. Let the doughnuts drain on paper towels, then fry the doughnut holes in the same way.

15. Dip the finished doughnuts in the warm glaze and let them cool on a wire rack. Glaze the doughnut holes in the same manner or simply toss them in powdered sugar.

Makes 24 doughnuts and doughnut holes

LA CREPERIE
Fresh Berry Crepes

LA CREPERIE RESTAURANT AT PARIS HOTEL AND CASINO IN LAS VEGAS FILLS ITS CREPES WITH A MIX OF RASPBERRIES, BLUEBERRIES, STRAWBERRIES, AND BLACKBER-RIES. YOU CAN USE ALL ONE KIND OR A MIX OF WHAT IS CURRENTLY IN SEASON. USING A FOOD PROCESSOR ENSURES A SMOOTH AND LIGHT BATTER.

Crepe Batter
2 cups all-purpose flour
2 tablespoons granulated sugar
2 teaspoons kosher salt
6 eggs
12 tablespoons (1½ sticks) unsalted butter, melted
2 cups milk
⅔ cup water
1 teaspoon vanilla extract

Raspberry Coulis
2 cups raspberries, fresh or thawed frozen

½ cup granulated sugar
Juice of ½ lemon
½ teaspoon vanilla extract

Whipped Cream
1 cup heavy cream
5 tablespoons powdered sugar

Filling and Garnish
Mixed fresh berries: 1 cup each raspberries, blackberries, blueberries, and strawberries

1. Make the crepe batter: Combine the flour, granulated sugar, and salt in the bowl of a food processor. Pulse once or twice to mix the ingredients.

2. Add the eggs, one at a time, pulsing after each addition.

3. Add the melted butter, milk, water, and vanilla extract. Pulse until the mixture is well combined.

4. Pour the batter into a covered container and refrigerate for 1 hour.

5. Make the raspberry coulis while the batter is resting in the refrigerator. Combine the raspberries, granulated sugar, lemon juice, and vanilla extract in a medium saucepan.

6. Bring the mixture to a boil, then reduce the heat and simmer for about 15 minutes.

7. Press the berries through a fine-mesh strainer and discard the seeds.

8. Make the whipped cream for the finished crepes: Whip the heavy cream to soft peaks.

9. Add the powdered sugar and whip the mixture to stiff peaks. Keep refrigerated until ready to use.

10. Cook and fill the crepes: Coat a small skillet or crepe pan with cooking spray and heat over medium heat.

11. Ladle enough batter to coat the bottom of the pan. Tip the skillet to coat it evenly.

12. Cook until the top of the crepe begins to bubble and the bottom is just lightly browned.

13. Flip the crepe over and cook the other side. Keep the crepes warm in a low oven while you are making the rest of them. Use up all the batter in this manner. As each crepe is done, transfer it to a parchment paper–lined sheet pan. Cover each layer with parchment.

14. Fill each crepe with a spoonful of the mixed berries and some of the raspberry coulis. Fold it up and place on a warmed dessert plate.

15. Garnish each of the filled crepes with more of the berries and a dollop of whipped cream. Pour a little of the coulis on the plate next to the crepes.

Serves 8 to 10

LA MADELEINE
Strawberries Romanoff

GET YOUR BERRIES AND CREAM IN A WHOLE NEW WAY, WITH BROWN SUGAR, SOUR
CREAM, AND BRANDY. THIS IS A GREAT WAY TO SERVE A SIMPLE DESSERT WITH MAXI-
MUM FLAIR. SUBSTITUTE VANILLA EXTRACT FOR THE BRANDY IF DINNER IS NOT AN
ADULTS-ONLY GATHERING.

½ cup sour cream
¼ cup packed golden brown
 sugar
2 tablespoons brandy

½ cup heavy cream
¼ cup powdered sugar
2 pints strawberries, hulled

1. Whisk together the sour cream and brown sugar. Stir until the sugar is
   incorporated.
2. Stir in the brandy.
3. Whip the heavy cream until soft peaks form.
4. Add the powdered sugar and whip until the cream forms stiff peaks.
5. Using a rubber spatula, fold the whipped cream into the sour cream
   mixture until the two mixtures are well blended. Serve with the fresh
   strawberries.

Serves 4 to 8

*This recipe can be used with any fresh berries of the season,
or other fruits such as pineapple and melon.
If you don't have brandy on hand, try another liqueur such as
Grand Marnier, triple sec, or sherry.*

LIBERTY TREE TAVERN
Caramel Apple Tart

LIBERTY TREE TAVERN AT MAGIC KINGDOM THEME PARK IN FLORIDA PRIDES ITSELF ON BEING AUTHENTICALLY REPRESENTATIVE OF REVOLUTIONARY NEW ENGLAND. THESE INDIVIDUAL APPLE TARTS MAY OR MAY NOT HAVE A PLACE IN OUR NATION'S HISTORY, BUT THEY DO DESERVE A PLACE ON YOUR MENU.

Caramel Sauce

2 cups granulated sugar

½ cup water

¾ cup heavy cream

2 tablespoons unsalted butter

Apple Pie Filling

6 apples, peeled, cored, and sliced

I cup granulated sugar

¼ cup cornstarch

½ teaspoon ground cinnamon

¼ teaspoon ground nutmeg

¼ teaspoon ground cloves

¼ teaspoon ground allspice

½ cup water

2 tablespoons fresh lemon juice

Shortbread Crust

½ pound (2 sticks) unsalted butter, softened

⅓ cup granulated sugar

2 eggs

2½ cups all-purpose flour

Pinch of kosher salt

I egg white, lightly beaten

2 tablespoons decorating sugar

Vanilla ice cream, for serving

1. To make the caramel sauce, combine the granulated sugar and the water in a heavy-bottomed saucepan over medium-high heat.

2. Cook the sugar until it is dissolved and the syrup begins to darken around the edges of the pan.

3. Remove the pan from the heat and whisk in ½ cup of the heavy cream and the butter. The caramel will bubble up as soon as the cream and butter make contact—just keep stirring with the whisk or a wooden spoon.

4. Once the bubbles subside, add the remaining ¼ cup heavy cream and stir until the sauce is smooth.

5. Transfer the sauce to a bowl and let it cool at room temperature. It will thicken as it cools.

6. To make the apple pie filling, combine the apples and granulated sugar in a large saucepan over medium heat, stirring to coat the apples evenly.

7. Whisk together the cornstarch, cinnamon, nutmeg, cloves, and allspice. Add the water and stir the mixture into a paste.

8. Add the cornstarch mixture to the pan with the apples and simmer until the apples are cooked through and the sauce has thickened.

9. Stir in the lemon juice and adjust the sugar if the apple mixture needs more sweetness. Let the apples cool until ready to use.

10. To make the shortbread crust, cream the butter and sugar with an electric mixer until light and fluffy.

11. Add the eggs, one at a time, beating well after each addition.

12. Whisk together the flour and salt. Gradually stir the dry ingredients into the creamed mixture and mix until blended.

13. Form the dough into a ball, then flatten it into a disk. Wrap it in plastic and refrigerate for at least 1 hour.

14. Preheat the oven to 350°F.

15. To make the tarts, divide the dough into 6 pieces.

16. On a floured surface, roll each piece of the dough into a circle and fit it into a muffin cup or small pie pan.

17. Fill each tart with a portion of the apple pie filling.

18. Bring the sides of the dough up and over the filling, folding the edges in a random manner.

19. Brush each tart with the beaten egg white and sprinkle with the decorating sugar.

20. If using small pie pans, arrange them on a baking sheet before putting them in the oven.

21. Bake the tarts for 15 to 20 minutes, until the crusts are golden brown.

22. Let the tarts cool, then put them on dessert plates and spoon over some of the caramel sauce.

23. Serve with a scoop of vanilla ice cream next to each tart and more caramel sauce.

Serves 6

LIBERTY TREE TAVERN
Lemon-Strawberry Trifle

MADE WITH POUND CAKE AND FRESH STRAWBERRIES, THIS TRIFLE IS A DELECTABLE ANYTIME DESSERT. THE LEMON CURD IS RICH AND CREAMY, BUT BALANCED WITH THE CITRUSY TANG OF FRESH LEMON JUICE.

Lemon Pound Cake

½ pound (2 sticks) unsalted butter, softened
1 cup granulated sugar
4 eggs
2 teaspoons vanilla extract
1½ cups all-purpose flour
1 teaspoon baking powder
½ teaspoon kosher salt
¼ cup fresh lemon juice

Lemon Curd

5 egg yolks
1 cup granulated sugar
⅓ cup fresh lemon juice
2 tablespoons finely grated lemon zest
8 tablespoons (1 stick) cold unsalted butter, cut into pieces

Whipped Cream

1 cup heavy cream
1 teaspoon vanilla extract
1 tablespoon powdered sugar

1 pint strawberries, hulled and sliced

1. Preheat the oven to 350°F. Coat a 5 by 9-inch loaf pan with butter or cooking spray and line with parchment or waxed paper.

2. To make the pound cake, cream the butter and sugar with an electric mixer until light and fluffy. Add the eggs, one at a time, beating well after each addition. Add the vanilla extract.

3. Whisk together the flour, baking powder, and salt. On low speed, add the dry ingredients alternately with the lemon juice to the creamed mixture, beating well after each addition.

4. Pour the batter into the prepared loaf pan and bake in the hot oven for 1 hour to 1 hour and 15 minutes. A toothpick inserted in the center of the cake should come out clean.

5. Let the cake cool on a wire rack before turning it out of the pan.

6. When cool, cut the cake into 1-inch squares.

7. To make the lemon curd, in a medium bowl, beat the egg yolks and the sugar with an electric mixer until light and foamy.

8. Set the bowl over a pan of simmering water and whisk until the mixture starts to thicken.

9. Whisk in the lemon juice and lemon zest, then stir the mixture until lightened and thickened, 8 to 10 minutes. The mixture should coat the back of a spoon.

10. Remove the curd from the heat and start stirring in the butter, one piece at a time, letting each piece melt before adding the next one.

11. Pour the curd into a clean bowl and set aside until needed. A piece of plastic wrap laid directly on top of the curd will keep a skin from forming.

12. To make the whipped cream, whip the heavy cream to soft peaks.

13. Add the vanilla extract and powdered sugar. Continue whipping until the cream forms stiff peaks.

14. Keep the whipped cream refrigerated until ready to use.

15. To assemble the trifle, pour portions of the lemon curd into glass mugs, or pour into a straight-sided glass bowl so that the bottom of the bowl is coated by ½ inch of curd.

16. Place a layer of sliced strawberries over the curd.

17. Make a layer of the cubed pieces of pound cake.

18. Repeat the process with the lemon curd, strawberries, and pound cake until the mugs are three quarters filled.

19. Place a dollop of whipped cream in each mug and garnish with strawberry slices if you have some extra. Refrigerate before serving.

Makes 8 to 10 individual servings or 1 large trifle

LIBERTY TREE TAVERN
Ooey-Gooey Toffee Cake

THIS EXTRAVAGANZA IS THE MOST POPULAR DESSERT AT THE LIBERTY TREE TAVERN. IT HAS GONE THROUGH A COUPLE OF TRANSFORMATIONS, BUT STILL RETAINS THE INVITING COMBINATION OF CAKE, CANDY, AND CHOCOLATE CHIPS.

Cake Batter
One 18.25-ounce box yellow cake mix
1 egg
4 tablespoons (½ stick) unsalted butter, softened

Topping
8 tablespoons (1 stick) unsalted butter, softened

One 8-ounces package cream cheese, softened
3 eggs
1 teaspoon vanilla extract
2 cups powdered sugar
One 10-ounce bag toffee candy pieces, broken up
1 cup semisweet chocolate chips

1. Preheat the oven to 325°F. Grease and flour a 13 by 9-inch baking pan.

2. To make the cake batter, follow the directions on the cake mix box. Beat in the egg and the softened butter with the wet ingredients called for in the cake mix directions. Pour the batter into the prepared pan.

3. To make the topping, in a medium bowl, cream the butter and cream cheese with an electric mixer.

4. Add the eggs, one at a time, beating well after each addition. Stir in the vanilla extract.

5. Gradually beat in the powdered sugar.

6. Using a wooden spoon, stir in the toffee pieces and chocolate chips, just blending them in—don't overmix the topping.

7. Carefully spread the topping over the cake batter and bake in the hot oven for 30 to 35 minutes until a long skewer inserted in the center of the cake comes out clean.

8. Let the cake cool before cutting into portions.

Makes 8 to 20 portions, depending on the size of each piece

LOCA LUNA

Cream Cheese Turtle Cake

THIS IS A VERY NUTTY CHOCOLATE CAKE THAT IS GREAT FOR A LARGE GROUP OR BUFFET. THE ICING IS A RICH COMBINATION OF COCOA, BUTTER, AND CARAMEL SAUCE.

Cake Batter
½ cup slivered almonds
½ cup chopped pecans
One 18.25-ounce box German chocolate cake mix
1¼ cups water
⅓ cup vegetable oil
3 eggs

Topping
8 tablespoons (1 stick) unsalted butter, softened
3½ cups powdered sugar
One 8-ounce package cream cheese, softened
½ cup slivered almonds
½ cup chopped pecans

Icing
¼ cup milk
4 tablespoons (½ stick) unsalted butter, softened
1¾ cups powdered sugar
2 tablespoons unsweetened cocoa powder
¾ cup semisweet chocolate chips
1 teaspoon vanilla extract
½ cup caramel sauce

1. Preheat the oven to 350°F. Coat a 9 x 13-inch baking pan with butter or cooking spray and flour.

2. To make the cake batter, sprinkle the almonds and pecans over the bottom of the pan.

3. Combine the cake mix with the water, oil, and eggs.

4. Beat at low speed with an electric mixer just until all the ingredients are combined, then increase the speed to medium and mix for about 2 minutes.

5. Pour the batter into the prepared pan and set aside.

6. To make the topping, melt the butter in a medium saucepan over low heat. Stir in the powdered sugar gradually, so that any lumps are dissolved.

7. Stir in the softened cream cheese and stir until smooth, about 1 minute. Make sure there are no lumps in the topping. Add a little milk if the mixture is too thick.

8. Pour the topping mixture in long rows over the cake batter, then swirl it into the batter, taking care not to overmix it.

9. Bake the cake in the hot oven for about 50 minutes, or until a toothpick comes out clean.

10. Top the cake with the almonds and pecans and set on a wire rack to cool.

11. To make the icing, combine the milk and butter in a heavy-bottomed saucepan and bring to a simmer over medium heat. Reduce the heat to low and whisk in the powdered sugar and cocoa powder.

12. When the powdered sugar has been incorporated, stir in the chocolate chips until they are melted and the mixture is smooth. Stir in the vanilla extract.

13. Drizzle the icing over the cake and let it set for 1 to 2 hours.

14. To serve, cut the cake into squares and drizzle with the caramel sauce.

Serves 12

Serve with a scoop of vanilla ice cream on each plate, if desired.

LUBY'S CAFETERIA
Chocolate Chess Pie

LUBY'S IS A WELCOME DESTINATION IN TEXAS AND BORDERING STATES. THE RESTAURANT'S REPUTATION FOR FRESH, HIGH-QUALITY FOOD HAS GROWN WITH ITS EXPANSION.

8 tablespoons (1 stick) unsalted butter, softened
1½ cups sugar
3 extra-large eggs
2 teaspoons vanilla extract
⅓ cup all-purpose flour
1 tablespoon unsweetened cocoa powder

One 14-ounce can evaporated milk
¼ cup light corn syrup
¼ cup semisweet chocolate chips, melted
One 9-inch piecrust, homemade (see page xxii) or purchased

1. Preheat the oven to 375°F.

2. Cream the butter and sugar with an electric mixer until light and fluffy. Add the eggs, one at a time, beating well after each addition. Stir in the vanilla extract.

3. Whisk together the flour and cocoa powder. Stir the dry ingredients into the creamed mixture.

4. Stir in the evaporated milk, corn syrup, and the melted chocolate chips. Mix well until all the ingredients are thoroughly blended.

5. Pour the batter into the piecrust and bake for 45 to 50 minutes. A toothpick inserted in the center of the pie should come out clean. Let the pie cool before serving.

Serves 8

Top each portion with whipped cream and chopped nuts, if desired.

LUBY'S CAFETERIA
Hawaiian Pie

THIS VERSION OF PINEAPPLE PIE HAS AN INTERESTING TEXTURE, DUE IN PART TO THE
ADDITION OF CORNMEAL USED TO THICKEN THE PIE FILLING. THIS PIE HOLDS UP VERY
WELL IN THE REFRIGERATOR AND CAN BE SERVED EITHER WARM OR CHILLED.

6 tablespoons (¾ stick) unsalted
  butter, softened
1½ cups sugar
3 eggs
1 teaspoon vanilla extract
2 tablespoons all-purpose flour
2 tablespoons cornmeal

One 14-ounce can crushed
  pineapple, drained
1½ cups sweetened shredded
  coconut
One 9-inch piecrust, homemade
  (see page xxii) or purchased

1. Preheat the oven to 350°F.

2. Cream the butter and sugar with an electric mixer until light and fluffy.
   Add the eggs, one at a time, beating well after each addition. Stir in the
   vanilla extract.

3. Whisk together the flour and cornmeal and gradually beat into the
   creamed mixture. Stir in the crushed pineapple and coconut.

4. Pour the filling into the piecrust. Bake the pie in the center of the oven
   for 45 minutes, or until a toothpick inserted in the center comes out
   clean.

Serves 8

*Fill a pastry bag with whipped cream
and pipe a decorative border around the rim of the pie
for an elegant presentation.*

LUBY'S CAFETERIA
Chocolate Icebox Pie

KEEP THIS LUBY'S FAVORITE IN MIND WHEN YOU WANT A RICH AND CREAMY PIE, BUT
DON'T WANT TO TURN ON THE OVEN. LET YOUR REFRIGERATOR DO ALL THE WORK. A
STORE-BOUGHT PIECRUST HELPS TO SAVE A LITTLE TIME.

2½ cups milk
1¼ cups sugar
¼ cup unsweetened cocoa
   powder
1 tablespoon unsalted butter,
   softened
½ cup cornstarch
½ cup cold water

1 teaspoon vanilla extract
3 extra-large egg yolks
1 cup mini marshmallows
1 prebaked 9-inch piecrust,
   homemade (see page 47)
   or purchased
Whipped cream and chocolate
   curls (optional)

1. Whisk together 2 cups of the milk and the sugar, cocoa powder, and
   the butter in a saucepan over medium heat and bring to a boil, stirring
   frequently. Reduce the heat to low and simmer.

2. Make a paste of the cornstarch and water. Whisk in the remaining ½ cup
   milk.

3. Add the vanilla extract and egg yolks to the cornstarch mixture and
   whisk until all the ingredients are smooth.

4. Very gradually whisk the cornstarch mixture into the simmering milk
   mixture, stirring constantly.

5. Cook until the mixture is thickened and smooth, whisking constantly,
   about 2 minutes.

6. Add the mini marshmallows to the saucepan and stir until they are
   melted and the mixture is smooth once again.

7. Take the pan off the heat and let the mixture cool for 1 minute, then
   pour the filling into the pie shell. Smooth the surface with a metal
   spatula and cover it with a sheet of plastic wrap sitting directly on the
   custard, to prevent a film from forming.

8. Refrigerate the pie for at least 2 hours.

9. Garnish each slice with whipped cream and chocolate curls, if desired.

Serves 8

MAGGIANO'S LITTLE ITALY
Italian Trifle with Seasonal Fruit

BE SURE TO USE INDIVIDUAL GLASSES OR A GLASS BOWL FOR THIS DESSERT. THE MIXED
FRUIT MAKES A BEAUTIFUL DISPLAY BETWEEN THE LAYERS OF BUTTERY POUND CAKE
AND VANILLA CUSTARD.

Pastry Cream

¾ cup milk

2 eggs

¼ cup granulated sugar

I teaspoon vanilla extract

I tablespoon cornstarch

Trifle

I pound cake, homemade
   or purchased

2 cups heavy cream

½ cup powdered sugar

Fruit Mix

I cup cubed pineapple

I cup red or green seedless
   grapes

I cup blueberries

I cup quartered strawberries

I cup orange sections

Fresh mint leaves, for garnish

1. To make the pastry cream, place a medium saucepan over medium heat
   for about 30 seconds, then pour in the milk. Let the milk scald until a
   skin forms on top.

2. Using an electric mixer, whisk together the eggs and sugar until light and
   foamy. Stir in the vanilla extract.

3. Whisk the cornstarch into the simmering milk. Once the mixture has
   thickened, take the pan off the heat.

4. Whisking constantly, slowly pour the milk mixture into the egg mixture.
   When it has been completely combined, pour the mixture back into the
   saucepan over low heat, whisking until it comes to a boil and thickens.

5. Remove the pastry cream from the heat and pour it into a clean bowl. Cover with a piece of plastic wrap sitting directly on the surface and let cool at room temperature.

6. Refrigerate for several hours.

7. To assemble the trifle, cut the pound cake into 1-inch-thick slices and then cut into 1-inch cubes.

8. Beat the heavy cream to soft peaks, then add the powdered sugar and beat to stiff peaks. Fold the whipped cream into the chilled pastry cream and blend well.

9. Mix all the fruit together in one bowl.

10. For each serving, place a couple of cubes of pound cake in a parfait glass or other tall clear glass.

11. Top the cake with ¼ cup of the pastry cream. Divide the mixed fruit on top.

12. Put more cubes of cake on the fruit and gently press down.

13. Top with the remaining pastry cream and garnish with a mint leaf.

Serves 6

You can also make one large trifle in a straight-sided glass bowl. Make several layers of the cake, pastry cream, and fruit, ending with the cream and garnishing the trifle with the remaining fruit.

MAGGIANO'S LITTLE ITALY
Spiced Pear Crostada

THESE FLAKY PASTRIES ARE DELICATELY FLUTED AROUND A FILLING OF FRESH PEARS
SPICED WITH CINNAMON AND NUTMEG. ONCE BAKED, THEY CAN BE SERVED WARM OR
AT ROOM TEMPERATURE, IDEAL FOR AN ELEGANT DINNER MENU.

Filling
3 ripe pears
2 teaspoons fresh lemon juice
2 tablespoons unsalted butter
½ teaspoon ground cinnamon
¼ teaspoon ground nutmeg
½ cup packed golden brown
   sugar

Crostadas
Piecrust dough for four 8-inch
   crusts, homemade (see
   page xxii) or purchased
2 tablespoons heavy cream
2 tablespoons granulated sugar

Ice cream (optional)

1. To make the filling, peel the pears, then core them. Cut the pears into
   ¼-inch slices and toss them in a bowl with the lemon juice.

2. Melt the butter in a large skillet over medium heat. When the butter
   begins to brown, add the sliced pears. Toss to coat them with the butter.

3. Simmer the pears in their juices until heated through, then add the cinnamon, nutmeg, and brown sugar. Toss them again to evenly coat, then
   simmer until the juices are thickened.

4. Remove the pan from the heat and let the pears cool to room temperature. Refrigerate the pears.

5. To make the crostadas, flour a clean work surface and divide the dough
   into 4 pieces. Roll each piece into a 9-inch circle and place on ungreased
   sheet pans.

6. Place a portion of the pear filling in the center of each pastry circle.
   Gently fold the edges of the dough toward the center, forming pleats in
   the dough as you work your way around the filling.

7. Put the crostadas in the refrigerator for 1 hour before baking.

8. Preheat the oven to 350°F.

9. When the oven is hot, brush each crostada with heavy cream and sprinkle with the granulated sugar.

10. Bake for 25 minutes, or until the pastry is golden brown. Let the crostadas cool on the sheet pans.

11. Cut each crostada into 4 pieces and set on a platter or on dessert plates. Serve with a scoop of ice cream, if desired.

Serves 16

MAIN STREET CAFE
Holiday Banana Split

HERE IS A VARIATION OF A TRIED-AND-TRUE AMERICAN CLASSIC. BANANA SPLITS
WITH PEPPERMINT ICE CREAM ARE FUN FOR THE HOLIDAYS OR ANY DAY THAT YOU
HAVE BANANAS, NUTS, AND CHOCOLATE IN THE HOUSE.

Whipped Cream
1 cup heavy cream
2 tablespoons powdered sugar
1 teaspoon vanilla extract

1½ quarts peppermint ice cream

4 ripe bananas, split lengthwise, then cut in half crosswise
½ cup hot fudge sauce or chocolate syrup
½ cup chopped nuts or slivered almonds

1. To make the whipped cream, with an electric mixer, whip the heavy cream to soft peaks.

2. Add the powdered sugar and vanilla extract, then whip to stiff peaks.

3. Keep refrigerated until ready to use.

4. To assemble the banana splits, put 3 scoops of ice cream in each of four shallow bowls.

5. Stand up 4 slices of banana around the edges of each bowl.

6. Spoon some of the fudge sauce over the ice cream.

7. Put a scoop of whipped cream over the ice cream and sprinkle with the chopped nuts. Serve immediately.

Serves 4

MAMA MELROSE'S RISTORANTE ITALIANO
Cappuccino Crème Brûlée

SEVERAL SPOONFULS OF FREEZE-DRIED COFFEE GRANULES GIVE THIS CREAMY CUSTARD A DISTINCTIVE MOCHA TWIST.

4 cups heavy cream
¼ cup freeze-dried coffee granules
1 vanilla bean, split
¾ cup granulated sugar
6 egg yolks

1 egg
¼ cup bittersweet chocolate shavings
2 teaspoons dark brown sugar

1. Preheat the oven to 250°F.

2. Combine the heavy cream and coffee granules in a bowl set over a saucepan of simmering water. Scrape the seeds out of the vanilla bean and add them to the cream mixture.

3. When bubbles start to form at the edges of the mixture, add the granulated sugar and stir to dissolve it.

4. Whisk together the egg yolks and the whole egg. Whisk ½ cup of the cream mixture into the eggs, then slowly whisk the egg mixture into the cream mixture. Reduce the heat to a simmer, and continue to stir the mixture constantly, until slightly thickened.

5. Strain the custard through a fine-mesh strainer into a pitcher. Sprinkle the chocolate shavings evenly among twenty 4-ounce soufflé cups, then transfer the cups to a large baking pan and fill them with the custard. Add enough hot water to the pan to come halfway up the sides of the soufflé cups.

6. Bake the custards in the hot oven for 2 hours, or until set. Let cool for 1 hour, then refrigerate until ready to serve.

7. Sprinkle the tops of the custards with the brown sugar and pass them under the broiler or use a kitchen torch to melt the sugar and caramelize the tops.

Serves 20

MAMA MELROSE'S RISTORANTE ITALIANO
Mama's Fruit Salad

MAMA MELROSE'S RISTORANTE ITALIANO AT DISNEY'S HOLLYWOOD STUDIOS THEME PARK SERVES THIS TERRIFIC FRUIT SALAD IN A CASUAL ITALIAN SETTING. SUBSTITUTE WHAT IS FRESHEST IF YOU CAN'T GET ALL THE FRUIT THAT IS LISTED.

1 cup Asti Spumante or prosecco sparkling wine
1 cup amaretto
2 tablespoons sugar
2 tablespoons fresh lemon juice
2 cups sliced strawberries
1 cup red or green seedless grapes
2 apples, cored and diced
2 pears, cored and diced
2 bananas, peeled and cut into ½-inch-thick slices
2 figs, peeled and sliced

1. Combine ½ cup of the wine with the amaretto, sugar, and lemon juice in a large serving bowl.
2. Add the prepared fruit and gently toss so that all the fruit is moistened.
3. Cover the bowl and refrigerate for a least 1 hour.
4. Just before serving, pour in the remaining ½ cup wine and toss.
5. Serve the fruit salad in parfait glasses or shallow bowls.

Serves 6 to 8

MARIE CALLENDER'S
Sour Cream–Blueberry Pie

THIS IS A DELICIOUS ALTERNATIVE TO A BAKED FRUIT PIE. USE FRESH OR FROZEN BLUEBERRIES, OR CANNED AS HERE. THE SOUR CREAM TOPPING IS REFRESHING AND NOT OVERLY SWEET.

Pie

1 red or green apple, peeled, cored, and cut into small dice
½ cup sugar
¼ teaspoon kosher salt
3 tablespoons cornstarch
¼ cup water
1 teaspoon fresh lemon juice
One 15-ounce can blueberries in heavy syrup, drained and syrup reserved
½ teaspoon ground cinnamon
1 prebaked 9-inch piecrust, homemade (see page 149) or purchased

Sour Cream Topping

½ teaspoon unflavored powdered gelatin
2 tablespoons water
1 cup sour cream
½ cup sugar
1 tablespoon cream cheese
1 teaspoon vanilla extract

Whipped cream (optional)

1. To make the pie, combine the diced apples, sugar, and salt in a saucepan over medium heat and simmer until the apples are cooked through but still firm.

2. Make a paste of the cornstarch and water.

3. Add the lemon juice and reserved berry syrup to the apple mixture, then stir in the cornstarch paste. Simmer until thickened, stirring frequently.

4. Stir in the blueberries and cinnamon, then let the mixture cool to room temperature.

5. Pour the filling into the prepared piecrust and refrigerate.

6. To make the sour cream topping, dissolve the gelatin in the water and set aside.

7. Whisk together the sour cream, sugar, and cream cheese in a bowl set over a saucepan of simmering water until well blended and smooth. Stir in the vanilla extract.

8. Slowly add the gelatin mixture and whisk until the sour cream mixture begins to firm up. Remove the bowl from the pan of simmering water and let cool to lukewarm, stirring frequently.

9. Spoon the sour cream topping over the blueberry filling and smooth it over. Refrigerate the pie until well chilled. Serve with whipped cream, if desired.

Serves 8

MAX AND ERMA'S
Banana Cream Pie

EVERYONE HAS A FAVORITE RESTAURANT WHEN IT COMES TO BANANA CREAM PIE, BUT MAX AND ERMA'S SEEMS TO HAVE WON FIRST PLACE IN THE "BEST EVER" CATEGORY. TRY THIS EASY NO-BAKE PIE FOR THOSE WHO DON'T CARE FOR A LOT OF ADDED SUGAR.

2 cups half-and-half
4 cups heavy cream
1½ cups instant vanilla pudding mix
4 bananas, cut into ¼-inch-thick slices

Two 9-inch vanilla wafer piecrusts, homemade or purchased
1 cup chocolate syrup

1. Combine the half-and-half, 2 cups of the heavy cream, and the vanilla pudding mix in a large bowl.

2. Using an electric mixer, beat on low speed for 1 minute to combine all the ingredients. The mixture should just start to thicken.

3. Increase the speed to medium for another minute as it thickens a bit more.

4. Bring the speed of the mixer up to high and beat for another minute or so. Do not overmix, or the filling will deflate.

5. Using one quarter of the bananas slices, arrange a single layer of banana in each pie shell. Spoon just enough of the filling into the shells to cover the banana slices.

6. Arrange another quarter of the bananas slices over the filling and spoon some filling over it. Repeat this process one more time, so that there are 3 layers of banana and 3 layers of filling in each pie.

7. Using a metal spatula dipped in water, mound the top layer of filling slightly toward the center of each pie so that it is a little higher than the crust.

8. Whip the remaining 2 cups heavy cream and spoon it over the pies. Drizzle the chocolate syrup over the whipped cream and garnish with the remaining banana slices.

Makes 2 pies, each serving 8

MCDONALD'S
Apple Muffin

THESE MUFFINS ARE A BREEZE TO PUT TOGETHER WITH STORE-BOUGHT MIXES, AND THE RESULTS ARE VERY CLOSE TO THE ORIGINAL MCDONALD'S APPLE MUFFIN. THE RECIPE MAKES TWO DOZEN MUFFINS, SO KEEP SOME FROZEN FOR AN URGENT SNACK ATTACK.

3 eggs
2 teaspoons apple pie spice, homemade (recipe follows) or purchased

One 18.25-ounce box yellow cake mix
One 21-ounce can apple pie filling

1. Preheat the oven to 350°F. Line 24 muffin cups with paper cupcake liners.
2. Beat the eggs with an electric mixer on medium speed until light and foamy. Stir in the apple pie spice and mix.
3. Combine the yellow cake mix and apple pie filling in a large bowl and stir to blend.
4. Stir in the egg mixture and mix so that all the ingredients are well incorporated.
5. Fill each muffin cup about two-thirds full.
6. Bake the muffins in the hot oven for 25 to 30 minutes, until a toothpick inserted in the center comes out clean.

Makes 24 muffins

Apple Pie Spice

1 tablespoon ground cinnamon
1 teaspoon ground nutmeg

1 teaspoon ground allspice
½ teaspoon ground cloves

Combine all the ingredients, mix them well together, and store in an airtight container.

MCDONALD'S
Fruit Smoothie

USE YOUR FAVORITE BERRIES FOR THIS SMOOTHIE. SEEDLESS FRUIT IS BEST. US-
ING NONFAT YOGURT WILL HELP KEEP THE CALORIES DOWN, JUST IN CASE YOU'RE
COUNTING.

¾ cup fresh berries
½ cup sliced peach or melon
½ banana, chopped
I teaspoon honey

¼ cup plain or vanilla yogurt
½ cup grape or apple juice
4 ice cubes
Fresh mint leaves (optional)

1. Combine the berries, peach, banana, honey, yogurt, juice, and ice in a
   blender and pulse until the ice is crushed. Serve the smoothie as is or
   keep blending until it reaches the consistency you prefer.
2. Pour into a tall glass and garnish with a fresh mint leaf, if desired.

Serves 1 or 2

MRS. K'S RESTAURANT
Toll House Pecan Pie

THIS PECAN PIE COMES TOGETHER VERY QUICKLY WHEN USING A READY-MADE PIE SHELL. ALL THE INGREDIENTS FOR THE FILLING EXCEPT THE PECANS ARE MIXED IN ONE BOWL AND POURED INTO THE SHELL, READY TO BE BAKED.

1½ cups chopped pecans
One 9-inch piecrust, homemade
  (see page xxii) or purchased
1½ cups dark corn syrup
¾ cup sugar
6 tablespoons (¾ stick) unsalted
  butter, melted

4 eggs, beaten
1 teaspoon vanilla extract
¼ teaspoon kosher salt
Whipped cream (optional)

1. Preheat the oven to 400°F.

2. Sprinkle the chopped pecans over the bottom of the pie shell.

3. Combine the corn syrup, sugar, melted butter, eggs, vanilla extract, and salt in a large bowl. Mix until all the ingredients are completely incorporated.

4. Pour the mixture into the pie shell and bake for 10 minutes.

5. After 10 minutes, reduce the oven temperature to 375°F and bake for 30 minutes, or until the filling is set.

6. Let the pie cool before cutting. Serve with whipped cream, if desired.

Serves 8

MULATE'S

Homemade Bread Pudding with Butter-Rum Sauce

IF YOUR GUESTS DON'T RECOGNIZE THE TEXTURE OF THIS BREAD PUDDING, THE
SURPRISE IS THE BREAD—IT'S HAMBURGER BUNS. DON'T GET ANYTHING FANCY, AND
NO SESAME SEEDS. GREAT USE OF BARBECUE LEFTOVERS.

Bread Pudding
1 tablespoon unsalted butter, softened
6 hamburger buns, torn into pieces
½ cup raisins, soaked in warm water and drained
6 eggs
2 cups milk
2 cups half-and-half

1 cup sugar
1 teaspoon vanilla extract
½ teaspoon ground cinnamon

Butter-Rum Sauce
4 tablespoons (½ stick) unsalted butter
¼ cup sugar
½ cup heavy cream
½ cup dark spiced rum

1. Preheat the oven to 350°F. Coat a 9 by 13-inch baking pan with the butter.

2. To make the bread pudding, sprinkle the hamburger bun pieces over the bottom of the prepared pan. Sprinkle the soaked raisins over the bread.

3. Whisk the eggs until well beaten. Whisk in the milk, half-and-half, sugar, vanilla extract, and cinnamon. Whisk thoroughly or beat with an electric mixer until very well combined.

4. Pour the egg mixture over the bread and raisins in the pan. Gently press down on the bread so that it is completely soaked.

5. Bake in the hot oven for 45 minutes, or until the pudding is firm to the touch. Let cool for about 15 minutes before serving with the butter-rum sauce.

6. To make the butter-rum sauce, melt the butter in a small saucepan over medium heat. Whisk in the sugar and continue stirring until the sugar is dissolved.

7. Add the heavy cream and stir until it begins to thicken. Stir in the rum, then let the mixture come to a simmer and thicken up again. Serve warm with the bread pudding.

Serves 10

OLD KEY LIME HOUSE
Key Lime Pie

OLD KEY LIME HOUSE DOES KEY LIME PIE BETTER THAN ANYBODY. THIS IS AN ALL-FROM-SCRATCH RECIPE, INCLUDING THE GRAHAM CRACKER CRUST. USE FRESH OR A GOOD-QUALITY BOTTLED KEY LIME JUICE FOR THE MOST AUTHENTIC FLAVOR.

Crust

1 sleeve graham crackers

3 tablespoons granulated sugar

¼ teaspoon kosher salt

6 tablespoons (¾ stick) unsalted butter, melted

Filling

3 egg yolks

3 tablespoons granulated sugar

One 14-ounce can sweetened condensed milk

¼ teaspoon kosher salt

⅔ cup fresh Key lime juice

3 tablespoons fresh lemon juice

Topping

1½ cups heavy cream

3 tablespoons powdered sugar

1 teaspoon vanilla extract

1. Preheat the oven to 350°F.
2. To make the crust, grind the graham crackers in a food processor until finely ground, enough for 1½ cups.
3. Combine the crumbs with the granulated sugar, salt, and melted butter.
4. Stir to make sure all the crumbs are moistened.
5. Press the crumb mixture evenly across the bottom and up the sides of a 9-inch pie plate.
6. Bake in the hot oven for 5 minutes, or until golden brown. Remove from the oven.
7. Reduce the oven temperature to 275°F.
8. To make the filling, beat the egg yolks and granulated sugar with an electric mixer until light and foamy.
9. Stir in the sweetened condensed milk and salt; mix well.
10. Whisk in the Key lime juice and lemon juice.

11. When everything is well combined and the oven has cooled down, pour the filling into the prepared crust and bake the pie in the center of the oven for 20 to 25 minutes, until set in the center.

12. Let the pie cool to room temperature, then refrigerate until cold.

13. To make the topping, whip the heavy cream to soft peaks.

14. Add the powdered sugar and vanilla extract.

15. Whip to stiff peaks and refrigerate until ready to use.

16. Serve the pie with a dollop of whipped cream on top.

Serves 8

OLIVE GARDEN
Apple-Praline Cheesecake

THIS IS ALMOST LIKE THREE DESSERTS IN ONE: APPLE PIE FILLING IS MIXED WITH CHEESECAKE AND BAKED IN A GRAHAM CRACKER CRUST UNDER A CRUNCHY PECAN TOPPING. THERE IS DEFINITELY SOMETHING FOR EVERYBODY.

Crust
1½ cups graham cracker crumbs
2 tablespoons granulated sugar
4 tablespoons (½ stick) unsalted butter, melted

Apple-Cheesecake Filling
4 tablespoons (½ stick) unsalted butter
2 pounds sweet red apples, peeled, cored, and cut into ½-inch chunks
½ cup packed light brown sugar
1 teaspoon ground cinnamon
½ teaspoon ground nutmeg
¼ teaspoon kosher salt

2 tablespoons fresh lemon juice
½ cup granulated sugar
Two 8-ounce packages cream cheese, softened
3 eggs
1 cup heavy cream

Pecan Topping
8 tablespoons (1 stick) unsalted butter, softened
1½ cups packed dark brown sugar
2 tablespoons heavy cream
1 cup pecan halves, coarsely chopped

1. To make the crust, combine the graham cracker crumbs with the granulated sugar and mix well.

2. Stir in the melted butter and blend until the crumbs are moistened.

3. Press the crumb mixture evenly across the bottom of a 9-inch springform pan.

4. To make the apple-cheesecake filling, melt the butter in a large saucepan over low heat and sauté the apples with the brown sugar, cinnamon, nutmeg, salt, and lemon juice. Simmer the apples in their juices just until they have softened but not browned.

5. Set the apple mixture aside to cool.

6. Combine the granulated sugar and the cream cheese and beat with an electric mixer until smooth and creamy. Add the eggs, one at a time, beating well after each addition. Slowly pour in the heavy cream and beat until the mixture is thick and creamy.

7. Gently fold the cheesecake mixture into the cooked apples and blend well.

8. Preheat the oven to 350°F.

9. To make the pecan topping, beat together the butter and brown sugar with an electric mixer until light and fluffy. Mix in the heavy cream and stir to blend.

10. Stir in the chopped pecans.

11. Pour the apple-cheesecake mixture into the prepared springform pan.

12. Spread the pecan topping over the filling and set the pan on a baking sheet.

13. Bake in the hot oven for 1 hour and 20 minutes to 1 hour and 30 minutes, until set. Let cool before removing the sides of the pan.

Serves 8

OLIVE GARDEN
Brownie Banana Fantastico

A DESSERT THAT IS BOTH A CHOCOLATE BROWNIE AND A BANANA SPLIT IS A GREAT
IDEA FOR A KIDS' PARTY OR A CASUAL SUMMER BUFFET. PACKAGED ITEMS MAKE THIS
CROWD-PLEASER QUICK TO PULL TOGETHER AND LEAVE PLENTY OF ROOM FOR YOUR
OWN IMAGINATION.

One 18.4-ounce box brownie mix
One 2.6-ounce envelope whipped
  dessert topping mix
1½ cups milk
One 5.1-ounce box instant
  banana pudding mix

Pineapple topping
4 ripe bananas, split
Whipped cream
Chocolate syrup
Chopped nuts
Maraschino cherries

1. Prepare and bake the brownie according to the package directions.

2. Whip the dessert topping mix with ½ cup of the milk on high speed for
   5 minutes, or until thickened.

3. Combine the banana pudding mix and the remaining 1 cup milk and
   beat on low speed for 2 minutes, or until well combined.

4. Fold the whipped topping into the banana pudding using a rubber spatula
   and blending gently. Refrigerate the banana mousse until ready to use.

5. Cut the baked brownie into 4 or 6 portions and put each one in a shallow bowl.

6. To assemble the dessert, spread pineapple topping over each brownie and
   put a banana half on either side of the brownie.

7. Put a large spoonful of the banana mousse on top of the pineapple, then
   top the mousse with whipped cream, chocolate syrup, chopped nuts,
   and a cherry. Serve immediately.

Serves 4 or 6

*If you have an extra very ripe banana or two, mash it up and
combine it with the mousse mixture to intensify the banana flavor.*

OLIVE GARDEN
Chocolate Ricotta Pie

A VERY LIGHT TEXTURE WITH PLENTY OF CRUNCH IS AN ODD BUT DELICIOUS COM-
BINATION IN THIS OLIVE GARDEN CUSTOMER FAVORITE. DON'T SKIP TOASTING THE
ALMONDS—IT GIVES THEM A VERY DISTINCTIVE DEPTH THAT MATCHES WELL WITH
THE SEMISWEET CHOCOLATE AND SILKY RICOTTA CHEESE.

1 cup blanched almonds
1½ cups graham cracker crumbs
2 tablespoons granulated sugar
8 tablespoons (1 stick) unsalted
  butter, melted
2 cups ricotta cheese

¾ cup powdered sugar
1 teaspoon vanilla extract
½ cup semisweet chocolate
  chips
1½ cups heavy cream

1. Preheat the oven to 375°F.

2. Put the almonds in an ovenproof skillet and toast them in the hot oven, shaking the pan frequently, until they are lightly golden. Take them out of the oven and put them on paper towels to cool down.

3. Combine the graham cracker crumbs and the granulated sugar and whisk together. Pour in the melted butter and stir to make sure all the crumbs are moistened. Press the mixture evenly across the bottom and up the sides of a 9-inch pie plate.

4. Bake the graham cracker crust for 7 to 8 minutes, until golden brown, then let it cool completely.

5. Combine the ricotta and powdered sugar and beat with an electric mixer until smooth and creamy. Stir in the vanilla extract and blend well.

6. Put the chocolate chips and toasted almonds in the bowl of a food processor and pulse a few times, until the ingredients are broken down but not ground.

7. Stir the chopped chocolate and almonds into the ricotta mixture and refrigerate for about 30 minutes.

8. Whip the heavy cream to soft peaks, then stir it into the ricotta mixture. Pour the mixture into the prepared crust and refrigerate until ready to serve, at least 1 hour.

Serves 8 to 12

OLIVE GARDEN
Raspberry Mousse Cheesecake

RASPBERRY PRESERVES GIVE THE MOUSSE ITS FLAVOR AND COLOR. A GARNISH OF FRESH RASPBERRIES ON EACH PORTION WILL ENHANCE THE FLAVOR.

Filling and Pie
Two 8-ounce packages cream cheese, softened
½ cup sugar
2 eggs
1 teaspoon vanilla extract
One 9-inch chocolate cookie crumb piecrust, homemade or purchased

Mousse
1½ teaspoons unflavored powdered gelatin
1½ tablespoons cold water
½ cup seedless raspberry preserves
1 cup heavy cream
2 tablespoons sugar

1. Preheat the oven to 325°F.

2. To make the filling, beat the cream cheese and sugar with an electric mixer, until smooth and creamy. Add the eggs, one at a time, beating well after each addition. Stir in the vanilla extract and blend well.

3. Pour the mixture into the cookie crumb crust and bake in the hot oven for 25 minutes. Let the pie cool to room temperature, then refrigerate until ready to use.

4. To make the mousse, sprinkle the gelatin powder over the cold water and let it soften. Microwave the mixture on high for 15 to 30 seconds, until the gelatin is completely dissolved. Whisk the raspberry preserves into the gelatin and refrigerate for about 10 minutes.

5. Whip the heavy cream to soft peaks, then stir in the sugar. Whip to stiff peaks and reserve about ½ cup to use for garnish.

6. Using a rubber spatula, fold the raspberry-gelatin mixture into the whipped cream. Spread the mousse over the cheesecake mixture in the

piecrust. Mound the mousse slightly in the center, then refrigerate for at least 1 hour.

7. Serve with a dollop of the reserved whipped cream on each slice.

Serves 8

For a nice contrast, grind an ounce or two of dark chocolate in a food processor or coffee grinder and sprinkle it around the rim or over the top of the mousse.

OUTBACK STEAKHOUSE
Candied Cinnamon Pecans

THESE ADDICTIVE PECANS ARE TOSSED INTO THE RESTAURANT'S CHOPPED BLUE CHEESE SALAD. IF YOU CAN STOP SNACKING ON THEM, THEY CAN DRESS UP YOUR FAVORITE SALAD AS WELL.

½ cup pecan halves, chopped
1 tablespoon unsalted butter, melted

1 tablespoon dark brown sugar
1 teaspoon ground cinnamon

1. Preheat the oven to 375°F. Line a sheet pan with parchment paper.
2. Toss the pecans in a bowl with the melted butter.
3. Combine the brown sugar and the cinnamon and toss with the buttered pecans.
4. Arrange the coated pecans on the sheet pan, and bake in the hot oven for 6 to 8 minutes, until the sugar is caramelized.
5. Remove the pan from the oven and let the pecans cool on the parchment paper.
6. The candied pecans can be stored in an airtight container once they have cooled completely at room temperature.

Makes ½ cup

This recipe is easily expanded—you may want to make a much larger batch to keep on hand.

OUTBACK STEAKHOUSE
Sweet Potato

WITH CINNAMON AND HONEY, A WELL-BAKED SWEET POTATO CAN TASTE LIKE CANDY—SWEET AND LUSCIOUS.

1 medium sweet potato
2 tablespoons olive oil
2 to 3 tablespoons kosher salt
¼ cup honey

4 tablespoons (½ stick) unsalted butter, softened
½ teaspoon ground cinnamon

1. Preheat the oven to 350°F.

2. Scrub the skin of the sweet potato and dry it with paper towels. Prick the skin all over with the tip of a small, sharp knife.

3. Rub the skin with the olive oil and salt, then bake the potato in the hot oven for 45 to 60 minutes, depending on the size. It should be very soft to the touch.

4. Whip together the honey and butter. Split open the sweet potato and rough it up with a fork, then spread with the honey-butter mixture.

5. Sprinkle with the cinnamon and serve hot.

Serves 1

OUTBACK STEAKHOUSE
Sydney's Sinful Sundae

CONFIRMATION IS PENDING ON WHETHER OR NOT SYDNEY, AUSTRALIA, REALLY HAS SINFUL SUNDAES, BUT THIS SNOWBALL OF ICE CREAM AND COCONUT WITH HOT FUDGE SAUCE AND STRAWBERRIES WOULD CERTAINLY QUALIFY.

1 cup sweetened shredded coconut	1 teaspoon vanilla extract
1 cup heavy cream	8 strawberries, hulled
2 tablespoons sugar	1 cup hot fudge sauce
	4 scoops vanilla ice cream

1. Preheat the oven to 300°F.

2. Put four dessert plates in the freezer.

3. Spread the shredded coconut out in a single layer on a sheet pan and toast in the hot oven, stirring occasionally, until golden brown; watch carefully so it doesn't burn. Let cool before using.

4. Whip the heavy cream to soft peaks, then add the sugar and vanilla extract and beat to stiff peaks. Refrigerate until ready to use.

5. Quarter 4 of the strawberries lengthwise, leaving the remaining 4 strawberries whole.

6. Heat the fudge sauce. Pour 2 tablespoons in the center of each dessert plate.

7. Roll each scoop of ice cream in the toasted coconut until completely covered. Place a coated ice cream ball in the fudge sauce in the center of each plate and spoon 2 tablespoons of the remaining hot fudge over the top of the ball.

8. Spoon a dollop of whipped cream onto each ball. Arrange 4 strawberry slices around each ball and put a whole strawberry on top. Serve immediately.

Serves 4

PACI RESTAURANT
Coconut Cake

THIS UNUSUALLY RICH COCONUT CAKE HAS A SURPRISINGLY FLAVORFUL FROSTING—DOUBLE ESPRESSO REDUCED WITH CHOCOLATE AND CREAM. IT COMPLEMENTS THE CAKE PERFECTLY, RATHER LIKE HAVING YOUR CAKE AND COFFEE TOGETHER.

Coconut Cake
½ pound (2 sticks) unsalted butter, softened
1½ cups sugar
3 eggs
1 teaspoon vanilla extract
2 cups all-purpose flour
1 teaspoon baking powder
½ teaspoon kosher salt
1 cup milk
1½ cups sweetened flaked coconut

Chocolate-Espresso Sauce
4 double espressos (1½ cups)
1 cup heavy cream
4 cups semisweet chocolate chips

1. Preheat the oven to 350°F. Butter and flour a 10-inch cake pan and line the bottom with a circle of parchment paper.

2. Make the cake: Cream the butter and sugar with an electric mixer until light and fluffy. Add the eggs, one at a time, beating well after each addition. Stir in the vanilla extract.

3. Whisk together the flour, baking powder, and salt. Alternately add the dry ingredients and the milk to the creamed mixture, ending with the flour mixture. Blend well.

4. Stir in the coconut and mix until all the ingredients are well blended.

5. Pour the batter into the prepared cake pan and bake in the hot oven for 55 to 60 minutes, until the cake springs back when touched lightly in the center.

6. Let the cake cool on a rack, then turn it over and remove the paper from the bottom. Set it upright on a cake plate before frosting.

7. Make the frosting while the cake is baking. Put the espresso coffee in a small saucepan and simmer until it is reduced by half, about 20 minutes.

8. Whisk in the heavy cream and bring the mixture back to a simmer. Let the mixture simmer for 5 to 6 minutes, then remove from the heat. Let cool at room temperature.

9. Melt the chocolate chips in a bowl set over a saucepan of simmering water, stirring occasionally.

10. When the chocolate is melted and smooth, slowly whisk in the cream-espresso mixture, whisking constantly. The sauce should be thick enough to coat a spoon.

11. Let the sauce cool until it hardens just a bit, then frost the coconut cake.

Serves 10 to 12

PAPPADEAUX SEAFOOD KITCHEN

Key Lime Pie

PAPPADEAUX EXCELS AT FRESH NEW ORLEANS—INSPIRED SEAFOOD FOR LUNCH AND DINNER. IT LIKES TO SERVE ITS KEY LIME PIE WITH A SCATTERING OF FRESH BERRIES WHEN IN SEASON.

Crust

¾ cup graham cracker crumbs

I cup finely ground pecans

3 tablespoons sugar

I teaspoon ground cinnamon

4 tablespoons (½ stick) unsalted butter, melted

Filling

One 8-ounce package cream cheese, softened

One 14-ounce can sweetened condensed milk

3 egg yolks, well beaten

⅔ cup water

½ cup all-purpose flour

¼ teaspoon kosher salt

I tablespoon finely grated Key lime zest

⅓ cup Rose's lime juice

⅓ cup fresh Key lime juice

Raspberry Sauce

¾ cup seedless raspberry preserves

¼ cup water

Whipped cream (optional)

Lime slices (optional)

1. Preheat the oven to 350°F.

2. To make the crust, whisk together the graham cracker crumbs and ground pecans, then add the sugar and cinnamon. Pour the melted butter over the mixture and combine until everything is well moistened.

3. Press the mixture evenly across the bottom and up the sides of a 9-inch pie plate. Bake in the hot oven for about 10 minutes, then set aside to cool.

4. To make the Key lime filling, beat the cream cheese with an electric mixer until light and fluffy. Stir in the sweetened condensed milk, then beat until well combined.

5. Whisk together the egg yolks and water, then whisk in the flour and salt. Add the lime zest, Rose's lime juice, and the Key lime juice and whisk thoroughly.

6. Put the bowl over a saucepan of simmering water and whisk until the mixture thickens to almost a pudding-like consistency. Whisk in the cream cheese mixture, stirring constantly until thickened and blending well.

7. Pour the filling into the prepared crust and refrigerate for at least 4 hours.

8. To make the raspberry sauce, heat the raspberry preserves and stir in the water. Whisk until well blended and simmer for a few minutes, then let the sauce cool.

9. To serve, put a slice of the pie in the center of a dessert plate and spoon the sauce on either side. Garnish with a dollop of whipped cream and a slice of lime, if desired.

Serves 8 to 12

PAYARD PATISSERIE AND BISTRO

Milk Chocolate Truffles à l'Ancienne

MAKING THESE CLASSIC CONFECTIONS WILL TAKE A BIT OF ADVANCE PLANNING, BUT THE FINAL RESULTS WILL MORE THAN JUSTIFY ALL THE EFFORT.

Fondant
2 cups sugar
½ cup heavy cream
¼ cup milk
Pinch of kosher salt
1 tablespoon light corn syrup

Ganache
12 tablespoons (1½ sticks)
  unsalted butter, cut into pieces
  and softened

¾ cup praline paste
1½ cups chopped milk chocolate,
  melted

Truffle Coating
1½ cups chopped milk chocolate
½ cup almonds, toasted and
  coarsely ground

1. First make the fondant, as it needs time to firm up. Combine the sugar, heavy cream, milk, and salt in a medium saucepan.

2. Bring the mixture to a boil, stirring constantly.

3. Put a lid on the pan and turn the heat down to medium-high. Let the mixture cook for 1½ minutes.

4. Add the corn syrup and stir it in well with a clean spoon. Wipe away the crystals of sugar that form on the sides of the pan with a wet pastry brush.

5. Cook the fondant until it reaches 228° to 230°F on a candy thermometer.

6. Pour the mixture onto a marble or other clean solid surface and let cool.

7. When the fondant is just a little warmer than your fingers, fold it in on itself, using a bench scraper or an offset metal spatula. When it thickens, knead it with your hands.

8. Once the fondant is firm, wrap it in plastic and refrigerate until ready to use.

9. Make the ganache: Line a baking sheet with plastic wrap.

10. Weigh out 3 ounces of the fondant and put it in the bowl of an electric mixer fitted with the paddle attachment. Beat it on low speed until it is softened.

11. Add the butter, a couple of pieces at a time, beating well after each addition.

12. Add the praline paste, beating until well incorporated.

13. When the mixture is smooth, add the melted milk chocolate and mix until it is just combined. Pour the mixture onto the prepared pan and cover it with another sheet of plastic wrap.

14. Refrigerate the ganache until it firms up, about 1 hour. Stir it about every 15 minutes so that it develops the consistency of a heavy frosting.

15. Line a baking sheet with parchment paper and fill a pastry bag with the ganache. Use a small round tip or work without a tip.

16. Pipe mounds about the size of a quarter and less than an inch high onto the parchment paper, leaving space between them.

17. Refrigerate the ganache for another 15 to 30 minutes, until the mounds are firm enough to be handled.

18. Form and coat the truffles: Melt the chopped milk chocolate for the coating and stir until it is smooth and has cooled down.

19. Line a sheet pan with waxed paper.

20. Roll each ganache mound between your palms into a round ball. Work quickly so that the heat from your hands doesn't start to melt the ganache.

21. When all the ganache has been rolled into balls, refrigerate the truffles briefly, about 15 minutes, to firm them up.

22. Dip each truffle into the melted chocolate using just your thumb and forefinger and place on the prepared sheet pan. Let the coated truffles set for about 20 minutes.

23. Stir the ground almonds into the remaining melted milk chocolate and dip the truffles again in the mixture. Line a sheet pan with a clean sheet of waxed paper. Return the truffles to the sheet pan to set, about 20 minutes, before storing in an airtight container. Keep them in a cool, dry place, and they will last up to 3 weeks.

Makes 40 to 50 truffles

Fondant can last for months in the freezer
if well wrapped in plastic.

PICCADILLY CAFETERIA
Carrot Soufflé

EVERYTHING ABOUT THIS DISH SAYS DESSERT, EXCEPT FOR THE MAIN INGREDIENT—
CARROTS! TO SERVE IT AS A SIDE DISH, ELIMINATE THE DUSTING OF POWDERED SUGAR
ON TOP.

2 pounds carrots, peeled and chopped	¼ cup all-purpose flour
8 tablespoons (1 stick) unsalted butter, melted	1 teaspoon baking powder
	1 teaspoon vanilla extract
1 cup granulated sugar	3 eggs, well beaten
	Powdered sugar, for dusting

1. Preheat the oven to 350°F.
2. Cook the carrots in boiling salted water until very tender.
3. Drain the carrots and mash them with a fork or pass them through a food mill.
4. Combine the mashed carrots with the melted butter, granulated sugar, flour, baking powder, vanilla extract, and beaten eggs. Stir until the ingredients are well blended.
5. Spoon the carrot mixture into a 2-quart casserole and sprinkle with enough powdered sugar to lightly cover the surface.
6. Bake in the hot oven for 30 minutes. Serve immediately, dusted with powdered sugar.

Serves 8

You can also make individual portions using 6 to 8 ramekins and filling them three-quarters full. Place the ramekins on a sheet pan and then bake them for about 20 minutes.

PICCADILLY CAFETERIA
Pecan Delight

POPULAR THROUGHOUT THE SOUTH, PICCADILLY OFFERS A HUGE NUMBER OF DES-
SERTS. ITS SOUTHERN FLAIR FOR COMFORT FOOD IS PROUDLY REPRESENTED BY ITS
PECAN DELIGHT.

½ cup finely chopped pecans
½ cup coarsely chopped pecans
3 egg whites
1 teaspoon vanilla extract
½ teaspoon cream of tartar

¾ cup sugar
½ cup finely crushed Ritz
   crackers
1½ cups frozen whipped topping,
   thawed

1. Preheat the oven to 350°F.

2. Spread the finely chopped pecans and the coarsely chopped pecans in separate sections on a sheet pan and toast them for 5 to 6 minutes. Remove
   when they are lightly golden brown, and set aside, separately, to cool.

3. Reduce the oven temperature to 275°F. Coat a 10-inch pie plate with
   cooking spray.

4. Using an electric mixer, beat the egg whites to soft peaks. Add the vanilla
   extract and the cream of tartar and beat to stiff peaks. Slowly add the
   sugar and beat until the whites are very stiff and the sugar is incorporated.

5. Fold in the finely chopped pecans and the Ritz crackers.

6. Spread the meringue mixture evenly across the bottom and up the sides
   of the prepared pie plate in a 1-inch-thick layer. Make a dime-sized hole
   in the center of the meringue mixture to help with even baking.

7. Bake the pie shell for 1 hour, or until the meringue turns light tan. Turn
   the oven off and let the shell sit for another hour, until completely dry.
   Remove the shell from the pie plate and let cool.

8. Spoon the whipped topping carefully into the meringue shell and sprinkle with the coarsely chopped pecans. Chill thoroughly before serving.

Serves 8 to 12

PLANET HOLLYWOOD
White Chocolate Bread Pudding

THE WHITE CHOCOLATE GIVES THIS TRADITIONALLY HOMEY DESSERT THE STAR TREATMENT. RICH WITH CREAM AND EGGS, THE FINAL TOUCH IS A SPLASH OF JIM BEAM BOURBON WHISKEY SAUCE.

Bread Pudding
4 cups French bread, crusts trimmed, cut into 1-inch cubes (about ⅔ loaf)
9 egg yolks
2 cups sugar
1 cup milk
2 cups heavy cream
1 teaspoon vanilla extract
5 eggs, well beaten
2¼ cups white chocolate chips

4 tablespoons (½ stick) unsalted butter, softened

Jim Beam Sauce
1 pound plus 4 tablespoons (4½ sticks) unsalted butter
4 cups sugar
1½ cups Jim Beam bourbon whiskey
5 eggs, well beaten

1. Preheat the oven to 450°F.

2. Make the bread pudding: Arrange the bread cubes on one or two baking sheets and put them in the oven while it heats up. The bread should be dried out, not toasted. Set it aside and turn off the oven.

3. Using an electric mixer, beat the egg yolks with 1 cup of the sugar until light and smooth.

4. Combine the milk, the remaining 1 cup sugar, the heavy cream, and the vanilla extract in a medium saucepan over medium heat, whisking constantly. Whisk until the mixture comes to a boil, then turn down the heat.

5. Add ½ cup of the cream mixture to the egg yolk mixture, whisking constantly so that the heat doesn't cause the eggs to cook, then slowly whisk the egg yolk mixture into the cream mixture.

6. Slowly whisk the beaten whole eggs into the cream mixture and stir for about 5 minutes, or until the custard is thickened. Stir in the white chocolate chips and continue to stir while they melt.

7. Put the dried bread into a large bowl and pour the white chocolate custard over it. Push the cubes down into the custard, making sure the bread absorbs all the liquid. Cover the bowl and set it aside until all the custard is absorbed, at least 1 hour.

8. Preheat the oven to 450°F.

9. Butter a 9 by 13-inch baking pan with the softened butter. Pour the bread pudding into the prepared pan and cover it with plastic wrap and then a sheet of foil.

10. Put the pan with the pudding into a larger pan, such as a roasting pan. Fill the larger pan with enough hot water to come halfway up the sides of the pudding pan.

11. Bake in the hot oven for 45 minutes, or until the custard is set. Take the foil and plastic off and let the pudding cool.

12. Make the sauce while the pudding is baking. Melt the butter in a large heavy-bottomed saucepan. Add the sugar and simmer on low heat. Don't stir the sugar and don't let it boil.

13. After about 5 minutes, stir in the Jim Beam with a wooden spoon. Let the mixture cook over low heat just until bubbles begin to appear around the sides of the pan. Remove the sauce from the heat.

14. Add ½ cup of the sauce to the beaten eggs, whisking constantly, then slowly whisk the egg mixture into the sauce, whisking constantly for 3 to 5 minutes or until the sauce thickens. For a smoother sauce, strain the mixture through a sheet of cheesecloth.

15. Serve the bread pudding in shallow bowls with the sauce poured over and around it.

Serves 9

This bread pudding also goes well with a scoop of vanilla ice cream on the side or a dollop of whipped cream on top.

THE PLAZA RESTAURANT

Walt's Favorite Chocolate Soda

YOU'LL HAVE TO BUY SOME SELTZER WATER, BUT THERE'S NO OTHER WAY TO GET THE OLD-FASHIONED FIZZ IN THIS ICE CREAM SODA.

½ cup chocolate syrup
2 scoops vanilla ice cream

¾ cup seltzer water
1 maraschino cherry

1. Refrigerate a tall soda glass that can hold at least 16 ounces.
2. Pour the chocolate syrup into the bottom of the chilled glass and top with 1 scoop of the ice cream.
3. Slowly pour in the seltzer water, filling the glass three quarters of the way.
4. Add the remaining 1 scoop ice cream and top with the cherry.

Serves 1

Variations

TRY THESE EQUALLY DELICIOUS COMBINATIONS.

Rocky road ice cream and cream soda
Pineapple sherbet and ginger ale
Chocolate chip ice cream and Coca-Cola
Butter pecan ice cream and root beer

PORTOBELLO
White Chocolate Crème Brûlée

LOVERS OF TRADITIONAL CRÈME BRÛLÉE WILL GO NUTS FOR THIS VARIATION. WHITE CHOCOLATE IS MELTED INTO THE VANILLA CUSTARD. YOU'LL FIND IT ELEGANT ENOUGH FOR SPECIAL OCCASIONS AND EASY ENOUGH FOR ONCE A WEEK!

5 egg yolks
½ cup plus 2 tablespoons sugar
2 cups heavy cream

⅓ cup white chocolate chips
1 teaspoon vanilla extract

1. Preheat the oven to 300°F.

2. Combine the egg yolks with ¼ cup of the sugar and beat with an electric mixer until light and foamy.

3. In a small saucepan over medium heat, combine the heavy cream and another ¼ cup of sugar. Bring the mixture to a boil, then reduce the heat to low and let simmer.

4. Stir in the white chocolate chips, a little at a time, stirring well after each addition.

5. Whisk ½ cup of the cream mixture into the egg yolk mixture, whisking constantly. When the cream is thoroughly incorporated, slowly whisk in the remaining cream mixture, stirring until everything is very well blended.

6. Stir in the vanilla extract.

7. Fill four 6-ounce ramekins with the custard. Set the ramekins in a large baking pan and pour in enough hot water to come halfway up the sides of the ramekins.

8. Bake in the hot oven for about 1 hour, or until the custards are set in the center. Let them cool before wrapping in plastic and refrigerating for at least 1 hour.

9. To serve, sprinkle the 2 tablespoons sugar evenly over the custards. Pass the custards under the broiler until the sugar begins to bubble and caramelize. You can also use a kitchen torch—move it rapidly over the sugar to caramelize.

Serves 4

A simple garnish on top of the caramelized sugar would make an impressive presentation. Scatter a few white chocolate shavings over the top, or center a cluster of fresh raspberries with a mint leaf, before serving.

PRANTL'S BAKERY
Burnt Almond Torte

PRANTL'S BAKERY HAS BEEN IN OPERATION JUST OUTSIDE OF PITTSBURGH FOR OVER FORTY YEARS. IT IS DEVOTED TO PRODUCING BAKED GOODS IN THE GERMAN TRADITION AND IS FAMOUS FOR ITS BURNT ALMOND TORTE. IT CAME ABOUT BECAUSE A GLUT IN CALIFORNIA ALMONDS ONE YEAR INSPIRED FOUNDER HENRY PRANTL TO PRODUCE A RECIPE FOR THE STATE'S ALMOND BOARD. IT HAS BEEN A BELOVED FAVORITE EVER SINCE.

Honey-Almond Brittle
½ cup granulated sugar
3 tablespoons honey
1½ tablespoons water
½ cup slivered almonds, toasted
1 tablespoon unsalted butter
¼ teaspoon baking soda

Cake
12 tablespoons (1½ sticks)
  unsalted butter, softened
1¼ cups granulated sugar
4 eggs
2 teaspoons vanilla extract
2½ cups cake flour
1½ teaspoons baking powder
½ teaspoon baking soda
½ teaspoon kosher salt
1 cup buttermilk

Custard
3 egg yolks
⅓ cup granulated sugar
2 tablespoons cornstarch
1 cup milk
1 tablespoon unsalted butter
1 teaspoon almond extract

Whipped Cream
½ cup heavy cream
3 tablespoons powdered sugar
1 teaspoon vanilla extract

1. Make the brittle first, so it will be ready when you need it. Combine the granulated sugar, honey, and water in a medium saucepan and stir just to dissolve the sugar. Bring the mixture to a boil, but do not stir it anymore.

2. Boil until the sugar begins to caramelize and turn a deep golden brown.

3. Immediately remove the pan from the heat and use a wooden spoon to stir in the toasted almonds, the butter, and the baking soda. The syrup will begin to foam up—just keep stirring until the butter melts and the foam subsides.

4. Pour the honey-almond mixture onto a buttered sheet pan, smoothing it a little, and let cool.

5. Once the brittle has hardened, break it into pieces and put it in a resealable plastic bag. Hit the brittle with a small hammer or mallet, or roll over it with a rolling pin, until it is well crushed.

6. Refrigerate until ready to use.

7. Preheat the oven to 350°F. Coat two 8-inch square cake pans with butter or cooking spray.

8. Make the cake: Cream the butter and sugar with an electric mixer until light and fluffy. Add the eggs, one at a time, beating well after each addition. Stir in the vanilla extract.

9. Whisk together the flour, baking powder, baking soda, and salt. Add the dry ingredients to the creamed mixture alternately with the buttermilk, stirring well after each addition and ending with the flour mixture.

10. Divide the batter between the prepared pans and tap the pans on the counter to settle the contents. Bake the cake layers in the hot oven for about 30 minutes, or until a toothpick inserted in the center comes out clean.

11. Let the layers cool in the pans on wire racks for 30 minutes, then turn them out of the pans and continue to let the layers cool.

12. Make the custard while the cake is baking. Beat the egg yolks and granulated sugar with an electric mixer until smooth. Add the cornstarch and mix well.

13. Bring the milk to a simmer over low heat in a heavy saucepan. Whisk ½ cup of the hot milk into the beaten egg mixture, whisking constantly.

14. When the milk is completely incorporated, whisk the remaining milk into the egg mixture, whisking constantly. Return the custard mixture to the saucepan. Increase the heat to medium, and whisk until the custard has thickened.

15. Remove the pan from the heat and stir in the butter and almond extract.

16. Pour the custard into a bowl and cover with a piece of plastic wrap set directly on the surface to prevent a skin from forming. Refrigerate until chilled.

17. When the custard is chilled, make the whipped cream. Whip the heavy cream to soft peaks.

18. Add the powdered sugar and vanilla extract, then beat to stiff peaks.

19. Fold the whipped cream into the custard, using a rubber spatula to gently but thoroughly mix it in.

20. Cover and refrigerate until ready to use.

21. Assemble the torte: Place one of the cake layers on a large serving platter.

22. Cover the top of the cake with the chilled custard and sprinkle with some of the brittle bits.

23. Place the second cake layer on top of the first one, and spread the remaining custard over the top and sides of the torte.

24. Refrigerate the cake for 1 hour to set the custard. Finish the cake by pressing the brittle into the sides of the torte, using the palm of your hand, and by sprinkling the remainder on top.

25. Refrigerate once more before serving.

Serves 8

RAGLAN ROAD
Bread and Butter Pudding

THIS FAVORITE OF VISITORS TO DOWNTOWN DISNEY, PLEASURE ISLAND, IS A CROSS BETWEEN BREAD PUDDING AND FRENCH TOAST. BUTTERED SLICES OF WHITE BREAD ARE SOAKED IN A CREAMY VANILLA CUSTARD, EXCEPT FOR THE PIECES ON TOP, WHICH TOAST IN THE OVEN WHEN THE PUDDING IS PUT IN TO BAKE. LEFTOVERS MAKE AN EXCELLENT BREAKFAST WITH MAPLE SYRUP!

8 tablespoons (1 stick) butter, softened
12 slices white bread, crusts trimmed
¼ cup seedless raisins, soaked and drained
2 cups heavy cream

1 cup milk
4 egg yolks
¼ cup sugar

Optional Garnishes
Dessert sauce of your choice
Ice cream
Whipped cream

1. Butter a 9 by 13-inch baking dish with 1 tablespoon of the softened butter.

2. Butter both sides of the white bread with the remaining 7 tablespoons butter and cut the slices into quarters.

3. Arrange about one third of the buttered bread in the prepared baking dish, overlapping the pieces slightly so they all fit in.

4. Scatter the raisins over the bread in the dish.

5. Cover with another layer of bread pieces, reserving the leftover pieces.

6. Combine the heavy cream and milk in a saucepan over medium heat and let the mixture just come to a boil. Remove it immediately.

7. Combine the egg yolks and sugar in a large bowl and set the mixture over a saucepan of simmering water. Whisk constantly until the mixture thickens and can coat the back of a spoon.

8. Whisk ½ cup of the cream mixture into the eggs and sugar. When it is completely incorporated, slowly whisk the remaining cream into the egg mixture, whisking constantly.

9. Pour two thirds of the custard over the layers of bread in the baking dish. Press down the bread so that it is submerged in the custard. Let the dish set for about 30 minutes, or until the custard has been absorbed.

10. Preheat the oven to 350°F while the bread is soaking.

11. Pour the remaining custard over the pudding and arrange the reserved pieces of buttered bread on top. Gently press the bread down into the custard so that the liquid comes halfway up the sides of the bread.

12. Bake in the hot oven for 30 minutes, or until the custard is set and the top is toasted a golden brown. Serve with your choice of dessert sauce, ice cream, or whipped cream.

Serves 4 to 6

This bread pudding can also be made in individual ramekins or custard cups.

RAINFOREST CAFE
Coconut Bread Pudding

THE RAINFOREST CAFE GOES TROPICAL WITH COCONUT AND APRICOTS TO FLAVOR ITS BREAD PUDDING. A HEALTHY DOSE OF COCO LÓPEZ ENHANCES THE COCONUT AND GIVES THE WHOLE DISH A BIT OF A CARIBBEAN ESSENCE.

1 loaf Pullman bread, crusts trimmed, cut into 1-inch cubes
½ cup thinly sliced dried apricots
½ cup sweetened shredded coconut
Two 15-ounce cans Coco López cream of coconut
2 cups milk

2 teaspoons vanilla extract
1½ cups sugar
6 eggs

Optional Garnishes
Vanilla ice cream
Chocolate shavings
Whipped cream
Toasted coconut

1. Preheat the oven to 350°F.

2. Line a 9 by 13-inch baking dish with half of the bread cubes. Layer ¼ cup of the sliced apricots and ¼ cup of the coconut over the bread.

3. Layer the remaining bread cubes on top and repeat the layering of the apricots and coconut.

4. Combine the Coco López, milk, vanilla extract, and sugar in a medium saucepan over medium heat and stir until the sugar dissolves.

5. Thoroughly whisk the eggs in a large bowl. Pour ½ cup of the warm coconut cream mixture into the eggs, whisking constantly. When it is well combined, whisk in the remaining coconut cream mixture.

6. Pour the coconut cream–egg mixture over the bread in the baking dish, making sure all the pieces are moistened.

7. Cover the dish with a sheet of plastic wrap and then a sheet of foil.

8. Put the baking dish into a larger pan and pour in enough hot water to come halfway up the sides of the baking dish.

9. Bake in the hot oven for about 1 hour. Remove the foil and plastic wrap, and bake for another 10 minutes, or until the top is golden brown.

10. Serve with a choice of garnishes, if desired.

Serves 8

RAINFOREST CAFE
Volcano

THIS IS A GREAT, HEAPING MOUND OF CHOCOLATE BROWNIE AND ICE CREAM, DRIP-
PING WITH HOT FUDGE AND CARAMEL, TOPPED OFF WITH WHIPPED CREAM. IT'S A
GREAT IDEA FOR A KIDS' PARTY, OR ANY TIME YOU WANT TO SERVE A BODACIOUS
DESSERT WITHOUT HAVING TO COOK.

Four 4 by 4-inch chocolate
  brownies, homemade or
  purchased
I quart vanilla ice cream
½ cup hot fudge sauce, warmed

½ cup caramel sauce, warmed
I cup heavy cream, whipped to
  stiff peaks with 3 tablespoons
  powdered sugar and
  I teaspoon vanilla extract

1. Cut each brownie into 4 equal strips.

2. Mound 2 scoops of ice cream into the center of each of four chilled dessert plates.

3. Arrange 4 brownie pieces at the base of the ice cream, pushing them into
the base to make a volcano shape.

4. Drizzle the hot fudge sauce down one side of the "volcano" and the caramel sauce down the other.

5. Top the "crater" with whipped cream and more sauce, if desired. If you're
celebrating a festive occasion, light a sparkler and put it on top—but
outdoors only!

Serves 4

*This dessert can be made as one large volcano. Use a large dessert
platter or a large, shallow bowl to assemble the ingredients and
serve with extra sauces and whipped cream on the side.
You can build your volcano with different ice creams,
such as rocky road and toffee, and get as creative as you wish.*

RATHER SWEET BAKERY AND CAFE
Tuxedo Cake

THE LONG STRIPES OF CHOCOLATE GLAZE OVER A SMOOTH WHIPPED-CREAM BASE MAY GIVE THIS TOWERING CAKE ITS NAME, BUT IT IS THE MOIST AND FLAVORFUL COMBINATION OF QUALITY INGREDIENTS THAT WILL IMPRESS YOU.

Triple-Layer Cake
4 cups granulated sugar
1 cup unsweetened cocoa powder
4 cups all-purpose flour
1 tablespoon baking soda
½ teaspoon kosher salt
½ pound (2 sticks) unsalted butter, cut into large pieces
2 cups water
1 cup canola oil
4 eggs
2 teaspoons vanilla extract
1 cup buttermilk

Whipped Cream Frosting
4 cups heavy cream
1½ cups powdered sugar
2 teaspoons vanilla extract

Chocolate Glaze
¾ cup chopped bittersweet chocolate
½ cup heavy cream
¼ cup light corn syrup
2 teaspoons vanilla extract

1. Position the racks in the lower third and center of the oven. Preheat the oven to 350°F. Butter and flour or spray three 9-inch cake pans. Line the bottoms with parchment paper.

2. To make the cake, in a large bowl, whisk together the granulated sugar, cocoa powder, flour, baking soda, and salt. Set aside.

3. Combine the butter pieces, water, and canola oil in a medium saucepan over medium heat. Simmer until the butter melts, stirring occasionally.

4. Pour the melted butter mixture into the dry ingredients and whisk thoroughly until smooth and creamy.

5. Add the eggs, one at a time, beating well with an electric mixer after each addition. Stir in the vanilla extract.

6. Whisk in the buttermilk and stir until everything is very well incorporated.

7. Pour equal amounts of the batter into each of the three prepared pans. Put one pan in the center of the bottom rack and two pans on either side of the higher rack.

8. Bake the cake layers for 35 to 40 minutes. A toothpick inserted in the center of the cake should come out clean.

9. Let the layers cool in the pans on wire racks for 15 minutes, then turn them out of the pans, remove the paper liners, and let cool completely before assembling, at least 2 hours.

10. To make the frosting, whip the heavy cream until it forms soft peaks.

11. Add the powdered sugar and vanilla extract.

12. Beat to stiff peaks and refrigerate until ready to use.

13. To make the chocolate glaze, put the chopped chocolate into a bowl.

14. Heat the heavy cream in a small saucepan until it just begins to steam, but not boil.

15. Pour the hot cream over the chocolate and stir to melt the chocolate.

16. Stir in the corn syrup and vanilla extract and blend well.

17. Pour the glaze into a pitcher and let it cool. If it hardens before you finish the cake, warm it just slightly so that it maintains its pouring consistency.

18. To assemble the cake, put one of the layers on a large platter. Coat the top and sides with the whipped cream frosting, then follow with the second and third layers, frosting the top and sides of the second layer. When all three are stacked, spread the top and sides with the remaining frosting. Use a metal spatula to give the sides a smooth finish.

19. Refrigerate the frosted cake for 1 hour to set the whipped cream.

20. Start pouring the glaze in the center of the cake and let it drip naturally over the sides in long drips, tilting the platter just a little if you need to,

to make sure the glaze will flow all the way to the edge and over. You
want the white frosting to show between the drizzles of glaze.

21. Refrigerate the cake to let the glaze set, about 1 hour.

22. To serve, slice the portions with a serrated cake knife dipped in hot water.

Serves 8 to 12

*Make a simple garnish to finish the top of the cake. A cluster of fresh
strawberries with mint leaves in the center, curled white and dark
chocolate shavings scattered all over, or small macaroons studded
along the top edge would all make an impressive presentation.*

RED LOBSTER
Bananas Foster Cheesecake

THIS IS A HUGE FAVORITE AT SEVERAL OF THE RED LOBSTER LOCATIONS. A PECAN CRUST IS FILLED WITH FRESH BANANA CHEESECAKE, BAKED WITH A LAYER OF SOUR CREAM, AND FINISHED WITH CARAMEL-RUM SAUCE AND MORE BANANAS. IT CAN STAY IN THE REFRIGERATOR UNTIL READY TO SERVE, MAKING IT A GOOD CHOICE FOR SPECIAL OCCASIONS AND PARTIES.

Pecan Crust
¾ cup finely chopped pecans
¾ cup all-purpose flour
3 tablespoons granulated sugar
3 tablespoons golden brown sugar
2 teaspoons vanilla extract
4 tablespoons (½ stick) unsalted butter, melted

Banana Cheesecake
Four 8-ounce packages cream cheese, softened
3 eggs
4 or 5 ripe bananas, pureed
1 cup sour cream
2 tablespoons fresh lemon juice
1 teaspoon vanilla extract

2 teaspoons ground cinnamon
¼ teaspoon kosher salt
1¼ cups granulated sugar
2 tablespoons cornstarch

Sour Cream Topping
1 cup sour cream
¼ cup granulated sugar
1 teaspoon vanilla extract

Caramel-Rum Sauce
One 17-ounce jar caramel sauce
¼ cup dark rum

Garnish
2 ripe bananas, cut into ¼-inch slices

1. Preheat the oven to 350°F.

2. To make the crust, combine the chopped pecans, flour, granulated sugar, brown sugar, and the vanilla extract. Pour in the melted butter and stir to moisten all the ingredients.

3. Press the mixture evenly across the bottom and halfway up the sides of a 9-inch springform pan. Fashion a strip of heavy-duty foil 3 inches high and wrap it around the pan.

4. To make the cheesecake, beat the softened cream cheese with an electric mixer until smooth and creamy. Add the eggs, one at a time, beating well after each addition.

5. Add the pureed bananas, sour cream, lemon juice, vanilla extract, cinnamon, salt, sugar, and cornstarch. Mix until well combined.

6. Spoon the mixture into the prepared crust and put the foil-wrapped pan into a larger roasting pan. Fill the roasting pan with enough hot water to come 1 inch up the sides of the springform pan.

7. Bake in the center of the oven for 1 hour and 15 minutes to 1 hour and 20 minutes, until the cake is just set in the center.

8. Remove the cake from the water bath and set it aside—do not turn off the oven.

9. To make the sour cream topping, whisk together the sour cream, sugar, and vanilla extract, blending well. Spread the mixture over the top of the cheesecake.

10. Set the cake directly on the rack in the center of the oven and bake for 10 minutes, or just until set. Turn off the heat and let the cake cool inside the oven.

11. Wrap the cooled cheesecake, still in the pan, in plastic and refrigerate for at least 4 hours.

12. To make the caramel-rum sauce and serve the cake, remove the plastic wrap and foil from around the springform pan and release the ring from the sides. Transfer the cake to a large dessert platter.

13. Heat the caramel sauce in a small saucepan over low heat, stirring to loosen it up.

14. Stir the rum into the caramel and whisk to blend it with the sauce.

15. Drizzle some of the sauce over the cake, then arrange the sliced bananas over the top. Serve with extra caramel-rum sauce on the side.

Serves 10

RED ROBIN GOURMET BURGERS
Gingerbread Milkshake

MAKE A GINGER SYRUP AND MIX IT WITH VANILLA ICE CREAM AND GRAHAM CRACKER CRUMBS, AND YOU HAVE A DEEPLY FLAVORFUL MILKSHAKE SOPHISTICATED ENOUGH FOR GROWN-UPS.

2 cups water
1½ cups sugar
1 tablespoon ground ginger
1 teaspoon vanilla extract
½ teaspoon ground cinnamon

¼ cup milk
1 pint vanilla ice cream, softened
¼ cup graham cracker crumbs
Whipped cream and gingersnap
  cookies (optional)

1. Combine the water, sugar, ginger, vanilla extract, and cinnamon in a medium saucepan. Bring the mixture to a boil, then reduce the heat and simmer for 15 minutes. Transfer to a covered container and cool to room temperature.

2. Whisk together the milk and ice cream. Add ½ cup of the ginger syrup, adding more or less to taste, and blend well. Pour into glasses and top with the graham cracker crumbs.

3. Garnish with whipped cream and gingersnap cookies, if desired.

Serves 4

RESTAURANT MARRAKESH
Apple Crepes

A TOUCH OF HONEY IN THE APPLE FILLING OF THESE CREPES BLENDS NICELY WITH THE SAUCE THAT IS SPOONED OVER THEM BEFORE THEY ARE BAKED. BAKING NOT ONLY HEATS THE FILLING, BUT GIVES THE CREPES A DEEPER, RICHER FINISH.

Crepe Batter
1 cup all-purpose flour
½ teaspoon kosher salt
2 eggs, beaten
1 cup milk
2 tablespoons unsalted butter, melted

Apple Filling
2 tablespoons honey
1 teaspoon ground cinnamon
2 cups apple pie filling, homemade or purchased

Sauce
1 cup honey
1 tablespoon ground cinnamon
4 tablespoons (½ stick) unsalted butter, melted

Garnish
Vanilla ice cream
Ground cinnamon

1. To make the crepe batter, whisk together the flour and salt in a medium bowl. Make a well in the middle of the flour and pour in the beaten eggs. Whisk with a fork until the eggs are blended with the flour.

2. Add enough milk to make a smooth paste, then whisk in the remaining milk. Stir in the melted butter. Let the batter sit for about 15 minutes.

3. To make the filling, stir the honey and cinnamon into the apple pie filling. Set aside.

4. To make the sauce, combine the honey and cinnamon in a small saucepan, stirring over low heat. When the honey mixture is warm, stir in the melted butter. Set the sauce aside and keep warm.

5. Preheat the oven to 350°F. Butter a sheet pan and set it aside.

6. To make the crepes, heat a small nonstick skillet over medium heat. Coat with butter or cooking spray.

7. Ladle just enough of the crepe batter to cover the bottom of the skillet. Tilt the pan to distribute the batter evenly.

8. Cook until bubbles rise on the surface and the edges and bottom are browned. Flip the crepe over and cook for another minute or two. Repeat with the remaining batter.

9. Remove the cooked crepes to a plate until all the batter has been used.

10. Spoon ¼ cup of the apple filling down the center of each crepe and roll the crepe up.

11. Place the crepes, seam side down, on the prepared sheet pan.

12. Pour most of the honey sauce over the crepes, then bake the crepes in the hot oven for 6 to 8 minutes.

13. To serve, place 2 crepes per person on warmed dessert plates. Drizzle with the juices from the baking pan.

14. Put a scoop of ice cream next to the crepes, drizzle with the remaining honey sauce, and sprinkle with cinnamon.

Serves 6 to 8

THE RITZ-CARLTON
Chocolate Chip Cookies

THESE ARE *BIG* COOKIES, SOFT AND CHEWY. BECAUSE THEY SPREAD WHILE BAKING, YOU'LL NEED MORE THAN ONE BAKING SHEET.

1¼ pounds (5 sticks) unsalted butter, softened
2 cups granulated sugar
2 cups packed dark brown sugar
5 eggs

1 tablespoon vanilla extract
6 cups all-purpose flour
1 teaspoon baking soda
1 teaspoon kosher salt
4 cups semisweet chocolate chips

1. Preheat the oven to 350°F.

2. Cream the butter and the granulated and brown sugars with an electric mixer until light and fluffy. Add the eggs, one at a time, beating well after each addition. Stir in the vanilla extract and blend well.

3. Whisk together the flour, baking soda, and salt. Gradually stir the dry ingredients into the creamed mixture until fully incorporated. Stir in the chocolate chips.

4. Use a ½-cup measuring cup to scoop the dough onto the cookie sheets, placing the scoops at least 3 inches apart. Gently press down the mounds of dough with the back of a spoon.

5. Bake for 10 to 12 minutes in the hot oven, until the edges are firm, and let the cookies cool on wire racks.

Makes about 24 large cookies

To make smaller cookies, roll the dough into a 2-inch-thick cylinder, wrap it in plastic, and refrigerate it for 1 hour. Cut the log into 1-inch-thick slices. Place the cookies 2 inches apart and bake for about 8 minutes.

ROSE AND CROWN PUB AND DINING ROOM
Baileys Irish Coffee Trifle

GOOD STRONG COFFEE FLAVORS THE CHOCOLATE FILLING IN THIS DAZZLING TRIFLE. SERVED IN TALL PARFAIT OR BEVERAGE GLASSES, THE TRIFLE CONSISTS OF LAYERS OF THE CUSTARD BETWEEN PIECES OF MOIST, TENDER CHOCOLATE CAKE. TOPPED WITH WHIPPED CREAM INFUSED WITH BAILEYS IRISH CREAM, THIS TRIFLE ACTUALLY IMPROVES WITH AGE, IF YOU CAN KEEP IT AROUND THAT LONG!

Chocolate Cream Filling
1½ cups granulated sugar
¾ cup unsweetened cocoa powder
½ cup cornstarch
¼ teaspoon kosher salt
3 cups milk
3 cups half-and-half
⅓ cup strong coffee
⅓ cup chopped bittersweet chocolate
2 tablespoons vanilla extract

Chocolate Cake
1¾ cups all-purpose flour
1¾ cups packed light brown sugar
¾ cup unsweetened cocoa powder
1½ teaspoons baking powder
1½ teaspoons baking soda
¼ teaspoon kosher salt
2 eggs
1 teaspoon vanilla extract
¼ cup canola oil
1 cup boiling water
1¼ cups buttermilk

Baileys Whipped Cream
⅔ cup heavy cream
2 tablespoons powdered sugar
2 tablespoons Baileys Irish Cream

1. Make the filling first (it can be made up to 2 days ahead and kept covered and refrigerated). Whisk together the granulated sugar, cocoa powder, cornstarch, and salt.

2. Slowly pour in the milk, whisking constantly.

3. Slowly pour in the half-and-half, whisking constantly.

4. Pour the mixture through a fine-mesh strainer into a medium saucepan.

5. Bring the mixture to a gentle boil over medium heat, whisking constantly, for about 2 minutes, then remove the pan from the heat. Fill a large bowl with ice cubes and water and set aside.

6. Stir the coffee, chocolate, and vanilla extract into the filling. Set the saucepan in the bowl with the ice water and let the filling chill, stirring occasionally. Refrigerate, covered, until ready to use.

7. Preheat the oven to 350°F.

8. To make the cake, coat a half sheet pan (12 by 17 inches) with butter or cooking spray.

9. Whisk together the flour, brown sugar, cocoa powder, baking powder, baking soda, and salt.

10. In a separate large bowl, beat the eggs with an electric mixer until foamy, then stir in the vanilla extract, canola oil, and the boiling water. Whisk the mixture until well blended.

11. Gradually stir the dry ingredients alternately with the buttermilk into the egg mixture. Stir until all the ingredients are well blended.

12. Pour the batter into the prepared sheet pan and bake for 25 to 30 minutes, until the cake springs back when touched in the center.

13. Let the cake cool, then cut into pieces shaped to fit in your dessert glasses.

14. To make the Baileys whipped cream, whip the heavy cream to soft peaks. Add the powdered sugar and Baileys Irish Cream. Whip to stiff peaks. Transfer to a pastry bag fitted with a fluted tip.

15. Put a piece of the chocolate cake in each dessert glass, then spoon some of the chocolate filling on top. Repeat the layers until the glass is three-quarters full.

16. Pipe the Baileys whipped cream on top of the trifle and serve immediately, or refrigerate for up to 2 hours.

Serves 14 to 16

Chocolate shavings, a dusting of cocoa powder, or a mixture of powdered sugar and instant coffee would make attractive finishing touches.

ROSE AND CROWN PUB AND DINING ROOM
Sticky Toffee Pudding

DO TRY TO FIND INDIVIDUAL FLUTED DESSERT MOLDS FOR THIS BAKED PUDDING. AS SERVED AT EPCOT, THE PUDDING COMES IN A HIGH-SIDED BOWL, WITH THE PUD-DING SITTING ON BOTH A VANILLA CUSTARD SAUCE AND A BUTTER-RUM SAUCE. THE CURVES OF THE BUNDT-STYLE PUDDING CATCH THE SAUCES AS THEY ARE POURED OVER AND AROUND, MAKING EVERY BITE SENSATIONAL.

Pudding
1½ cups chopped dried dates
1 cup hot water
8 tablespoons (1 stick) unsalted
  butter, softened
1½ cups granulated sugar
2 eggs
1 vanilla bean
2 cups all-purpose flour
2 teaspoons baking powder
2 teaspoons baking soda
¼ teaspoon kosher salt

Custard Sauce
8 egg yolks
⅓ cup granulated sugar
1 vanilla bean
1 cup milk
1 cup heavy cream

Butter-Rum Toffee Sauce
2 tablespoons unsalted butter
⅓ cup packed dark brown sugar
½ cup heavy cream
1 tablespoon dark rum

1. Preheat the oven to 325°F.

2. Make the pudding first: Put the chopped dates in the hot water to soak.

3. Cream the butter and granulated sugar with an electric mixer until light and fluffy. Add the eggs one at a time, beating well after each addition. Split the vanilla bean and scrape out the seeds. Stir the seeds into the creamed mixture.

4. Whisk together the flour, baking powder, baking soda, and salt. Stir the dry ingredients into the creamed mixture alternately with the hot water and dates. Mix until well blended. Add additional hot water if the batter is too thick.

5. Coat six to eight pudding molds with butter or cooking spray and fill them halfway with the batter. Set the molds on a sheet pan and bake the puddings in the hot oven for 15 minutes. Let the puddings cool thoroughly before unmolding.

6. Make the custard sauce: Beat the egg yolks and granulated sugar with an electric mixer until light and foamy.

7. Split the vanilla bean and scrape out the seeds. Combine the seeds with the milk and heavy cream in a medium saucepan, then bring the mixture to a boil and remove from the heat.

8. Set the bowl with the egg yolk mixture over a saucepan of simmering water.

9. Whisk in ½ cup of the hot cream mixture, whisking constantly.

10. Slowly add the rest of the cream mixture to the egg yolk mixture and whisk over the simmering water until the sauce thickens—be careful not to let the mixture get too hot, or the yolks will overcook.

11. Remove the bowl from the pan once the custard sauce has thickened. Set it in the refrigerator and stir frequently until the sauce is chilled. Cover with a piece of plastic wrap set directly on the surface of the sauce to keep a skin from forming. This sauce can be served cold or warm.

12. Make the butter-rum toffee sauce: Combine the butter and brown sugar in a small saucepan over medium heat. Whisk until the sugar dissolves. Stir in the heavy cream and bring to a boil, then remove the pan from the heat. Stir in the rum. Set the sauce aside and keep warm.

13. Assemble the pudding: Pour a little of the custard sauce and the butter-rum toffee sauce in the bottom of each dessert bowl. Unmold the pudding, and put it on top of the sauces. Pour a little of the custard sauce and the butter-rum toffee sauce over the top of the pudding and serve immediately.

Serves 6 to 8, depending on the size of the molds

A dollop of fresh whipped cream on top of the pudding makes an excellent finishing touch.

RUBY TUESDAY
Apple Pie

THIS IS THE MOST UNIQUE WAY OF CUSTOMIZING A FROZEN PIE THAT YOU WILL COME ACROSS.

¾ pound plus 4 tablespoons (3½ sticks) unsalted butter
1 unbaked 9-inch deep-dish apple pie, homemade (see page 149) or purchased
1 cup packed light brown sugar
2 tablespoons ground cinnamon
¼ teaspoon ground allspice
¼ teaspoon ground cloves
2 teaspoons fresh lemon juice
¾ cup all-purpose flour
½ cup granulated sugar
1½ cups chopped walnuts

1. Put 2½ sticks of the butter in the freezer and let them get hard, about 1 hour.

2. Thaw the apple pie at room temperature for about 30 minutes, if frozen.

3. Preheat the oven to 350°F.

4. Melt the remaining 1 stick butter in a small saucepan with ½ cup of the brown sugar, 1 tablespoon of the cinnamon, the allspice, cloves, and lemon juice. Stir with a wooden spoon until well blended and the sugar is dissolved.

5. Cut a cross in the center of the top crust of the pie, folding back some of the pastry. Transfer the melted butter mixture to a measuring cup and pour into the pie through the center hole you created. Wet your fingers and replace the folded crust and seal the dough, leaving the other vents in the crust as is.

6. Bake the pie for 30 minutes in the hot oven. Place a sheet pan on the bottom rack to catch any drips. Remove the pie to a cooling rack and reduce the oven temperature to 275°F.

7. Grate the 2½ sticks frozen butter into a bowl. Toss with the flour, granulated sugar, walnuts, the remaining 1 tablespoon cinnamon, and the remaining ½ cup brown sugar.

8. Fashion a strip of foil around the edges of the pie, creating a high lip. Using your hands, spread the butter topping all over the pie. The foil strip should be secure enough to keep the topping from falling off.

9. Return the pie to the oven and bake for another 30 to 40 minutes, until the topping is golden brown. Let the pie rest for 10 minutes before serving.

Serves 8

**Serve with a scoop of vanilla ice cream or whipped cream,
if desired.**

RUBY TUESDAY

Smurf Punch

THIS IS A REFRESHING WAY TO END A SUMMER MEAL WHEN SOMETHING LIGHT AND EASY IS CALLED FOR.

Crushed ice (optional)
½ cup ginger ale
2 to 3 drops blue food coloring

Whipped cream
1 maraschino cherry

Fill a tall glass with crushed ice, if using, then add the ginger ale and blue food coloring. Stir with a long spoon and top with whipped cream and the cherry.

Serves 1

RUGGLES GRILL

Reese's Peanut Butter Cup Cheesecake

BE PREPARED FOR AN ONSLAUGHT OF PEANUT AND CHOCOLATE. THIS CHEESECAKE MADE FROM PEANUT BUTTER AND REESE'S PEANUT BUTTER CUPS SITS IN A CRUST OF OREO COOKIE CRUMBS AND CHOPPED PEANUTS. IF YOU ARE A PEANUT AND CHOCOLATE FANATIC, IT WON'T GET MUCH BETTER THAN THIS.

Crust
24 Oreo cookies (without the filling; 48 wafers), crushed
1 cup roasted peanuts
8 tablespoons (1 stick) unsalted butter, melted

Cheesecake
Four 8-ounce packages cream cheese, softened
5 eggs
1½ cups packed golden brown sugar

1 cup creamy or chunky peanut butter
½ cup heavy cream
1 teaspoon vanilla extract
12 Reese's peanut butter cups, cut into small pieces

Topping
½ cup sour cream
½ cup granulated sugar

1. To make the crust, put the Oreo cookies and peanuts in a food processor and pulse until the mixture is the texture of crumbs.

2. Pour the melted butter into the crumb mixture and pulse until it is well blended.

3. Press the mixture evenly across the bottom and halfway up the sides of a 10-inch springform pan. Refrigerate until ready to use.

4. Preheat the oven to 300°F.

5. To make the cheesecake, beat the cream cheese with an electric mixer until fluffy.

6. Add the eggs, one at a time, beating well after each addition. Add the brown sugar, peanut butter, heavy cream, and vanilla extract and beat until thoroughly blended.

7. Using a rubber spatula, fold in the pieces of peanut butter cups.

8. Spoon the cheesecake mixture into the prepared crust and smooth the top. Fashion a strip of heavy-duty foil 3 inches high and wrap it around the pan.

9. Put the cheesecake pan inside a larger roasting pan and pour in enough hot water to come halfway up the sides of the springform pan.

10. Bake for 1½ hours, or until the cheesecake is set in the center. Remove the roasting pan with the cheesecake, but leave the oven on.

11. To make the topping, whip the sour cream and granulated sugar until smooth.

12. Using a metal spatula, spread the sour cream mixture over the cheesecake.

13. Put the cheesecake back in the hot oven directly on the rack and bake for about 5 minutes.

14. Let the cheesecake cool in the pan on a wire rack before loosening the sides of the crust from the pan and then releasing the ring.

15. Refrigerate the cake for at least 4 hours before serving.

Serves 10

S&W CAFETERIA
Egg Custard Pie

A CHAIN OF CAFETERIAS SERVING THE SOUTH SINCE THE 1920S, S&W BECAME KNOWN AS A PLACE TO GET STRAIGHTFORWARD AMERICAN FOOD AT REASONABLE PRICES. THIS EGG CUSTARD PIE IS AN AUTHENTIC EXAMPLE OF OLD-FASHIONED SOUTHERN EXCELLENCE.

1¼ cups sugar
2 tablespoons unsalted butter, softened
½ teaspoon kosher salt
4 eggs

1 teaspoon vanilla extract
2 cups milk
One 9-inch deep-dish piecrust, homemade (see page 149) or purchased

1. Preheat the oven to 425°F.
2. Cream the sugar, butter, and salt with an electric mixer until smooth. Add the eggs, one at a time, beating well after each addition. Stir in the vanilla extract.
3. Decrease the speed of the mixer and gradually pour in the milk.
4. When the mixture is well combined, pour it into the piecrust.
5. Bake in the hot oven for 30 to 40 minutes, until the custard begins to set in the center. The middle may still be wiggly. Because of the high oven temperature, the pie may brown too rapidly. If it does, cover the crust, or the whole pie, with foil and continue to bake.
6. Let the pie cool before serving.

Serves 8

SANDHILL INN
Cold Sabayon with Fresh Fruit

THIS CREAMY, CUSTARD-LIKE DESSERT SAUCE IS LIGHTLY FLAVORED WITH SWEET MARSALA WINE. LOOK IN SPECIALTY MARKETS OR WINE SHOPS—THERE REALLY IS NO SUBSTITUTE FOR ITS TAWNY FLAVOR.

1½ teaspoons unflavored powdered gelatin
¼ cup cold water
⅔ cup dry white wine
¼ cup Marsala wine
½ cup sugar
3 egg yolks

1 egg
2 tablespoons fresh lemon juice
1 tablespoon Grand Marnier liqueur
1 cup heavy cream, whipped to soft peaks
2 cups fresh berries

1. Sprinkle the gelatin over the water and let it dissolve.

2. Combine the gelatin mixture, white wine, Marsala, sugar, egg yolks, egg, lemon juice, and Grand Marnier in a bowl set over a saucepan of simmering water. Whisk constantly until the mixture thickens enough to coat the back of a spoon.

3. Fill a larger bowl with ice cubes and water, then set the bowl with the sabayon on top, whisking constantly until it has cooled.

4. Use a rubber spatula to fold in the whipped cream and blend it thoroughly.

5. Divide the berries among six to eight brandy glasses or small bowls, and top with the sabayon.

Serves 6 to 8

SHUTTERS AT OLD PORT ROYALE— DISNEY WORLD
Caribbean Sand Bars

PECANS AND WALNUTS GIVE THESE BAR COOKIES A SIGNIFICANT AMOUNT OF CRUNCH. CUT THEM INTO SMALLER SQUARES TO INCREASE YOUR YIELD.

12 tablespoons (1½ sticks) unsalted butter, softened
1¼ cups packed light brown sugar
2 eggs
1 teaspoon vanilla extract

1 cup all-purpose flour
½ teaspoon kosher salt
1 teaspoon baking powder
4 cups chopped pecans
1 cup chopped walnuts

1. Preheat the oven to 375°F. Grease or spray a 9 by 9-inch baking pan.

2. Using an electric mixer, cream the butter and brown sugar until smooth and creamy. Add the eggs, one at a time, beating well after each addition. Stir in the vanilla extract.

3. Whisk together the flour, salt, and baking powder. Gradually stir the dry ingredients into the egg mixture, blending thoroughly. Fold in the pecans and walnuts and mix well.

4. Spread the batter onto the bottom of the prepared baking pan and bake for 25 to 30 minutes, until a toothpick inserted in the center comes out clean.

5. Let the cookie cool completely before cutting into bars or squares.

Serves 8 to 16

THE SOURCE
Chocolate Soufflé

THIS SOUFFLÉ IS SERVED AS A PART OF A CHOCOLATE TRIO—CHOCOLATE SOUF-
FLÉ, CHOCOLATE SORBET, AND 10-YEAR CHOCOLATE SAUCE—AT THE SOURCE, AN
AWARD-WINNING WOLFGANG PUCK RESTAURANT IN WASHINGTON, D.C.

Soufflé
2 tablespoons unsalted butter,
   softened
¼ cup granulated sugar
½ cup chopped bittersweet
   chocolate
4 eggs, separated

¼ cup orange liqueur
3 egg whites
1 tablespoon fresh lemon juice

Garnish
½ cup powdered sugar
½ cup whipped cream

1. Preheat the oven to 400°F.

2. To make soufflé, coat six 8-ounce soufflé cups with the butter and
   sprinkle them with 2 tablespoons of the sugar. Refrigerate until ready
   to use.

3. Melt the chocolate in a bowl set over a saucepan of simmering water.
   Remove the bowl from the heat and let cool. Whisk in the 4 egg yolks
   and the orange liqueur. Mix well.

4. In a separate bowl, with an electric mixer, beat all 7 egg whites until they
   form soft peaks. Add the lemon juice and the remaining 2 tablespoons
   sugar. Beat until stiff peaks form.

5. With a rubber spatula, stir about one quarter of the egg white mixture
   into the melted chocolate mixture. When it is well combined, fold in
   the remaining egg white mixture.

6. Fill the prepared soufflé cups with the soufflé mixture. Make a shallow
   trench along the inside edge of each cup with your thumb. This will
   force the soufflé up into a little hat shape as it bakes.

7. Place the cups on a sheet pan and bake in the hot oven for 8 to 10 minutes. The edges should be set, but the centers should still be soft.

8. Transfer the soufflés to napkin-lined dessert plates and dust with the powdered sugar. Place a dollop of whipped cream in the center of each soufflé and serve immediately.

Serves 6

SPAGO
Cheesecake

SPAGO IS KNOWN FOR PLACING CALIFORNIA CUISINE ON THE CULINARY MAP. IT DRAWS CELEBRITIES AND HIGH-POWERED BUSINESS EXECS TO ITS BEVERLY HILLS LOCATION. ITS CLIENTELE EXPECTS NOTHING LESS THAN THE BEST RESULTS. TRY YOUR HAND AT WOLFGANG PUCK'S RUM-LACED CHEESECAKE TO SEE IF IT MEETS YOUR EXPECTATIONS.

Nut Crust
½ cup all-purpose flour
¼ teaspoon kosher salt
½ cup finely chopped pecans or hazelnuts
2 tablespoons dark brown sugar
4 tablespoons (½ stick) cold unsalted butter, cut into small pieces

Cheesecake
Three 8-ounce packages cream cheese, softened and cut into pieces
1¼ cups granulated sugar
¼ teaspoon kosher salt
¾ cup sour cream
1 tablespoon fresh lemon juice
2 teaspoons vanilla extract
1 tablespoon dark rum
3 eggs

1. Preheat the oven to 350°F.

2. To make the crust, whisk together the flour, salt, nuts, and brown sugar. With your hands or a pastry cutter, cut in the butter and mix until the mixture resembles small peas.

3. Press the dough evenly across the bottom and halfway up the sides of a 9-inch springform pan. Fashion a strip of heavy-duty foil 3 inches high around the bottom of the pan and twist the ends to tighten it.

4. Bake in the hot oven for 8 to 10 minutes, until the crust is lightly golden brown. Remove from the oven but leave the oven on.

5. To make the cheesecake, beat together the softened cream cheese, granulated sugar, and salt with an electric mixer until smooth and creamy.

6. Stir in the sour cream, lemon juice, vanilla extract, and rum and beat until well incorporated.

7. Add the eggs, one at a time, beating well after each addition.

8. Spoon the mixture into the prepared crust and smooth the top.

9. Put the foil-wrapped pan into a larger roasting pan and fill the roasting pan with enough hot water to come halfway up the sides of the spring-form pan.

10. Bake for 1 hour and 10 minutes to 1 hour and 15 minutes, until the top is lightly golden and the cheesecake is firm in the center.

11. Let the cake cool in the pan on a wire rack for about 1 hour, then cover it with plastic wrap and refrigerate for at least 4 hours, and preferably overnight.

12. Loosen the crust from the pan by running a knife around the edges, then release the ring.

13. Use a thin, sharp knife to cut into slices.

Serves 8 to 10

A few fresh berries on top or on the side of the cheesecake make an elegant garnish.

SPAGO
Dessert Pancakes

THESE GOLDEN PUFFS COME TOGETHER VERY QUICKLY AND SHOULD BE SERVED HOT OFF THE GRIDDLE.

1½ cups all-purpose flour
2 teaspoons baking powder
1 teaspoon baking soda
¼ cup granulated sugar
¼ teaspoon kosher salt
1½ cups buttermilk
2 eggs, well beaten

4 tablespoons (½ stick) unsalted butter, melted, plus more for the griddle
2 teaspoons vanilla extract
1 cup apricot jam, slightly warmed
½ cup powdered sugar

1. Heat a heavy griddle or cast-iron skillet over medium-high heat.

2. Sift together the flour, baking powder, baking soda, granulated sugar, and salt.

3. Whisk the buttermilk into the beaten eggs, then add the melted butter and vanilla extract.

4. Whisk the flour mixture into the buttermilk mixture until the ingredients just come together in a batter. The batter will still be a little lumpy, but it should not be overmixed.

5. Melt some butter on the griddle, and place a heaping tablespoon of batter on the griddle for each pancake. The pancakes should puff up within seconds. When golden brown on the bottom, flip over and cook the other side. Repeat with the remaining batter.

6. Place the pancakes on warm plates and spread with the apricot jam. Dust them with the powdered sugar and serve warm.

Serves 5

A dollop of whipped cream or crème fraîche on top of the pancakes adds a cool and creamy touch.

SPAGO
Pot de Crème

THINK OF THIS DESSERT AS CHOCOLATE PUDDING FOR GROWN-UPS. NOTHING IN-STANT IN THIS RECIPE—BITTERSWEET CHOCOLATE IS GENTLY BAKED WITH CREAM AND EGGS IN INDIVIDUAL CUSTARD CUPS AND THEN TOPPED WITH A SWIRL OF WHITE CHOCOLATE WHIPPED CREAM. ONCE THEY ARE MADE, THE *POTS DE CRÈME* CAN STAY COVERED IN THE REFRIGERATOR FOR AT LEAST 3 DAYS.

3 ounces bittersweet chocolate, cut into small pieces
3½ cups heavy cream
½ cup milk
5 egg yolks
¼ cup sugar
¼ teaspoon kosher salt
¼ cup finely chopped white chocolate
½ teaspoon vanilla extract

1. Preheat the oven to 375°F.

2. Chop the bittersweet chocolate into small pieces, saving a portion to finely grate for garnish. Melt the chopped chocolate in a bowl set over a saucepan of simmering water. Take the chocolate off the heat when it is almost completely melted. Set aside.

3. Heat a medium saucepan and scald 2 cups of the heavy cream and the milk, being careful not to burn the mixture. Set aside.

4. Combine the egg yolks, sugar, and salt. Beat with an electric mixer until light and smooth, dissolving the sugar.

5. Slowly pour the hot cream mixture into the yolk mixture, whisking con-stantly until cooled.

6. Set a fine-mesh strainer over the bowl of melted chocolate and pour the cream and egg mixture through the strainer and into the chocolate. Whisk until well mixed.

7. Line the bottom of a high-sided baking pan with kitchen towels—the towels will steady the *pots de crème.*

8. Divide the chocolate mixture evenly among six custard cups and place the cups on the towels. Fill the baking pan with enough hot water to come halfway up the sides of the cups.

9. Cover the pan with foil and bake for about 35 minutes in the hot oven. The custards should still be a little wiggly when you take them out.

10. Let the custards cool to room temperature before covering them and putting them in the refrigerator for 2 to 3 hours, until chilled.

11. To serve, melt the white chocolate in a bowl set over a saucepan of simmering water, stirring occasionally. When the chocolate has melted, let it cool to room temperature.

12. Whip the remaining 1½ cups heavy cream to soft peaks. Add the vanilla extract and the melted white chocolate.

13. Whip to stiff peaks, and spoon over the chilled *pots de crème.*

14. Garnish with a little grated bittersweet chocolate on top of each serving.

Serves 6

SPRINGS CAFE
Crème Brûlée Tart

THIS VERSION OF CRÈME BRÛLÉE MAY END UP BEING YOUR FAVORITE. THE FAMIL-
IAR CREAMY VANILLA CUSTARD IS POURED OVER MIXED FRUITS ON A FLAKY TART
OF PUFF PASTRY. BE SURE TO USE THE FRESHEST FRUITS YOU CAN FIND, AND GIVE
YOURSELF ENOUGH TIME TO MAKE THE CUSTARD THE DAY BEFORE YOU NEED TO
BAKE THE TART.

Custard
6 egg yolks
½ cup sugar
3 cups heavy cream
1 vanilla bean, split lengthwise
½ pound (2 sticks) unsalted
    butter, softened and cut into
    pieces

Tart
8 ounces puff pastry, homemade
    or purchased
¾ cup chopped mixed fruits
    (pears, apricots, plums) and
    fresh berries
½ cup sugar

1. Make the custard a day ahead. Combine the egg yolks and sugar in a
    bowl set over a saucepan of simmering water. Whisk until the mixture
    is pale yellow and thickened. The mixture should form strings when
    drizzled from a spoon.

2. Remove the bowl from the saucepan and slowly whisk in the heavy cream.
    Scrape the seeds from the vanilla bean and add them to the mixture.

3. Put the bowl back over the simmering water and let the mixture cook
    for about 45 minutes, stirring frequently. The mixture should thicken
    enough to coat the back of a spoon.

4. When the custard has thickened, remove it from the heat and whisk in
    the butter, a couple of pieces at a time. When the butter has been com-
    pletely incorporated, strain the custard through a fine-mesh strainer into
    a bowl. Cover and refrigerate overnight or for at least 8 hours.

5. Make the tart: Roll out the puff pastry on a floured surface to a thickness
    of ¼ inch. Lay the dough over a 10-inch flan ring and move the ring
    onto a baking sheet lined with parchment paper.

6. Press the pastry down along the inside walls of the ring and onto the baking sheet on the bottom. Roll a rolling pin over the top of the ring and it will cut off the excess pastry. Refrigerate the pastry for 30 minutes.

7. Preheat the oven to 350°F.

8. Prick the tart shell all over with the tines of a fork. Line it with parchment paper and cover it with weights, such as beans or rice, to keep it from puffing up when it bakes.

9. Bake the pastry in the hot oven for 25 to 30 minutes, until the pastry is golden brown. Let the pastry cool down on a wire rack after baking, then remove the parchment paper and weights. Remove the pastry from the ring.

10. Spoon the chopped mixed fruits and berries over the bottom of the baked tart shell.

11. Pour the chilled custard over the fruit, smoothing it over the top with a metal spatula dipped in hot water.

12. Sprinkle the sugar over the top of the custard, making as even a layer as possible. Pass the tart under a hot broiler to caramelize the sugar, being careful not to burn the pastry. If you have a kitchen torch, you can position the flame directly over the sugar to melt it, making a thin but solid shell of sugar.

13. Use a sharp knife to cut the tart into wedges. Strike firmly to break through the hardened caramel.

Serves 8 to 10

A simple placement of 3 perfect fresh berries on a mint leaf is all the garnish this dessert needs.

STARBUCKS
Caramel Macchiato

ONE OF THE STARBUCKS TOP SELLERS CAN BE MADE AT HOME IF YOU HAVE AN ESPRESSO MACHINE.

I cup milk
Vanilla syrup
¾ cup freshly brewed coffee

2 tablespoons caramel sauce
Whipped cream

1. Steam the milk until it has the level of frothiness you prefer.

2. Pour vanilla syrup into an oversized mug or a heatproof glass. Add the steamed milk and top with the foam.

3. Pour the coffee into the mug through the foam. Add the caramel sauce, then stir well and top with whipped cream.

Serves 1

STARBUCKS
Chocolate-Espresso Pudding

YOU CAN SERVE THIS CHILLED PUDDING TO EVEN YOUR NON-COFFEE-DRINKING FRIENDS. STARBUCKS USES INSTANT ESPRESSO POWDER, BUT YOU CAN USE WHATEVER TYPE OF INSTANT YOU HAVE, EVEN DECAF.

2 cups nonfat soy milk
½ cup packed light brown sugar
3 tablespoons unsweetened cocoa powder
¼ cup cornstarch
1 tablespoon instant espresso powder

¼ teaspoon kosher salt
¼ cup chopped bittersweet chocolate
1 teaspoon vanilla extract

1. Combine the soy milk and brown sugar in a medium saucepan over medium heat, and stir until the sugar dissolves.

2. Whisk in the cocoa powder, cornstarch, espresso powder, and salt. Bring the mixture to a boil, then reduce the heat and simmer for 1 minute, or until thick.

3. Remove from the heat and stir in the chopped chocolate and the vanilla extract.

4. Pour equal amounts of the mixture into four dessert mugs or bowls. Put a piece of plastic wrap directly on the surface of the pudding to keep a film from forming.

5. Refrigerate for at least 4 hours, then remove the plastic wrap and serve.

Serves 4

Top the pudding with a dollop of whipped cream, if desired.

STARBUCKS
Cranberry Bliss Bars

THESE CHEWY TRIANGLES ARE THE PERFECT BITE-SIZED TREATS WITH A CUP OF COF-
FEE, TEA, OR HOT COCOA. THE RECIPE MAKES ABOUT 36 BARS, SO YOU CAN FREEZE
SOME TO ALWAYS HAVE THEM ON HAND FOR EMERGENCY SNACK ATTACKS.

Cranberry Blondie
½ pound (2 sticks) unsalted
   butter, softened
1 cup packed golden brown
   sugar
¼ cup granulated sugar
3 eggs
2 teaspoons vanilla extract
2 cups all-purpose flour
1½ teaspoons baking powder
¾ cup dried cranberries
¾ cup white chocolate chips

Frosting
Half an 8-ounce package cream
   cheese, softened
2 tablespoons unsalted butter,
   softened
1 tablespoon finely grated orange
   zest
1 teaspoon vanilla extract
3 cups powdered sugar

Toppings
¼ cup white chocolate chips
2 tablespoons finely grated
   orange zest
½ cup chopped dried cranberries

1. Preheat the oven to 350°F. Line a 10 by 15-inch baking pan with parchment paper or coat with cooking spray.

2. Make the cranberry blondie first: Cream the butter and the brown and
   granulated sugars with an electric mixer until light and fluffy. Add the
   eggs, one at a time, beating well after each addition. Stir in the vanilla
   extract.

3. Whisk together the flour and baking powder. Gradually stir the dry
   ingredients into the creamed mixture and blend well.

4. Fold in the dried cranberries and white chocolate chips. Mix thoroughly.

5. Pour the batter into the prepared pan and bake for about 25 minutes, or until a toothpick inserted in the center comes out clean. Check the blondie while baking—it is ready to come out when it turns light brown at the edges. If it overbakes, the bars will be dry.

6. Remove the blondie pan to a wire rack to cool.

7. Prepare the frosting while the blondie is baking. Beat together the cream cheese and butter with an electric mixer until light and fluffy.

8. Add the orange zest and the vanilla extract. Beat in the powdered sugar until the frosting is fluffy and smooth. If it is too thick to spread easily, add a little milk.

9. When the blondie has cooled down, spread the frosting evenly over the top and let it sit for about 15 minutes to let the frosting firm up.

10. To add the toppings, melt the white chocolate chips and drizzle over the top of the frosting.

11. Scatter the orange zest and chopped cranberries over the top.

12. Let the blondie sit for 1 hour for the white chocolate to firm up.

13. Cut into 4 by 4-inch squares, then cut each square in half to make a triangle, or cut into bar shapes or smaller squares.

Makes 36 bars

STARBUCKS
Heath Bars

PREPARE THESE CRUNCHY TOFFEE BARS FOR A QUICK SNACK OR DESSERT FOR A CROWD. MAKE THE EASY BATTER FROM PANTRY STAPLES, THEN USE WHITE AND DARK CHOCOLATE CHIPS AND COARSELY CHOPPED HEATH BARS FOR A SUPER BATCH OF DELICIOUS TREATS.

12 tablespoons (1½ sticks) unsalted butter, softened
12 tablespoons (1½ sticks) margarine, softened
1¼ cups granulated sugar
1¼ cups packed light brown sugar
3 eggs
2 teaspoons vanilla extract

4 cups all-purpose flour
1½ teaspoons baking soda
1 teaspoon kosher salt
1½ cups semisweet chocolate chips
1½ cups white chocolate chips
Eight 2.8-ounce Heath bars, coarsely chopped

1. Preheat the oven to 350°F. Coat a 15 by 19-inch baking pan with butter or cooking spray.

2. Cream the butter and margarine with an electric mixer until well blended, then add the granulated and brown sugars. Beat the mixture until light and fluffy.

3. Add the eggs, one at a time, beating well after each addition. Stir in the vanilla extract.

4. Whisk together the flour, baking soda, and salt. Gradually add the dry ingredients to the creamed mixture, blending thoroughly.

5. Fold in the semisweet and white chocolate chips and the coarsely chopped Heath bars.

6. Pour the batter into the prepared pan and bake for 20 to 25 minutes in the hot oven, until a toothpick inserted in the center comes out clean.

7. Let the blondie cool for 30 minutes before cutting. Cut into 12 bars, or large or small squares, if you desire.

Makes 12 bars

STARBUCKS
Iced Vanilla Latte

IT'S MOSTLY MILK, BUT STILL A COOL WAY TO HAVE AN ESPRESSO.

2 tablespoons vanilla syrup
Crushed ice

1¼ cups cold milk
¼ cup hot or cold espresso

1. Pour the vanilla syrup into the bottom of a large mug or tall heatproof glass. Add a full cup of ice or just as much as you prefer.
2. Pour in the cold milk, then the espresso. Stir and enjoy.

Makes 1 latte

STARBUCKS
Marble Pound Cake

MELTED SEMISWEET CHOCOLATE IS SWIRLED THROUGHOUT THIS ORANGE-SCENTED POUND CAKE. IT'S JUST AS GOOD FOR BREAKFAST AS IT IS FOR DESSERT.

1 pound (4 sticks) unsalted butter, softened
2½ cups sugar
10 eggs
2 teaspoons vanilla extract
2 tablespoons orange liqueur, such as Grand Marnier
2 tablespoons finely grated orange zest
4¼ cups cake flour, sifted
2 teaspoons baking powder
¼ teaspoon kosher salt
¾ cup semisweet chocolate chips, melted

1. Preheat the oven to 325°F. Coat a 10-inch tube pan with butter or cooking spray and line the bottom with a circle of waxed paper cut to fit. Flour the pan and remove any excess flour.

2. Cream the butter and sugar with an electric mixer until light and fluffy. Add the eggs, one at a time, beating well after each addition. Stir in the vanilla extract, orange liqueur, and orange zest. Mix until well blended.

3. Sift together the flour, baking powder, and salt. Gradually add the dry ingredients to the creamed mixture and blend thoroughly.

4. Pour half the batter into the prepared tube pan. Spoon the melted chocolate in big drops all around the batter, then run through with a dinner knife in a circular motion. Top with the remaining batter and smooth with the back of spoon, making a bit of a trench as you go around.

5. Bake for 1 hour and 15 minutes to 1 hour and 20 minutes. The cake is done when a toothpick inserted in the center comes out clean. Turn the pan once during baking and cover the cake with foil if it looks like the top is getting too brown.

6. Let the cake cool in the pan on a wire rack for 10 minutes, then invert it, remove the pan, peel off the waxed paper, and let the cake cool upside down for 20 minutes. Turn the cake right side up and let it cool for another 20 minutes.

7. Put the cake on a serving plate. Using a serrated knife, cut it into portions.

Serves 12 to 16

Serve the cake with some sweetened whipped cream or a scoop of ice cream on the side.

STARBUCKS
Old-Fashioned Coffee Cake

STARBUCKS IS THE LARGEST CHAIN OF COFFEE SHOPS IN THE WORLD. ALONG WITH ALL THAT COFFEE, IT MAKES AND SELLS A HUGE VARIETY OF PASTRIES AND BAKED ITEMS. ONE OF THE CUSTOMER FAVORITES OVER THE YEARS HAS BEEN THIS BUTTERY CAKE FILLED WITH A NUTTY GRAHAM CRACKER STREUSEL.

Streusel

1½ cups graham cracker crumbs
¾ cup chopped walnuts
¾ cup packed golden brown sugar
1 teaspoon ground cinnamon
½ teaspoon ground allspice
¼ teaspoon ground cardamom
8 tablespoons (1 stick) unsalted butter, melted

Cake

8 tablespoons (1 stick) unsalted butter, softened
1 cup granulated sugar
2 eggs
2 teaspoons vanilla extract
2 cups all-purpose flour
2½ teaspoons baking powder
½ teaspoon kosher salt
1 cup milk

1. To make the streusel, combine the graham cracker crumbs, chopped walnuts, brown sugar, cinnamon, allspice, and cardamom. Stir or whisk the ingredients until well blended.

2. Stir in the melted butter and mix to make sure all the ingredients are moistened. Set the streusel aside.

3. Preheat the oven to 350°F. Coat a 10-inch tube pan with butter or cooking spray and flour. Shake off any excess flour.

4. To make the cake, cream the butter and granulated sugar with an electric mixer until light and fluffy. Add the eggs, one at a time, beating well after each addition. Stir in the vanilla extract.

5. Whisk together the flour, baking powder, and salt. Gradually stir the dry ingredients into the creamed mixture and blend well. Slowly pour in the milk and mix thoroughly.

6. Pour half the cake batter into the prepared tube pan. Sprinkle the batter with half the streusel.

7. Pour in the remaining batter, and top with the remaining streusel.

8. Bake for about 50 minutes, or until a toothpick inserted in the cake comes out clean.

9. Let the cake cool on a wire rack for 30 minutes, then remove from the pan and serve.

Serves 10 to 12

STARBUCKS
Pumpkin–Cream Cheese Muffins

THESE ARE A GREAT SEASONAL ALTERNATIVE TO COOKIES AND PIES. THE MUFFINS ARE FLAVORED WITH TRADITIONAL PUMPKIN PIE SPICES AND FINISHED WITH PUMPKIN SEEDS FOR A LITTLE CRUNCH.

One 8-ounce package cream cheese, softened
2 cups canned pumpkin
2 cups sugar
4 eggs
1 teaspoon vanilla extract
3 cups all-purpose flour

4 teaspoons pumpkin pie spice
1 teaspoon ground cinnamon
1 teaspoon ground nutmeg
½ teaspoon ground cloves
½ teaspoon kosher salt
1 teaspoon baking soda
½ cup chopped pumpkin seeds

1. Preheat the oven to 350°F. Coat 24 muffin cups with butter or cooking spray, or use paper liners.

2. Using your hands, shape the softened cream cheese into a long, thin log and wrap it in plastic. Freeze it until ready to use.

3. Beat the canned pumpkin with the sugar with an electric mixer until smooth. Add the eggs, one at a time, beating well after each addition. Stir in the vanilla extract.

4. Whisk together the flour, pumpkin pie spice, cinnamon, nutmeg, cloves, salt, and baking soda. Gradually stir the dry ingredients into the pumpkin mixture and mix until well blended.

5. Unwrap the frozen cream cheese and cut the log into 24 pieces.

6. Pour the batter into the prepared muffin pans, filling the cups only half full.

7. Put 1 piece of cream cheese in the center of each muffin cup and press it gently into the batter. Sprinkle the tops with the pumpkin seeds.

8. Bake for 20 to 25 minutes, until a toothpick inserted in the center of a muffin comes out clean.

9. Let the muffins cool for 15 minutes before turning them out of the pans.

Makes 24 muffins

SUBWAY
Chocolate Chip Cookies

ALTHOUGH KNOWN PRIMARILY FOR ITS HEALTHFUL SPIN ON SANDWICHES, SUBWAY
MAKES SOME OUTSTANDING CHOCOLATE CHIP COOKIES.

½ pound (2 sticks) unsalted
  butter, softened
½ cup granulated sugar
1 cup packed golden brown sugar
2 eggs

2 teaspoons vanilla extract
2 cups self-rising flour
1½ cups semisweet chocolate
  chips

1. Cream the butter and the granulated and brown sugars with an electric mixer until light and fluffy. Add the eggs, one at a time, beating well after each addition. Stir in the vanilla extract and blend well.

2. Stir in the flour, ½ cup at a time, until all the flour has been completely incorporated. Stir in the chocolate chips. Cover the bowl and refrigerate the dough for 1 hour.

3. Preheat the oven to 350°F. Coat a baking sheet with cooking spray or line it with parchment paper.

4. Roll the dough into balls the size of walnuts and place them on the prepared sheet pan at least 2 inches apart.

5. Bake the cookies for 10 to 12 minutes, until golden brown and the edges are firm, then let cool on wire racks before storing in an airtight container.

Makes 12 to 18 cookies

TACO BELL
Caramel Apple Empanadas

THESE ARE AN EASILY MADE VERSION OF A POPULAR LATIN AMERICAN FOOD. THE
FILLINGS CAN BE EITHER SWEET OR SAVORY AND THE EMPANADAS CAN BE SERVED
COLD OR HOT.

1½ cups frozen diced apples,
thawed
1 tablespoon cornstarch
6 tablespoons (¾ stick) unsalted
butter
¼ cup packed light brown
sugar

¼ teaspoon ground cinnamon
¼ teaspoon ground allspice
1 cup heavy cream
3½ cups baking mix, such as
Bisquick

1. Preheat the oven to 400°F. Coat a sheet pan lightly with butter or cooking spray.

2. Mix the apples with the cornstarch.

3. Melt 4 tablespoons of the butter in a skillet and add the apples, brown sugar, cinnamon, and allspice. Cook over medium heat, stirring until the mixture thickens and the apples are softened.

4. Remove the pan from the heat and mash the apples with a fork, then set the mixture aside.

5. Stir the heavy cream into the baking mix with a fork until the mix is moistened. Knead the dough a couple of times on a floured surface, then roll it out to a 15 by 20-inch rectangle, ½ inch thick.

6. Cut the dough into twelve 5-inch squares. Fill the center of each square with a tablespoon of the mashed apples.

7. Fold over one side of the dough, either into a rectangle or triangle shape, and press the edges together with the tines of a fork.

8. Arrange the empanadas on the prepared sheet pan. Melt the remaining 2 tablespoons butter and brush onto the top of each empanada. Bake for 18 to 20 minutes, until golden brown. Serve warm.

Makes 12 empanadas

A light dusting of powdered sugar makes a nice finishing touch.

TACO BELL
Crispitos

THIS IS A VERSION OF A TRADITIONAL MEXICAN FRIED-PASTRY DESSERT, PERFECT FOR TIMES WHEN YOU HAVE FLOUR TORTILLAS THAT ARE BEGINNING TO DRY OUT. A DRIZZLE OF HONEY OVER THE WARM *CRISPITOS* IS A NICE VARIATION.

½ cup sugar
2 tablespoons ground cinnamon

Twelve 8-inch flour tortillas
2 cups canola oil

1. Whisk together the sugar and cinnamon.
2. Cut the tortillas into quarters.
3. Heat the oil in a large skillet over medium-high heat.
4. Fry the quartered tortillas, 3 or 4 pieces at a time, until they turn golden on the bottom, then flip them over and brown the other side. Be careful not to let them fry for too long, as they will continue to brown after they are removed from the oil.
5. Drain the tortillas on wire racks or paper towels, then toss with the sugar and cinnamon mixture. Serve hot.

Makes 48 crispitos

TED'S MONTANA GRILL
Strawberry Shortcake

LIKE MANY THINGS, THERE IS NEVER A SINGLE BEST RECIPE FOR STRAWBERRY SHORT-
CAKE. BUT THE PATRONS OF TED'S IN ATLANTA THINK THIS VERSION IS A WINNER.

1 pound strawberries, hulled and
sliced
1½ tablespoons granulated sugar

Shortcake
2 cups all-purpose flour
2½ teaspoons baking powder
1 teaspoon kosher salt
2 teaspoons granulated sugar
1¼ cups heavy cream

Whipped Cream
1 cup heavy cream
2 tablespoons powdered sugar
1 teaspoon vanilla extract

Häagen-Dazs vanilla ice cream

1. Toss the sliced strawberries with the granulated sugar and set them aside for a couple of hours.

2. Preheat the oven to 450°F. Lightly coat a baking sheet with butter or cooking spray.

3. Make the shortcake: Whisk together the flour, baking powder, salt, and granulated sugar. Stir in the heavy cream and mix until the ingredients are just combined.

4. Knead the dough on a floured surface just a couple of times, then separate the dough into 4 equal-sized biscuits. Place the biscuits on the prepared baking sheet.

5. Bake the biscuits in the hot oven for 10 to 15 minutes, until golden brown on the bottom and lightly golden on top.

6. While the biscuits are baking, make the whipped cream: Whip the heavy cream to soft peaks. Add the powdered sugar and vanilla extract.

7. Whip to stiff peaks and refrigerate until ready to use.

8. Assemble the strawberry shortcake: For each serving, split a warm biscuit and lay the bottom half in a shallow dessert bowl. Top the biscuit with a scoop of vanilla ice cream, then cover with a portion of the strawberries.

9. Replace the top half of the biscuit and spoon a big dollop of whipped cream over the shortcake.

10. Spoon some of the remaining strawberries, along with their juices, around the shortcake and serve the bowl with the strawberries.

Serves 4

Dust the top of the shortcake with a little powdered sugar, if desired.

T.G.I. FRIDAY'S
Brownie Obsession

YOU DON'T REALLY HAVE TO BE OBSESSED TO DIG INTO ONE OF T.G.I. FRIDAY'S
MONUMENTAL BROWNIES, BUT YOU HAD BETTER LEAVE PLENTY OF ROOM SO YOU
CAN FINISH EVERY SPOONFUL.

Brownies
8 tablespoons (1 stick) unsalted butter

Two 4-ounce bars Ghirardelli semisweet baking chocolate, coarsely chopped

1¾ cups granulated sugar

2 eggs

2 teaspoons vanilla extract

1½ cups all-purpose flour

½ teaspoon baking soda

½ teaspoon kosher salt

½ cup chopped walnuts (optional)

Chocolate Sauce
4 tablespoons (½ stick) unsalted butter

1½ (4-ounce) bars Ghirardelli milk chocolate baking chocolate, coarsely chopped

¼ cup granulated sugar

¾ cup heavy cream

Caramel Sauce
¾ cup packed dark brown sugar

4 teaspoons cornstarch

1 tablespoon unsalted butter

½ cup heavy cream

Topping
1 pint vanilla ice cream

1. Preheat the oven to 350°F. Coat a 9 by 13-inch baking pan with butter or cooking spray and lightly dust with flour.

2. Make the brownies first. Combine the butter and semisweet chocolate in a bowl set over a saucepan of simmering water and stir until melted. Add the granulated sugar and stir until it dissolves. Remove the bowl from the pan. Let cool slightly.

3. Add the eggs, one at a time, beating well with a wooden spoon after each addition. Stir in the vanilla extract.

4. Whisk together the flour, baking soda, and salt. Gradually stir the dry ingredients into the chocolate mixture and blend well. Stir in the chopped nuts, if using.

5. Pour the batter into the prepared pan and bake the brownie in the hot oven for 15 to 20 minutes, until a toothpick inserted in the center comes out slightly sticky.

6. Let cool in the pan on a wire rack, then cut into 6 or 8 individual brownies.

7. Make the chocolate sauce: Combine the butter and milk chocolate in a bowl set over a saucepan of simmering water and stir until melted. Add the granulated sugar and stir until it dissolves.

8. Whisk in the heavy cream and stir until the mixture is well combined. Remove the bowl from the pan and keep the sauce warm.

9. Make the caramel sauce: Combine the brown sugar, cornstarch, and butter in a saucepan over medium heat. Stir until the butter melts and is blended with the sugar.

10. Whisk in the heavy cream and bring the mixture to a boil, stirring constantly. Reduce the heat and simmer for 2 minutes.

11. Let the caramel sauce cool before using.

12. Assemble the dessert: Place each brownie in a shallow bowl. Spoon chocolate sauce over each one.

13. Put a scoop of vanilla ice cream on top of the chocolate sauce.

14. Drizzle caramel sauce over the ice cream.

Serves 6 to 8

For extra crunch, garnish with chopped walnuts on top of the brownies before serving.

T.G.I. FRIDAY'S
Ultimate Strawberry Daiquiri

ALTHOUGH NOT TECHNICALLY A DESSERT, IT IS BEST TO HAVE A FULL STOMACH BEFORE SIPPING THIS RUM-LACED COCKTAIL.

¼ cup Captain Morgan spiced rum

1 tablespoon strawberry liqueur

1 tablespoon grenadine

1 tablespoon Rose's lime juice

4 strawberries, hulled and coarsely chopped

1 tablespoon sugar

1 whole strawberry, for garnish

1. Combine the rum, strawberry liqueur, grenadine, lime juice, and chopped strawberries with 2 cups of crushed ice in a blender. Process until smooth.

2. Wet the rim of a martini or margarita glass and dip it into the sugar.

3. Make a slit in the whole strawberry from the bottom and slide it onto the rim of the glass.

4. Pour the daiquiri into the garnished glass and serve with a small bar straw.

Serves 1

THE LADY & SONS
Blueberry Cream Pie

THIS IS SUCH AN EASY PIE TO MAKE, YOU'LL SERVE IT ALL THROUGH THE SUMMER!

I cup chopped pecans
One 9-inch deep-dish piecrust,
   homemade (see page 47)
   or purchased
Two 3-ounce packages cream
   cheese, softened

I cup powdered sugar
I cup heavy cream
½ cup granulated sugar
I teaspoon vanilla extract
One 21-ounce can blueberry
   pie filling

1. Press the chopped nuts evenly across the bottom of the piecrust. Bake the shell according to the recipe or package directions. Let cool.

2. Beat together the cream cheese and powdered sugar with an electric mixer until creamy and smooth.

3. Whip the heavy cream to soft peaks. Add the granulated sugar and vanilla extract, then whip to stiff peaks.

4. Using a rubber spatula, fold the whipped cream into the cream cheese mixture.

5. Spoon the cream mixture into the prepared pie shell and top with the blueberry pie filling.

6. Refrigerate until well chilled.

Serves 6 to 8

For variety, use different chopped nuts, such as walnuts or hazelnuts, and try a different pie filling, like cherry or apple.

TIM HORTONS
Chocolate Cake Doughnuts

THESE CAKE DOUGHNUTS ARE MADE WITHOUT YEAST, SO THEY DON'T NEED TIME TO RISE, BUT THE DOUGH WILL NEED TO BE REFRIGERATED FOR AT LEAST AN HOUR. BE SURE TO GIVE YOURSELF ENOUGH TIME.

Doughnuts
2½ cups all-purpose flour

1 cup unsweetened cocoa powder

2 teaspoons baking powder

½ teaspoon kosher salt

4 eggs

1½ cups sugar

¼ cup buttermilk

8 tablespoons (1 stick) unsalted butter, melted

6 cups vegetable oil, for frying

Mocha Glaze
¾ cup semisweet chocolate chips

½ cup heavy cream

1 tablespoon unsalted butter

2 teaspoons light corn syrup

2 teaspoons instant espresso powder or instant coffee powder

1. To make the doughnuts, whisk together the flour, cocoa powder, baking powder, and salt.

2. In a separate bowl, with an electric mixer, beat the eggs with the sugar, buttermilk, and melted butter.

3. Stir the egg mixture into the dry ingredients and mix until well blended.

4. Refrigerate for at least 1 hour or up to 3 hours.

5. Roll the chilled dough out onto a floured surface and pat to a ½-inch thickness. Cut out 16 doughnuts with a floured 3-inch doughnut cutter and place them on a floured baking sheet.

6. Fill an electric fryer with the oil and heat to 375°F, or use a heavy-bottomed 5-quart saucepan and fill with 4 to 5 inches of oil, and heat to 375°F.

7. Slip 2 or 3 doughnuts into the oil. Cook each doughnut until the bottom is golden brown, then flip once, and cook until the other side is golden brown. Remove to paper towels to drain. Repeat with the remaining doughnuts, making sure to maintain an even oil temperature.

8. While the doughnuts drain, make the mocha glaze: Combine the chocolate chips, heavy cream, butter, corn syrup, and espresso powder in a bowl over a saucepan of simmering water. Stir the mixture frequently until smooth.

9. Dip the tops of the doughnuts in the mocha glaze and let the doughnuts rest on a platter for about 5 minutes before serving.

Makes 16 doughnuts

To use up the scraps of dough, roll them into ropes and braid 2 of the ropes together, then twist the ends to make doughnut twists. Fry them in the same manner as the doughnuts, and finish them in the mocha glaze.

TIM HORTONS
Oatmeal Muffins

EVERYONE NEEDS A GO-TO RECIPE FOR OATMEAL MUFFINS, AND TIM HORTONS HAS
ONE OF THE BEST.

1 cup milk	¼ cup sugar
1 cup quick-cooking oats	2 teaspoons baking powder
1 egg	1 teaspoon ground cinnamon
¼ cup canola oil	½ teaspoon kosher salt
1 cup all-purpose flour	

1. Preheat the oven to 425°F. Coat 12 muffin cups with butter or cooking spray, or insert paper liners.

2. Combine the milk and oats and let them set for about 15 minutes for the oats to soak.

3. Beat together the egg and oil with an electric mixer, then stir in the oat mixture and blend well.

4. Whisk together the flour, sugar, baking powder, cinnamon, and salt. Gradually stir the dry ingredients into the oat mixture and mix thoroughly.

5. Fill the muffin cups two-thirds full and bake for 20 to 25 minutes, until a toothpick inserted in the center of a muffin comes out clean. Serve warm or at room temperature.

Makes 12 muffins

For variation, add ¼ cup raisins and ¼ cup chopped walnuts, chocolate chips, or grated coconut.

TONY'S TOWN SQUARE RESTAURANT

Lemon Panna Cotta

THIS IS REALLY TWO DESSERTS IN ONE—A COOL AND LEMONY PANNA COTTA SERVED WITH A TRADITIONAL CANNOLI FILLED WITH SWEETENED RICOTTA AND DIPPED IN GROUND CHOCOLATE.

Lemon Panna Cotta

One .25-ounce envelope
  unflavored powdered gelatin
½ cup warm water
2 vanilla beans, split
4 cups heavy cream
2 tablespoons finely grated
  lemon zest
¼ cup fresh lemon juice
¾ cup granulated sugar

Cannoli Filling

1 cup high-quality ricotta cheese
½ teaspoon vanilla extract
¼ teaspoon ground cinnamon
½ cup powdered sugar
2 tablespoons finely grated
  lemon zest

Candied Lemon Zest

1¼ cups granulated sugar
1 cup water
Zest of 3 lemons, removed in
  thin strips

8 cannoli shells (available at
  Italian markets or online)

¼ cup ground dark chocolate

1. Make the panna cotta first: Dissolve the gelatin in the warm water.

2. Scrape the seeds from the 2 vanilla beans and add them to a saucepan with the heavy cream, grated lemon zest, lemon juice, and granulated sugar. Bring the mixture to a boil, then reduce the heat, stirring frequently.

3. Add the dissolved gelatin and stir until the mixture thickens.

4. Pour the custard into eight 5-ounce ramekins or tart dishes. Refrigerate for at least 4 hours.

5. Make the cannoli filling: Whisk together the ricotta cheese, vanilla extract, cinnamon, powdered sugar, and grated lemon zest. When the ingredients are well mixed, cover the bowl and refrigerate the filling until ready to use.

6. Make the candied lemon zest: Combine 1 cup of the sugar and the water in a saucepan over medium heat and stir until the sugar is dissolved.

7. Add the lemon zest and cook for 8 minutes, or until the zest is softened. Drain through a fine-mesh strainer, then toss with the remaining ¼ cup sugar while still warm. Let the candied zest dry at room temperature on paper towels for at least 1 hour.

8. To assemble the cannoli, fill a pastry bag with the cannoli filling and pipe the mixture into the cannoli shells. Dip the ends of the cannolis in the ground chocolate.

9. Serve the panna cotta with some candied lemon zest in the center of each ramekin and a cannoli on the side of a dessert plate lined with a doily or a folded napkin.

Serves 8

TREEBEARDS
Buttercake

TREEBEARDS HAS SEVERAL LOCATIONS IN HOUSTON, ALL IN UNIQUE LOCATIONS, INCLUDING A TUNNEL AND A CHURCH BASEMENT! ONE ITEM THE VARIOUS LUNCH SPOTS ALL HAVE IN COMMON IS THE BUTTERCAKE.

Cake Batter
One 18-ounce box yellow cake
  mix
8 tablespoons (1 stick) unsalted
  butter, melted
1 egg, beaten

Filling
5 cups powdered sugar
One 8-ounce package cream
  cheese, softened
2 eggs
2 teaspoons vanilla extract

1. Preheat the oven to 350°F. Coat a jelly roll pan with cooking spray.

2. To make the cake batter, combine the yellow cake mix with the melted butter and beaten egg. Beat with an electric mixer until well combined. Spoon the batter evenly across the bottom and up the sides of the prepared pan, then set aside.

3. To make the filling, beat 3½ cups of the powdered sugar with the cream cheese with an electric mixer until smooth and creamy. Add the eggs, one at a time, beating well after each addition. Stir in the vanilla extract and beat the cream cheese mixture at high speed until whipped, about 3 minutes.

4. Reduce the speed of the mixer and beat in the remaining 1½ cups powdered sugar. Beat at high speed for another 3 minutes.

5. Spread the filling evenly over the cake batter and bake for about 40 minutes, or until the cake is golden brown. Let cool to room temperature, then cut into squares.

Serves 8

This cake can be finished with almost any frosting before serving, including just plain whipped cream.

TUSKER HOUSE RESTAURANT

Banana–Cinnamon Bread Pudding with Vanilla Sauce

FILLED WITH RAISINS, PECANS, AND BANANAS, THIS VERSION OF BREAD PUDDING HITS ALL THE RIGHT SPOTS—IT HAS FLAVOR, TEXTURE, AND AN INCREDIBLE VANILLA SAUCE.

Bread Pudding
1 pound cinnamon bread, crusts trimmed, cut into 1-inch squares
6 ripe bananas
1½ cups milk
1 cup pasteurized egg product
½ cup packed light brown sugar
½ cup granulated sugar
1 tablespoon ground cinnamon
1 tablespoon vanilla extract
½ teaspoon ground nutmeg
½ cup raisins
½ cup chopped pecans

4 tablespoons (½ stick) unsalted butter, melted
¼ cup superfine sugar

Vanilla Sauce
4 tablespoons (½ stick) unsalted butter
2 tablespoons all-purpose flour
¾ cup granulated sugar
¼ teaspoon kosher salt
1¼ cups milk
1 cup heavy cream
1 egg, well beaten
1 tablespoon vanilla extract

1. Preheat the oven to 325°F.

2. To make the bread pudding, scatter the bread cubes in a 9-inch round cake pan.

3. Mash the bananas. Whisk together the milk, pasteurized egg product, brown sugar, granulated sugar, cinnamon, vanilla extract, nutmeg, raisins, and pecans. Whisk in the mashed bananas.

4. Pour the mixture into the pan with the cinnamon bread and let sit for 30 minutes, pressing down to make sure all the bread cubes get soaked.

5. Bake for 25 minutes, or until set. Brush the top with the melted butter and sprinkle with the superfine sugar.

6. To make the vanilla sauce, melt the butter in a medium saucepan over medium heat, then whisk in the flour and cook for 5 minutes, stirring constantly. If the flour begins to brown, lower the heat.

7. Whisk together the sugar, salt, milk, heavy cream, beaten egg, and vanilla extract. Stir this mixture into the butter mixture, and whisk constantly until the sauce thickens, about 5 minutes.

8. To serve, cut the bread pudding into 8 wedges and put each wedge in a shallow bowl. Ladle the warm vanilla sauce over the bread pudding and serve immediately.

Serves 8

Sweetened whipped cream or vanilla ice cream would be an easy finishing touch for this dessert.

WALDORF ASTORIA
Red Velvet Cake

THE TRUE ORIGINS OF RED VELVET CAKE ARE SOMEWHAT OF A MYSTERY. THE WAL-
DORF ASTORIA CONNECTION SEEMS TO ORIGINATE WITH A LADY FROM SAN JOSE, A
BILL FOR $350 FROM THE CHEF AT THE WALDORF ASTORIA, AND FREE COPIES OF THE
RECIPE GIVEN AWAY ON A BUS. DESPITE THESE MURKY DETAILS, IT IS A MOIST AND
TENDER CAKE.

Red Velvet Cake
8 tablespoons (1 stick) unsalted
    butter, softened
1½ cups granulated sugar
2 eggs
¼ cup red food coloring
2 tablespoons unsweetened
    cocoa powder
½ teaspoon kosher salt
1 cup buttermilk
2¼ cups all-purpose flour

1 teaspoon vanilla extract
1 tablespoon white vinegar
1 tablespoon baking soda

Boiled Milk Frosting
⅔ cup all-purpose flour
2 cups milk
1 pound (4 sticks) unsalted
    butter
2 cups powdered sugar
2 teaspoons vanilla extract

1. Preheat the oven to 350°F. Coat two 8-inch cake pans with butter or cooking spray and flour.

2. To make the cake, cream the butter and granulated sugar with an electric mixer until light and fluffy. Add the eggs, one at a time, beating well after each addition.

3. Make a paste with the food coloring and the cocoa powder. Beat into the creamed mixture, then add the salt and buttermilk. Blend well.

4. Beat in the flour, vanilla extract, vinegar, and baking soda, in that order. Mix until all the ingredients are well incorporated.

5. Pour the batter into the two prepared pans and bake in the hot oven for 30 minutes, or until the cake springs back when touched in the center. Let the cake layers cool on wire racks before turning them out of the pans.

6. To make the frosting, whisk the flour into the milk in a saucepan over medium heat and cook until the mixture is thickened, then let cool. Cream the butter and powdered sugar with an electric mixer until light and fluffy. Stir in the vanilla extract.

7. Whisk the creamed mixture into the cooled milk mixture and stir until well blended and smooth.

8. To assemble and frost the cake, split the 2 cake layers and place 1 of the 4 layers on a plate. Frost the layer, then cover with another layer and frost it. Repeat the procedure with the remaining 2 layers, so there are 4 frosted layers. Using a metal spatula, spread the frosting around the sides of the cake and smooth out the top.

9. Let the cake sit for about 15 minutes before serving to let the frosting firm up. The cake can also be refrigerated overnight to let the frosting actually harden.

Serves 8 to 12

WENDY'S

Frosty

A DELICIOUS CHOCOLATE MILK AND ICE CREAM BLEND. DOUBLE OR TRIPLE THE RECIPE, AND KEEP IN THE REFRIGERATOR FOR HOT DAYS.

1 pint vanilla ice cream
1 cup milk
¼ cup chocolate syrup

1 teaspoon vanilla extract
2 tablespoons frozen whipped topping

1. Combine the ice cream and milk in a blender and process until smooth.
2. Add the chocolate syrup and vanilla extract. Blend on medium speed just until the ingredients are well incorporated—do not overmix.
3. Add the whipped topping and slowly blend.
4. Serve in tall, chilled glasses.

Serves 2

The same type of Frosty can be made with strawberry ice cream (omit the chocolate syrup) or chocolate ice cream.

THE WILLOWS
Coconut Cream Pie

THIS ALL-AMERICAN CLASSIC COUNTS FRESH COCONUT AS ITS MOST OUTSTANDING
INGREDIENT. USE PACKAGED ONLY IF YOU CAN'T FIND A PIECE OF FRESH COCONUT
IN YOUR MARKET.

Filling
2 cups milk
½ cup sugar
½ teaspoon kosher salt
¼ cup cornstarch
4 egg yolks
½ cup grated fresh coconut
1 teaspoon vanilla extract

Meringue
4 egg whites
1 teaspoon vanilla extract
¼ cup sugar

1 baked 9-inch piecrust,
   homemade (see page 47)
   or purchased

1. Make the filling first: Combine the milk, sugar, and salt in a saucepan over medium heat. Let the mixture come to a boil, then reduce the heat.

2. Whisk in the cornstarch and the egg yolks, stirring constantly, and cook for a couple of minutes more.

3. Remove the pan from the heat and stir in the grated coconut and the vanilla extract. Let the custard cool before making the meringue.

4. Preheat the oven to 325°F.

5. To make the meringue, using an electric mixer, beat the egg whites to soft peaks. Add the vanilla extract and slowly add the sugar while continuing to run the mixer. Beat until stiff peaks form.

6. Fill the pie shell with the custard mixture. Lightly spoon the meringue in puffy mounds over the entire surface of the pie so that the custard is completely covered.

7. Bake in the hot oven for 15 to 18 minutes, until the meringue is nicely browned.

Serves 8

THE YARDARM
Rich Lemon Pie

A LONGTIME CAPE COD FAVORITE, THE YARDARM SERVES STRAIGHTFORWARD NEW ENGLAND FARE WITH A DISTINCTIVE FLAIR. ITS LEMON PIE IS A GOOD EXAMPLE.

12 tablespoons (1½ sticks) unsalted butter
1⅓ cups sugar
¼ cup fresh lemon juice
2 tablespoons finely grated lemon zest
3 eggs, separated

1 egg
1 or 2 slices white bread, crusts trimmed
1 baked (8-inch) piecrust, homemade (page 47) or purchased

1. Preheat the oven to 350°F.

2. Combine the butter and 1 cup of the sugar in a saucepan over low heat and stir until the butter is melted and the sugar is dissolved. Stir in the lemon juice and the lemon zest. Take the pan off the heat.

3. Whisk the egg yolks and the whole egg until frothy. Slowly whisk into the lemon mixture, stirring constantly. Whisk until the mixture has thickened and set it aside.

4. Using an electric mixer, beat the egg whites to soft peaks. Add the remaining ⅓ cup sugar and beat to stiff peaks. Set the meringue aside.

5. Cut the bread into cubes the size of large crumbs and scatter them over the bottom of the piecrust. Pour the lemon filling over the bread, making sure the cubes are all covered.

6. Spoon the meringue over the lemon filling, spreading it all the way out to the edges of the pie shell to seal them during baking.

7. Bake the pie in the hot oven just until the meringue begins to brown. Let cool before serving.

Serves 8

ZINGERMAN'S BAKEHOUSE
Whoopie Pies

A FAVORITE FOR KIDS AND GROWN-UPS, THESE HOMEMADE WHOOPIE PIES ARE NOTHING LIKE THE PACKAGED ONES. THE MARSHMALLOW CENTERS HAVE A UNIQUE TEXTURE, AND THE TOPS AND BOTTOMS ARE LIKE INDIVIDUAL CHOCOLATE CAKES.

Cakes
8 tablespoons (1 stick) unsalted butter, softened
1 cup packed light brown sugar
1 egg
1 teaspoon vanilla extract
2 cups all-purpose flour
½ cup unsweetened cocoa powder
1¼ teaspoons baking soda
½ teaspoon kosher salt
1 cup buttermilk
½ cup semisweet chocolate chips

Filling
4 regular marshmallows
2 teaspoons water

1. Preheat the oven to 350°F. Line a baking sheet with parchment paper.

2. To make the cakes, cream the butter and brown sugar with an electric mixer until light and fluffy. Add the egg and vanilla extract and beat into the mixture.

3. Whisk together the flour, cocoa powder, baking soda, and salt. Gradually stir the dry ingredients into the creamed mixture alternately with the buttermilk, beating well after each addition. Stir in the chocolate chips.

4. Make 12 mounds of dough on the prepared pan using a ¼-cup measuring cup. Make sure the mounds are placed at least 6 inches apart.

5. Bake for about 12 minutes. The cakes should be puffy and spring back when touched in the center. Let cool on wire racks before filling.

6. To make the filling, combine the marshmallows and water in a microwave-safe bowl and melt the marshmallows on high for 30 to 40 seconds.

7. Spread the filling on the flat sides of 6 of the cakes. Let the filling set for 5 to 10 minutes before topping with the remaining 6 cakes, flat sides to the filling. The marshmallow may firm up while you are filling the cakes—just microwave it for a few seconds to melt it again.

8. Let the pies sit for a few minutes to set before serving. They can be stored in an airtight container for up to 3 weeks or tightly wrapped in plastic and frozen for up to 1 month.

Serves 6

ZUNI CAFÉ
Scones

ZUNI CAFÉ IS STILL GOING STRONG AFTER DECADES IN SAN FRANCISCO. THESE SCONES REPRESENT ITS MOTTO THAT EXCELLENCE DOESN'T HAVE TO BE FANCY, JUST THE BEST THERE IS.

3 cups unbleached flour
4 teaspoons baking powder
¼ teaspoon kosher salt
1 cup sugar
½ pound (2 sticks) cold salted butter, cut into small pieces
½ cup mixed dried currants, barberries, and orange-flavored cranberries

1 tablespoon finely grated orange zest
1 egg
½ cup cold milk
2 teaspoons orange blossom water

1. Preheat the oven to 350°F. Line 2 sheet pans with parchment paper.

2. Whisk together the flour, baking powder, salt, and all but 1 tablespoon of the sugar. Mix well.

3. Cut in the butter, using a pastry cutter or your hands, until the butter is the size of small peas.

4. Add the dried fruits and orange zest and toss well.

5. Whisk together the egg, milk, and orange blossom water. Stir this mixture into the dry ingredients, and mix gently until the dough comes together and everything is well moistened.

6. Divide the dough in half and form each half into a ball. Flour a clean work surface and pat each ball into a flat 6- or 7-inch circle. Roll out each circle until it is ¾ inch thick. Cut each round into 8 wedges.

7. Arrange the wedges on the sheet pans without crowding. Sprinkle with the remaining 1 tablespoon sugar and bake for 20 to 25 minutes, until golden brown and firm to the touch. Serve warm.

Makes 16 scones

TRADEMARKS

- 1900 Park Fare is a registered trademark of 1900 Park Fare.
- '21' Club is a registered trademark of '21' Club.
- 2Bleu is a registered trademark of 2Bleu.
- Akershus Royal Banquet Hall is a registered trademark of Akershus Royal Banquet Hall.
- The American Club is a registered trademark of The American Club.
- Anthony's is a registered trademark of Anthony's.
- Applebee's is a registered trademark of Applebee's International, Inc.
- Arby's is a registered trademark of Arby's Restaurant Group, Inc.
- Babbo Ristorante is a registered trademark of Babbo Ristorante.
- Bahama Breeze is a registered trademark of Darden Concepts, Inc.
- Bakers Square is a registered trademark of Bakers Square Restaurants.
- Baskin-Robbins is a registered trademark of Baskin-Robbins.
- The Bazaar by José Andrés is a registered trademark of The Bazaar by José Andrés.
- Benihana is a registered trademark of Benihana, Inc.
- Biergarten Restaurant is a registered trademark of Disney Enterprises, Inc.
- Big Boy Restaurant is a registered trademark of Big Boy Restaurants International LLC.
- Bistro de Paris is a registered trademark of Bistro de Paris.
- BoardWalk Bakery is a registered trademark of BoardWalk Bakery.
- Boatwright's Dining Hall is a registered trademark of Boatwright's.
- Boma—Flavors of Africa is a registered trademark of Disney Enterprises, Inc.
- Boston Market is a registered trademark of Boston Market Corporation.

- Bouchon Bakery is a registered trademark of Bouchon Bakery.
- Boulangerie Patisserie is a registered trademark of Boulangerie Patisserie.
- Brennan's is a registered trademark of Brennan's Inc.
- California Pizza Kitchen is a registered trademark of California Pizza Kitchen, Inc.
- Carnival Cruise Lines is a registered trademark of Carnival Cruise Lines Inc.
- Carrabba's Italian Grill is a registered trademark of OSI Restaurant Partners, LLC.
- Chart House is a registered trademark of Chart House.
- The Cheesecake Factory is a registered trademark of The Cheesecake Factory, Inc.
- Cheryl's is a registered trademark of Cheryl & Co.
- Chili's is a registered trademark of Brinker International.
- CiCi's Pizza is a registered trademark of CICI Enterprises, LP.
- Cinderella's Royal Table is a registered trademark of Disney Enterprises, Inc.
- Cinnabon is a registered trademark of Cinnabon Inc.
- Citricos is a registered trademark of Citricos.
- Clinkerdagger is a registered trademark of Clinkerdagger.
- Coco's is a registered trademark of Coco's.
- Cold Stone Creamery is a registered trademark of Kahala Franchising LLC.
- Commander's Palace is a registered trademark of Commander's Palace.
- Coral Reef Restaurant is a registered trademark of Coral Reef Restaurant.
- Cracker Barrel is a registered trademark of CBOCS Properties, Inc.
- Dairy Queen is a registered trademark of International Dairy Queen, Inc.
- Denny's is a registered trademark of DFO, LLC.
- Dunkin' Donuts is a registered trademark of DD IP Holder LLC.
- Duquesne Club is a registered trademark of Duquesne Club.
- Eat'n Park is a registered trademark of Eat'n Park Hospitality Group, Inc.

- Edy's is a registered trademark of Edy's.
- El Chico is a registered trademark of Consolidated Restaurant Operations, Inc.
- El Torito is a registered trademark of El Torito Restaurants, Inc.
- Fannie May Candy is a registered trademark of Fannie May Candy.
- Fleming's Steakhouse is a registered trademark of Fleming's Steakhouse.
- Furr's Fresh Buffet is a registered trademark of Furr's Cafeteria.
- Ghirardelli Soda Fountain and Chocolate Shop is a registered trademark of Ghirardelli Soda Fountain and Chocolate Shop.
- Hardee's is a registered trademark of Hardee's Food Systems, Inc.
- House of Plenty is a registered trademark of House of Plenty.
- IHOP is a registered trademark of International House of Pancakes, Inc.
- Jack in the Box is a registered trademark of Jack in the Box, Inc.
- Jai by Wolfgang Puck is a registered trademark of Wolfgang Puck Worldwide Inc.
- Joe's Crab Shack is a registered trademark of Landry's Seafood Restaurants, Inc.
- Joe's Stone Crab Restaurant is a registered trademark of Joe's Stone Crab Restaurant.
- KFC is a registered trademark of Yum! Brands, Inc.
- Kringla Bakeri og Kafé is a registered trademark of Kringla Bakeri og Kafé.
- Krispy Kreme is a registered trademark of Krispy Kreme Doughnut Corporation.
- La Creperie is a registered trademark of La Creperie.
- La Madeleine is a registered trademark of La Madeleine.
- Liberty Tree Tavern is a registered trademark of Liberty Tree Tavern.
- Loca Luna is a registered trademark of Loca Luna.
- Luby's Cafeteria is a registered trademark of Luby's Inc.
- Maggiano's Little Italy is a registered trademark of Maggiano's Little Italy.
- Main Street Cafe is a registered trademark of Main Street Cafe.
- Mama Melrose's Ristorante Italiano is a registered trademark of Mama Melrose's Ristorante Italiano.

- Marie Callender's is a registered trademark of Marie Callender's.
- Max and Erma's is a registered trademark of Max and Erma's.
- McDonald's is a registered trademark of McDonald's Inc.
- Mrs. K's Restaurant is a registered trademark of Mrs. K's.
- Mulate's is a registered trademark of Mulate's.
- Old Key Lime House is a registered trademark of Old Key Lime House.
- Olive Garden is a registered trademark of Darden Restaurants, Inc.
- Outback Steakhouse is a registered trademark of Outback Steakhouse, Inc.
- Paci Restaurant is a registered trademark of Paci Restaurant.
- Pappadeaux Seafood Kitchen is a registered trademark of Pappadeaux Seafood Kitchen.
- Payard Patisserie and Bistro is a registered trademark of Payard Patisserie.
- Piccadilly Cafeteria is a registered trademark of Piccadilly Cafeteria.
- Planet Hollywood is a registered trademark of Planet Hollywood, Inc.
- The Plaza Restaurant is a registered trademark of Plaza Restaurant.
- Portobello is a registered trademark of Portobello Yacht Club.
- Prantl's Bakery is a registered trademark of Prantl's Bakery.
- Raglan Road is a registered trademark of Raglan Road.
- Rainforest Cafe is a registered trademark of Landry's Restaurants, Inc.
- Rather Sweet Bakery and Cafe is a registered trademark of Rather Sweet Bakery and Cafe.
- Red Lobster is a registered trademark of Darden Restaurants, Inc.
- Red Robin Gourmet Burgers is a registered trademark of Red Robin Gourmet Burgers, Inc.
- Restaurant Marrakesh is a registered trademark of Restaurant Marrakesh.
- The Ritz-Carlton is a registered trademark of The Ritz-Carlton Hotel Company LLC.
- Rose and Crown Pub and Dining Room is a registered trademark of Rose & Crown Dining Room.

- Ruby Tuesday is a registered trademark of Morrison Restaurant's, Inc.
- Ruggles Grill is a registered trademark of Ruggles Grill.
- S&W Cafeteria is a registered trademark of S&W Cafeteria.
- Shutters at Old Port Royale—Disney World is a registered trademark of Disney Enterprises, Inc.
- The Source is a registered trademark of The Source.
- Spago is a registered trademark of Spago.
- Springs Cafe is a registered trademark of Springs Cafe.
- Starbucks is a registered trademark of Starbucks Corporation.
- Subway is a registered trademark of Doctor's Associates, Inc.
- Taco Bell is a registered trademark of Yum! Brands, Inc.
- Ted's Montana Grill is a registered trademark of Ted's.
- T.G.I. Friday's is a registered trademark of T.G.I. Friday's, Inc.
- The Lady & Sons is a registered trademark of The Lady & Sons.
- Tim Hortons is a registered trademark of The TDL Marks Corporation.
- Tony's Town Square Restaurant is a registered trademark of Tony's Town Square Restaurant.
- Treebeards is a registered trademark of Treebeards.
- Tusker House Restaurant is a registered trademark of Tusker House.
- Waldorf Astoria is a registered trademark of Waldorf Astoria.
- Wendy's is a registered trademark of Wendy's International, Inc.
- The Willows is a registered trademark of The Willows.
- The Yardarm is a registered trademark of The Yardarm.
- Zingerman's Bakehouse is a registered trademark of Zingerman's Bakehouse.
- Zuni Café is a registered trademark of Zuni Café.

RESTAURANT WEBSITES

For restaurant trademark details and locations please visit:

1900 Park Fare	www.disneyworld.disney.go.com/dining
'21' Club	www.21club.com
2Bleu	www.2bleu.com
Akershus Royal Banquet Hall	www.disneyworld.disney.go.com/dining
The American Club	www.americanclubresort.com
Anthony's	www.vicandanthonys.com
Applebee's	www.applebees.com
Arby's	www.arbys.com
Babbo Ristorante e Enoteca	www.babbonyc.com
Bahama Breeze	www.bahamabreeze.com
Bakers Square	www.bakerssquare.com
Baskin-Robbins	www.baskinrobbins.com
The Bazaar	www.thebazaar.com
Benihana	www.benihana.com
Biergarten Restaurant	www.disneyworld.disney.go.com/dining
Big Boy Restaurant	www.bigboy.com
Bistro de Paris	www.disneyworld.disney.go.com/dining
BoardWalk Bakery	www.disneyworld.disney.go.com/dining
Boatwright's Dining Hall	www.disneyworld.disney.go.com/dining
Boma—Flavors of Africa	www.disneyworld.disney.go.com/dining
Boston Market	www.bostonmarket.com
Bouchon Bakery	www.bouchonbakery.com
Boulangerie Patisserie	www.disneyworld.disney.go.com/dining
Brennan's	www.brennansneworleans.com
Burton's Sunnybrook Restaurant	www.burtonsgrill.com

California Pizza Kitchen	www.cpk.com
Carnival Cruise Lines	www.carnival.com
Carrabba's Italian Grill	www.carrabbas.com
Chart House	www.chart-house.com
The Cheesecake Factory	www.thecheesecakefactory.com
Cheryl's	www.cheryls.com
Chili's	www.chilis.com
CiCi's Pizza	www.cicispizza.com
Cinderella's Royal Table	www.disneyworld.disney.go.com/dining
Cinnabon	www.cinnabon.com
Citricos	www.disneyworld.disney.go.com/dining
Clinkerdagger	www.clinkerdagger.com
Coco's	www.cocosbakery.com
Cold Stone Creamery	www.coldstonecreamery.com
Commander's Palace	www.commanderspalace.com
Coral Reef Restaurant	www.disneyworld.disney.go.com/dining
Cracker Barrel	www.crackerbarrel.com
Dairy Queen	www.dairyqueen.com
Denny's	www.dennys.com
Dunkin' Donuts	www.dunkindonuts.com
Duquesne Club	www.duquesne.org
Eat'n Park	www.eatnpark.com
Edy's	www.edys.com
El Chico	www.elchico.com
El Torito	www.eltorito.com
Fannie May Candy	www.fanniemay.com
Fleming's Steakhouse	www.flemingssteakhouse.com
Furr's Fresh Buffet	www.furrs.net
Ghirardelli Soda Fountain and Chocolate Shop	www.ghirardelli.com
Hardee's	www.hardees.com
House of Plenty	www.houseofplenty.net
IHOP	www.ihop.com
Jack in the Box	www.jackinthebox.com
Jai by Wolfgang Puck	www.wolfgangpuck.com/restaurants
Joe's Crab Shack	www.joescrabshack.com

Joe's Stone Crab Restaurant	www.joesstonecrab.com
KFC	www.kfc.com
Kringla Bakeri og Kafé	www.disneyworld.disney.go.com/dining
Krispy Kreme	www.krispykreme.com
La Creperie	www.parislasvegas.com
La Madeleine	www.lamadeleine.com
Liberty Tree Tavern	www.disneyworld.disney.go.com/dining
Loca Luna	www.loca-luna.com
Luby's Cafeteria	www.lubys.com
Maggiano's Little Italy	www.maggianos.com
Main Street Cafe	www.mainstreetcafe.com
Mama Melrose's Ristorante Italiano	www.disneyworld.disney.go.com/dining
Marie Callender's	www.mariecallenders.com
Max and Erma's	www.maxandermas.com
McDonald's	www.mcdonalds.com
Mrs. K's Restaurant	www.mrsks.com
Mulate's	www.mulates.com
Old Key Lime House	www.oldkeylimehouse.com
Olive Garden	www.olivegarden.com
Outback Steakhouse	www.outback.com
Paci Restaurant	www.pacirestaurant.com
Pappadeaux Seafood Kitchen	www.pappadeaux.com
Payard Patisserie and Bistro	www.caesarspalace.com
Piccadilly Cafeteria	www.piccadilly.com
Planet Hollywood	www.planethollywood.com
The Plaza Restaurant	www.disneyworld.disney.go.com/dining
Portobello	www.portobellorestaurant.com
Prantl's Bakery	www.prantlsbakery.com
Raglan Road	www.raglanroad.com
Rainforest Cafe	www.rainforestcafe.com
Red Lobster	www.redlobster.com
Red Robin Gourmet Burgers	www.redrobin.com
Restaurant Marrakesh	www.disneyworld.disney.go.com/dining
The Ritz-Carlton	www.ritzcarlton.com

Rose and Crown Pub and Dining Room	www.disneyworld.disney.go.com/dining
Ruby Tuesday	www.rubytuesday.com
Ruggles Grill	www.rugglesgrill.com
S&W Cafeteria	www.swcafeteria.com
Shutters at Old Port Royale—Disney World	www.disneyworld.disney.go.com/dining
The Source	www.wolfgangpuck.com/restaurants/fine-dining/3941
Spago	www.wolfgangpuck.com/restaurants
Springs Cafe	www.springspreserve.org
Starbucks	www.starbucks.com
Subway	www.subway.com
Taco Bell	www.tacobell.com
Ted's Montana Grill	www.tedsmontanagrill.com
T.G.I. Friday's	www.fridays.com
The Lady & Sons	www.ladyandsons.com
Tim Hortons	www.timhortons.com
Tony's Town Square Restaurant	www.disneyworld.disney.go.com/dining
Treebeards	www.treebeards.com
Tusker House Restaurant	www.disneyworld.disney.go.com/dining
Waldorf Astoria	www.waldorfastoria3.hilton.com
Wendy's	www.wendys.com
The Willows	www.willowshawaii.com
The Yardarm	www.yardarmrestaurant.com
Zingerman's Bakehouse	www.zingermansbakehouse.com
Zuni Café	www.zunicafe.com

INDEX

chocolate (*cont.*)
substitutions, xix
Trinidads, Fannie May Candy, 130–31
Turtle Pie, Baskin-Robbins, 38
Turtle Pie, House of Plenty, 138
Whoopie Pies, Zingerman's Bakehouse, 286–87
see also brownie(s); white chocolate
chocolate cake(s):
Black Forest, Biergarten Restaurant, 45–46
Double Fudge Coca-Cola, Cracker Barrel, 117–18
Doughnuts, Tim Hortons, 273–74
Flourless Torte, '21' Club, 5–6
Lava, Fleming's Steakhouse, 132
Melting, Carnival Cruise Lines, 75–76
Red Velvet, Waldorf Astoria, 281–82
Sachertorte, Babbo Ristorante e Enoteca, 32–33
Sin, Applebee's, 17–18
Slab Cake Batter Ice Cream, Cold Stone Creamery, 104
Soufflé Torte, Anthony's, 13–14
Triple-Chocolate Meltdown, Applebee's, 24–25
Tuxedo, Rather Sweet Bakery and Cafe, 222–24
Wave, Coral Reef Restaurant, 109–10
chocolate chip(s):
Cookies, Subway, 263
Cookies, The Ritz-Carlton, 230
Crumb Cakes, Boardwalk Bakery, 53–54
Heath Bars, Starbucks, 256
Mighty Ice Cream Pie, Chili's, 93
Ooey-Gooey Toffee Cake, Liberty Tree Tavern, 166–67
Pecan Cookies, Ghirardelli Soda Fountain and Chocolate Shop, 135–36
Ricotta Pie, Olive Garden, 193–94
chocolate glaze:
'21' Club, 5–6
Babbo Ristorante e Enoteca, 32–33
Rather Sweet Bakery and Cafe, 222–23
chocolate sauce:
Espresso, Paci Restaurant, 200–201
Holiday Banana Split, Main Street Cafe, 177
T.G.I. Friday's, 269–70
see also hot fudge sauce

cinnamon:
Apples, Boston Market, 61
Apple Turnovers, Applebee's, 19
Bread Pudding, Banana, with Vanilla Sauce, Tusker House Restaurant, 279–80
Candied Pecans, Outback Steakhouse, 197
Ice Cream, Joe's Crab Shack, 146–47
Roll, Cinnabon, 97–98
cobblers:
Apple and Raisin, Chili's, 90–91
Peach, Hardee's, 137
Coca-Cola Double Fudge Cake, Cracker Barrel, 117–18
Cocomisù, Boma—Flavors of Africa, 56–57
coconut:
Bread Pudding, Rainforest Cafe, 219–20
Cake, Paci Restaurant, 200–201
Carrot Cake Cheesecake, The Cheesecake Factory, 82–83
Cocomisù, Boma—Flavors of Africa, 56–57
Cream Pie, The Willows, 284
Crème Anglaise, Bahama Breeze, 35–36
Fruit Punch Jell-O Salad, Furr's Fresh Buffet, 133
Hawaiian Pie, Luby's Cafeteria, 170
Piña Colada Bread Pudding, Bahama Breeze, 35–36
Sydney's Sinful Sundae, Outback Steakhouse, 199
Trinidads, Fannie May Candy, 130–31
coffee:
Baileys Irish, Trifle, Rose and Crown Pub and Dining Room, 231–32
Cappuccino Crème Brûlée, Mama Melrose's Ristorante Italiano, 178
Caramel Macchiato, Starbucks, 252
Chocolate-Espresso Pudding, Starbucks, 253
Chocolate-Espresso Sauce, Paci Restaurant, 200–201
ice cream, in Chart House Mud Pie, 79
Iced Vanilla Latte, Starbucks, 257
Mocha Glaze, Tim Hortons, 273–74
see also Kahlúa coffee liqueur
Coffee Cake, Old-Fashioned, Starbucks, 260–61

302 | Index

marshmallows, miniature:
  Chocolate Icebox Pie, Luby's Cafeteria,
    171–72
  Double Fudge Coca-Cola Cake, Cracker
    Barrel, 117–18
  Fruit Punch Jell-O Salad, Furr's Fresh
    Buffet, 133
  Sweet Potato Casserole, Boston Market,
    62–63
mascarpone cheese, in Boma—Flavors of
  Africa Cocomisù, 56–57
meringue:
  Pie, Coconut Cream, The Willows,
    284
  Tart, Passion Fruit, Boma—Flavors of
    Africa, 58
Mighty Ice Cream Pie, Chili's, 93
Milk Chocolate Truffles à l'Ancienne,
  Payard Patisserie and Bistro,
  204–6
milkshakes, *see* shakes
mint:
  Girl Scout Thin Mint Cookie Ice Cream,
    Ed's, 126
  peppermint ice cream, in Main Street
    Cafe Holiday Banana Split, 177
Mocha Glaze, Tim Hortons, 273–74
mousse:
  Baileys and Jack Daniel's, Coral Reef
    Restaurant, 107–8
  Chocolate, Boulangerie Patisserie,
    67
  Chocolate, Carrabba's Italian Grill,
    78
  Kahlúa, El Torito, 128
  Pumpkin, Coco's, 101–2
  Raspberry, Cheesecake, Olive Garden,
    195–96
mud pies:
  Chart House, 79
  Everything, 2Bleu, 9
muffins:
  Apple, McDonald's, 183
  Blueberry-Cheese Buckle, Cinderella's
    Royal Table, 95–96
  Oatmeal, Tim Hortons, 275
  Pumpkin–Cream Cheese, Starbucks,
    262
  Pumpkin-Spice, Dunkin' Donuts,
    121
  Strawberry n' Crème, Eat'n Park,
    125

N

Napoleon, French Toast, The Cheesecake
  Factory, 80–81
nut(s):
  Crust, Spago, 245
  Three-, Torte, The American Club, 12
  see also specific nuts
Nutella Crepes, Coco's, 103

O

oatmeal:
  Cookie Crumble, 62
  Muffins, Tim Hortons, 275
Ooey-Gooey Toffee Cake, Liberty Tree
  Tavern, 166–67
Oreo crusts:
  Chart House, 79
  The Cheesecake Factory, 86
  Peanut, Ruggles Grill, 238

P

pancakes:
  Cheesecake, IHOP, 139–40
  Dessert, Spago, 247
  Sweet Potato, Boatwright's Dining Hall,
    55
panna cotta:
  Lemon, Tony's Town Square Restaurant,
    276–77
  Saffron, with Rhubarb *Marmellata*,
    Babbo Ristorante e Enoteca, 30–31
Parfait, Key Lime, Coral Reef Restaurant,
  111
Passion Fruit Meringue Tart, Boma—
  Flavors of Africa, 58
pastry(ies):
  Apple Strudel, Biergarten Restaurant,
    43–44
  Apple Turnovers, Arby's, 26–27
  Baked Apple Dumplings, Cracker Barrel,
    114–15
  Caramel Apple Empanadas, Taco Bell,
    264
  Cinnamon-Apple Turnovers, Applebee's,
    19
  Crispitos, Taco Bell, 266
  Spiced Pear Crostada, Maggiano's Little
    Italy, 175–76
  see also pies; puff pastry; tarts

Triple-Chocolate Meltdown, Applebee's, 24–25

truffle(s):
Milk Chocolate, à l'Ancienne, Payard Patisserie and Bistro, 204–6
White Chocolate, Coral Reef Restaurant, 109–10
White Chocolate–Raspberry, Cheesecake, The Cheesecake Factory, 86–87

turnovers:
Apple, Arby's, 26–27
Cinnamon-Apple, Applebee's, 19

Turtle Cake, Cream Cheese, Loca Luna, 167–68

turtle pies:
Baskin-Robbins, 38
House of Plenty, 138

Tuxedo Cake, Rather Sweet Bakery and Cafe, 222–24

U

Upside-Down Cheesecake, Pineapple, Boma—Flavors of Africa, 59–60

V

vanilla:
Custard Sauce, Rose and Crown Pub and Dining Room, 233–34
-Filled Doughnuts, Dunkin' Donuts, 122–23
Frosting, Cheryl's, 88–89
Latte, Iced, Starbucks, 257
Sauce, 1900 Park Fare, 2
Sauce, Tusker House Restaurant, 279–80

Volcano, Rainforest Cafe, 221

W

walnuts:
Apple Dapple, Burton's Sunnybrook Restaurant, 69–70
Caribbean Sand Bars, Shutters at Old Port Royale—Disney World, 242
Carrot Cake Cheesecake, The Cheesecake Factory, 82–83
Chocolate Brownie Sundae, Chili's, 92
Three-Nut Torte, The American Club, 12

Whiskey Sauce, Bread Pudding Soufflé with, Commander's Palace, 105–6

white chocolate:
Baileys and Jack Daniel's Mousse, Coral Reef Restaurant, 107–8
Bread Pudding, Planet Hollywood, 209–10
chips, in Applebee's Maple Butter Blondies, 20–21
chips, in Applebee's Triple-Chocolate Meltdown, 24–25
Cranberry Bliss Bars, Starbucks, 254–55
Crème Brûlée, Portobello, 212–13
Graham Cracker Crust, Boma—Flavors of Africa, 59–60
Heath Bars, Starbucks, 256
Raspberry Truffle Cheesecake, The Cheesecake Factory, 86–87
Trinidads, Fannie May Candy, 130–31
Truffle, Coral Reef Restaurant, 109–10

whole wheat flour, xxi

Whoopie Pies, Zingerman's Bakehouse, 286–87

Y

yeast, working with, xxiv
yogurt, in McDonald's Fruit Smoothie, 184